ISBN: 9781314131475

Published by:
HardPress Publishing
8345 NW 66TH ST #2561
MIAMI FL 33166-2626

Email: info@hardpress.net
Web: http://www.hardpress.net

W. R. M.
From
K. M. C. 189

AUTUMN: FROM THE JOURNAL
OF HENRY D. THOREAU

EDITED BY H. G. O. BLAKE

" This world is no blot for us
Nor blank ; it means intensely and means good ;
To find its meaning is my meat and drink."
BROWNING, *Fra Lippo Lippi.*

" In the last stage of civilization, poetry, religion and philosophy will be one, and there are glimpses of this truth in the first." — THOREAU, *December* 17, 1837.

BOSTON AND NEW YORK
HOUGHTON, MIFFLIN AND COMPANY
The Riverside Press, Cambridge
1892

The Riverside Press, Cambridge, Mass., U. S. A.
Electrotyped and Printed by H. O. Houghton & Company.

PREFACE.

WITH the present volume, the four seasons, as they are represented in Thoreau's journal, are nominally completed, though but a part of the Spring and Summer has been given, and much has been omitted in all the four volumes printed.

As I have said before, my own interest in the journal is in the character and genius of the writer, rather than in any account of the phenomena of nature. According to Thoreau's own view, such a journal is, in the strictest sense, an autobiography. "Our thoughts," he says, "are the epochs in our lives; all else is but as a journal of the winds that blew while we were here." And again in this volume, under October 21, 1857, "Is not the poet bound to write his own biography? Is there any other work for him but a good journal? We do not wish to know how his imaginary hero, but how he the actual hero, lived from day to day." As the "Week on the

Concord and Merrimack Rivers," though describing a voyage very limited as to time and distance, yet from its intermingling of thought with loving observation and poetic description seems a far-reaching journey, so these oft-repeated walks and boating excursions in and about Concord, to Fair Haven, the Cliffs, Conantum, etc., abound in more genuine life, more of the true spirit of travel, than the most varied adventures of ordinary travelers in distant lands. One may have visited other continents, and yet never gone so far.

In continuing to publish these volumes, I feel sure of an eager and earnest company of readers, though not a very large one. I have also the satisfaction of discharging a duty which seemed to devolve upon me by inheritance, thus making better known a life which has been to me for so many years of the deepest interest, which in the hurry and rush of our present civilization is certainly well worth attending to, a life which, however partial, as every finite life must be, points so clearly and steadily towards the highest ideal. Here was a young man, with a liberal education and little or no pecuniary means, who on entering the world determined not to throw obstacles in the way of his true life by attempting to earn such a living and such a position as the usages of society set before him. The cheerful serenity which appears in his writings, as it did in his manners and conversation, shows how successful was this plan for him, — how with simple wants and in obscurity he enjoyed the wealth of the world. He knew early, with little experience, through the intimations of his genius, how false the aims of society are; that real success is not in proportion to the property and distinction one acquires, but to the degree in which he finds heaven here upon earth, though this idea was not expressed by him in the language of religion. Many persons talk in this way, listen approvingly to such preaching, but fall in with the current. The remarkable thing about this man is that though not a church-goer, not caring for the institutions of religion, he yet regarded it as the clear dictate of wisdom thus to make the most of life, and acted upon his conviction. In view of these things, the charge of egotism and selfishness will at once spring to the lips of many.

But probably few of us know better than he did, that an unworthy self-regard is fatal to the object he had in view.

> "Renounce joy for my fellow's sake ? That's joy
> Beyond joy."

Though deeply interested and sometimes active in the cause of human freedom, he commonly took little part in works of philanthropy and reform. Had he done otherwise, we should probably have lost from his character somewhat of that strong personal element which, though more quiet in its operation than associated schemes of reform, is doubtless the most powerful influence in the progress of mankind.

THE EDITOR.

AUTUMN.

September 21, 1854. I sometimes seem to myself to owe all my little success, all for which men commend me, to my vices. I am perhaps more willful than others, and make enormous sacrifices even of others' happiness, it may be, to gain my own ends. It would seem as if nothing good could be accomplished without some vice to aid in it.

Sept. 21, 1859. Heard in the night a snapping sound, and the fall of some small body on the floor from time to time. In the morning I found it was produced by the witch-hazel nuts on my desk springing open and casting their seeds quite across my chamber, hard and stony as these nuts were. For several days they are shooting black seeds about my chamber. . . . I suspect that it is not when the witch-hazel nut first gapes open that the seeds fly out, for I see many, if not most of them, open first with the seeds in them; but when I release a seed, it being still held by its base, it flies, as I have said.

I think that its slippery base is compressed by
the unyielding shell which at length expels it,
just as I can make one fly by pressing it, and
letting it slip from between my thumb and
finger.   It appears to fit close to the shell at its
base, even after the shell gapes.

The ex-plenipotentiary refers in after speeches
with complacency to the time he spent abroad,
and the various lords and distinguished men he
met, as to a *deed done*, and an ever memorable occasion.   Of what account are titles and
offices and opportunities, if you do no memorable deed?

Sept. 21, 1860. . . . P. M.   To Easterbrook
country. . . . The pods of the broom are nearly
half of them open.   I perceive that one just ready
to open opens with a slight spring, on being
touched, and the pod curls a little.   I suspect
that such seeds as these, which the winds do not
transport, will turn out to be more sought by the
birds, etc., and so transported by them, than
those lighter ones which are furnished with a
pappus, and so transported by the wind; *i. e.*,
that those which the wind takes are less generally the food of birds and quadrupeds than the
heavier and wingless seeds.

Sept. 22, 1852. . . . In love we impart each
to each, in subtlest, immaterial form of thought
or atmosphere, the best of ourselves, such as

commonly vanishes or evaporates in aspirations, and mutually enrich each other. The lover alone perceives and dwells in a certain human fragrance. To him humanity is not only a flavor, but an aroma and a flavor also.

Sept. 22, 1854. . . . P. M. Over Nawshawtuck. The river is peculiarly smooth, and the water clear and sunny, as I look from the stone bridge. A painted tortoise, with his head out, outside of the weeds, looks as if resting in the air in that attitude, or suggests it, at an angle of 45°, with head and flippers outstretched. . . . As I look off from the hilltop, I wonder if there are any finer days in the year than these, the air is so fine and bracing. The landscape has acquired some fresh verdure withal. The frosts come to ripen the days like fruits, persimmons. . . . Crossing the hill behind Minott's just as the sun is preparing to dip below the horizon, the thin haze in the atmosphere north and south along the western horizon reflects a purple tinge, and bathes the mountains with the same, like a bloom on fruits. I wonder if this phenomenon is observed in warmer weather, or before the frosts have come. Is it not another evidence of the ripe day? I saw it yesterday. . . .

By moonlight all is simple. We are enabled to erect ourselves, our minds, on account of the fewness of objects. We are no longer distracted.

It is simple bread and water. It is simple as
the rudiments of an art, a lesson to be taken before sunlight, perchance, to prepare us for that.

Sept. 22, 1858. A clear, cold day. . . .
Leave Salem for Cape Ann on foot. . . . One
mile southeast of the village of Manchester
struck the beach of " musical sand," just this
side of a large, high, rocky point called Eagle
Head ! This is a curving beach ; may be one
third of a mile long and some twelve rods wide.
We found the same kind of sand on a similar
but shorter beach on the east side of Eagle
Head. We first perceived the sound when we
scratched with an umbrella or the finger swiftly
and forcibly through the sand ; also still louder
when we struck forcibly with our heels, " scuf-
fing " along. The wet or damp sand yielded no
peculiar sound, nor did that which lay loose and
deep next the bank, but only the more compact
and dry. The sound was not at all musical, nor
was it loud. Fishermen might walk over it all
their lives, as indeed they have done, without
noticing it. R———, *who had not heard it*, was
about right when he said it was like that made
by rubbing wet glass with your finger. I
thought it as much like the sound made in wax-
ing a table as anything. It was a squeaking
sound, as of one particle rubbing on another. I
should say it was merely the result of the fric-

tion of peculiarly formed and constituted particles. The surf was high and made a great noise,
yet I could hear the sound made by my companion's feet two or three rods distant, and if it
had been still, probably could have heard it five
or six rods.

Sept. 22, 1860. . . . Some of the early botanists, like Gerard, were prompted and compelled to describe their plants, but most nowadays only measure them, as it were. The
former is affected by what he sees, and so inspired to portray it ; the latter merely fills out a
schedule prepared for him, makes a description
pour servir. I am constantly assisted by the
books in identifying a particular plant and
learning some of its humbler uses, but I rarely
read a sentence in a botany which reminds me
of flowers or living plants. Very few, indeed,
write as if they had seen the thing which they
pretend to describe.

Sept. 23, 1855. 8 P. M. I hear from my
chamber a screech-owl about Monroe's house,
this bright moonlight night, — a loud, piercing
scream, much like the whinner of a colt, perhaps, a rapid trill, then subdued or smothered, a
note or two.

Sept. 23, 1859. . . . What an array of non-
producers society produces ! . . . Many think
themselves well employed as charitable dispens-

ers of wealth which somebody else earned, and these who produce nothing, being of the most luxurious habits, are precisely they who want the most, and complain loudest when they do not get what they want. They who are literally paupers, maintained at the public expense, are the most importunate and insatiable beggars. They cling like the glutton to a living man and suck his vitals up. To any locomotive man there are three or four deadheads clinging, as if they conferred a great favor on society by living upon it. Meanwhile, they fill the churches, and die and revive from time to time. They have nothing to do but sin and repent of their sins. How can you expect such blood-suckers to be happy?

Not only foul and poisonous weeds grow in our tracks, but our vileness and luxuriance make simple, wholesome plants rank and weed-like. All that I ever got a premium for was a monstrous squash, so coarse that nobody could eat it. Some of these bad qualities will be found to lurk in the pears that are invented in the neighborhood of great towns. "The evil that men do lives after them." The corn and pota-toes produced by excessive manuring may be said to have not only a coarse, but a poisonous quality. . . . What creatures is the grain raised in the cornfields of Waterloo for, unless it be

for such as prey upon men? Who cuts the
grass in the graveyard? I can detect the site
of the shanties that have stood all along the
railroad by the ranker vegetation. I do not go
there for delicate wild flowers. It is important,
then, that we should air our lives by removals,
excursions into the fields and woods. Starve
your vices. Do not sit so long over any cellar
hole as to tempt your neighbor to bid for the
privilege of digging saltpetre there. So live
that only the most beautiful wild flowers will
spring up where you have dwelt, harebells, violets, and blue-eyed grass.

Sept. 23, 1860. . . . I hear that a large owl,
probably a cat-owl, killed and carried off a full-
grown turkey in Carlisle, a few days ago.

Sept. 24, 1851. . . . 8 A. M. To Lee's Bridge
via Conantum. It is a cool and windy morning,
and I have donned a thick overcoat for a walk.
The wind is from the north, so that the telegraph harp does not sound where I cross. . . .
This windy, autumnal weather is very exciting
and bracing, clear and cold after the rain of yesterday, it having cleared off in the night. . . .
The river washes up stream before the wind,
with white streaks of foam on its dark surface
diagonally to its course, showing the direction
of the wind. Its surface, reflecting the sun, is
dazzlingly bright. The outlines of the hills are

remarkably distinct and fine, and their surfaces
bare and hard, not clothed with a thick air.   I
notice one red tree, a red maple, against the
woodside in Conant's meadow.   It is a far
brighter red than the blossoms of any tree in
summer, and more conspicuous.   The huckleberry bushes on Conantum are all turned red.

What can be handsomer for a picture than
our river scenery now!   First this smoothly
shorn meadow on the west side of the stream,
looking from Conantum Cliff, with all the
swaths distinct, sprinkled with apple-trees casting heavy shadows, black as ink, such as can be
seen only in this clear air, this strong light, one
cow wandering restlessly about in it, and lowing ; then the blue river, scarcely darker than,
and hardly to be distinguished from, the sky,
its waves driven southward or up stream by the
wind, making it to appear to flow that way,
bordered by willows and button bushes ; then
the narrow meadow beyond, with varied lights
and shades from its waving grass, which for
some reason has not been cut this year, though
so dry, now at length each grass-blade bending
south before the wintry blast, as if looking for
aid in that direction ; then the hill, rising sixty
feet to a terrace-like plain, covered with shrub
oaks, maples, etc., now variously tinted, clad all
in a livery of gay colors, each bush a feather in

its cap; and further in the rear, the wood-crowned cliff, some two hundred feet high, where gray rocks here and there project from amidst the bushes, with its orchard on the slope; and to the right of the cliff the distant Lincoln hills in the horizon; the landscape so handsomely colored, the air so clear and whole-some, and the surface of the earth so pleasingly varied that it seems rarely fitted for the abode of man.

Sept. 24, 1858. [Salem.] . . . Saw at the East India Marine Hall a Bay lynx killed in Danvers July 21st (I think in 1827); an-other killed in Lynnfield in March, 1832. These skins were now, at any rate, quite light, dirty whitish, or white wolfish color, with small pale brown spots. The animals much larger than I expected. Saw a large fossil turtle, some twenty inches in diameter, with the plates distinct, in a slate-colored stone from western New York; also a sword in its scabbard, found in the road near Concord, April 19, 1775, and supposed to have belonged to a British officer.

Sept. 24, 1859. P. M. To Melvin's Preserve. . . . I have many affairs to attend to, and feel hurried these days. Great works of art have endless leisure for a background, as the universe has space. Time stands still while they are created. The artist cannot be in a hurry. The earth moves round the sun with inconceivable rapidity, and yet the surface of the lake is not ruffled by it. It is not by compromise, it is not by a timid and feeble repentance, that a man will save his soul, and live at last. He must conquer a clear field, letting Repentance & Co. go, that well-meaning but weak firm that has assumed the debts of an old and worthless one. You are to fight in a field where no allowances will be made, no courteous bowing to one-handed knights. You are expected to do your duty, not in spite of every thing but *one*, but in spite of *every thing*. . . .

Going along this old Carlisle road — road for walkers, for berry-pickers, and no more worldly travelers ; road for Melvin and Clark, not for the sheriff, nor butcher, nor the baker's jingling cart; road where all wild things and fruits abound, where there are countless rocks to jar those who venture in wagons ; road which leads to and through a great but not famous garden, zoölogical and botanical, at whose gate you never arrive, — as I was going along there, I perceived the grateful scent of the Dicksonia fern now partly decayed. It reminds me of all up country, with its springy mountain sides and unexhausted vigor. Is there any essence of Dicksonia fern, I wonder ? Surely that giant who my neighbor expects is to bound up the Alleghanies will have his handkerchief scented with that. The sweet fragrance of decay! When I wade through by narrow cow-paths, it is as if I had strayed into an ancient and decayed herb garden. Nature perfumes her garments with this essence now especially. She gives it to those who go a-barberrying and on dank autumnal walks. The very scent of it, if you have a decayed frond in your chamber, will take you far up country in a twinkling. You would think you had gone after the cows there, or were lost on the mountains. It is the scent the earth yielded in the saurian period, before man was created and fell, before milk and water were invented, and the mints. *Rana sylvatica* passed judgment on it, or rather that peculiarly scented *Rana palustris*. It was in his reign it was introduced.

A man must attend to nature closely for many years to know when, as well as where, to look for his objects, since he must always anticipate her a little. Young men have not learned the phases of nature. They do not know what constitutes a year, or that one year is like another. I would know when in the year to expect certain thoughts and moods, as the sportsman knows when to look for plover.

Though you may have sauntered near to heaven's gate, when at length you return toward the village you give up the enterprise a little, and you begin to fall into the old ruts of thought, like a regular roadster. Your thoughts very properly fail to report themselves to headquarters. They turn toward night and the evening mail, and become begrimed with dust, as if you were just going to put up at (with?) the tavern, or had even come to make an exchange with a brother clergyman on the morrow.

That old Carlisle road, which leaves towns behind ; where you put off worldly thoughts ; where you do not carry a watch nor remember the proprietor ; where the proprietor is the only trespasser, looking after his apples, the only one who mistakes his calling there, whose title is not good ; where fifty may be a-barberrying, and you do not see one. It is an endless succession of glades where the barberries grow thickest, successive yards amid the barberry bushes where you do not see out. There I see Melvin and the robins, and many a nut-brown maid. The lonely horse in its pasture is glad to see company, comes forward to be noticed, and takes an apple from your hand. Others are called great roads, but this is greater than they all. It is only laid out, offered to walkers, not accepted by the town and the traveling world ; to be represented by a dotted line on charts, not indicated by guideboards, undiscoverable by the uninitiated, that it may be wild to a warm imagination.

Nature, the earth herself, is the only panacea. They bury poisoned sheep up to the neck in earth to take the poison out of them.

Sept. 25, 1840. Birds were very naturally made the subject of augury, for they are but borderers upon the earth, creatures of another and more ethereal element than our existence can be supported in, which seem to flit between us and the unexplored.

Prosperity is no field for heroism unless it endeavor to establish an independent and supernatural prosperity for itself. In the midst of din and tumult and disorder we hear the trumpet sound. Defeat is heaven's success. We cannot be said to succeed to whom the world shows any favor. In fact, it is the hero's *point d'appui*, which, by offering resistance to his action, enables him to act at all. At each step he spurns the world. He vaults the higher in proportion as he employs the greater resistance of the earth. It is fatal when an elevation has been gained by too wide a concession, retaining no point of resistance; for the hero, like the aeronaut, must float at the mercy of the winds, or cannot sail and steer himself for calm weather. When we rise to the step above, we tread hardest on the step below.

My friend must be my tent companion.

Sept. 25, 1851. I am astonished to find how

much travelers both in the east and west permit themselves to be imposed on by a name ; that the traveler in the east, for instance, presumes so great a difference between one Asiatic and another, because one bears the title of Christian, and the other not. At length he comes to a sect of Christians, Armenians or Nestorians, predicates of them a far greater civilization, civility, and humanity than of their neighbors, I suspect not with much truth. At that distance, and therefore impartially viewed, I see but little difference between a Christian and a Mahometan, and thus I perceive that European and American Christians are precisely like these heathenish Armenian and Nestorian Christians ; not Christians, of course, in any true sense, but one other heathenish sect in the west, the difference between whose religion and that of the Mahometans is very slight and unimportant. That nation is not Christian where the principles of humanity do not prevail, but the prejudice of race. I expect the Christian not to be superstitious, but to be distinguished by the clearness of his knowledge, the strength of his faith, the breadth of his humanity. A man of another race, an African, for instance, comes to America to travel through it, and he meets with treatment exactly similar to or worse than that which the American meets with among the Turks,

Arabs, and Tartars. The traveler in both cases finds the religion to be a mere superstition and frenzy or rabidness.

Examined a hornets' nest suspended from contiguous huckleberry bushes. The tops of the bushes appearing to grow out of it, little leafy sprigs, had a pleasing effect. It was an inverted cone, eight or nine inches by seven or eight. I found no hornets buzzing about it. Its entrance appeared to have been enlarged, so I concluded it had been deserted, but, looking nearer, I discovered two or three dead hornets, men of war, in the entry way. Cutting off the bushes which sustained it, I proceeded to open it with my knife. First there were half a dozen layers of waved brownish paper resting loosely on one another, occupying nearly an inch in thickness, for a covering. Within were the six-sided cells in three stories, suspended from the roof and from one another by one or two suspension rods only, the lower story much smaller than the rest; and in what may be called the attic of the structure were two live hornets, appearing partially benumbed with cold, but which in the sun seemed rapidly recovering themselves. Most of the cells were empty, but in some were young hornets still, their heads projecting, apparently still-born, perhaps overtaken unexpectedly by cold weather. These insects appear to be very sensible to cold. The inner circles were of whitish, the outer of grayish, paper.

In these cooler, windier, crystal days, the note of the jay sounds a little more native. Standing on the cliffs, I see them flitting and screaming from pine to pine beneath. Hawks, too, I perceive, sailing about in the clear air, looking white against the green pines, like the seeds of the milkweed. There is almost always a pair of hawks. Their shrill scream and that of the owls and wolves are related to each other.

Sept. 25, 1852. The scarlet of the dogwood is the most conspicuous and interesting of the autumnal colors at present. You can now easily detect them at a distance. Every one in the swamps you have overlooked is revealed. The smooth sumach and the mountain ash are a darker, deeper, bloodier red. Found the fringed gentian November 7th last year.

Sept. 25, 1854. I suspect that I know on what the brilliancy of the autumnal tints will depend. On the greater or less drought of the summer. If the drought has been uncommonly severe, as this year, I should think it would so far destroy the vitality of the leaf that it would attain only to a dull, dead color in autumn ; that to become brilliant in autumn, the plant should be full of sap and vigor to the last.

Do I see a *Fringilla hiemalis* in the Deep Cut? It is a month earlier than last year.

I am detained by the very bright red blackberry leaves strewn along the sod, the vine being inconspicuous. How they spot it !

On the shrub oak plain as seen from the Cliffs, the red at least balances the green. It looks like a rich, shaggy rug now, before the woods are changed.

There was a splendid sunset while I was on the water, beginning at the Clamshell reach. All the lower edge of a very broad dark slate cloud, which reached backward almost to the zenith, was lit up through and through with a dun golden fire, the sun being below the horizon, like a furze plain densely on fire a short distance above the horizon. There was a clear pale robin's-egg sky beneath, and some little clouds, on which the light fell, high in the sky, but nearer, seen against the upper part of the distant, uniform, dark slate one, were of a fine grayish silver color, with fine mother-of-pearl tints, unusual at sunset (?). The furze gradually burnt out on the lower edge of the cloud, changed into a smooth, hard, pale pink vermilion, which gradually faded into a gray, satiny pearl, a fine Quaker color. All these colors were prolonged in the rippled reflection to five or six times their proper length. The effect was particularly remarkable in the case of the reds, which were long bands of red perpendicular in the water.

Sept. 25, 1855.   In the evening went to Welch's (?) circus with C——.   Approaching, I perceived the peculiar scent which belongs to such places, a certain sourness in the air, suggesting trodden grass and cigar smoke.   The curves of the great tent, at least eight or ten rods in diameter, the main central curve, and wherever it rested on a post, suggested that the tent was the origin of much of the Oriental architecture, — the Arabic, perhaps.   There was the pagoda in perfection.   It is remarkable what graceful attitudes feats of strength and agility seem to require.

Sept. 25, 1859.   P. M.   To Emerson's Cliff. Holding a white pine needle in my hand and turning it in a favorable light as I sit upon this cliff, I perceive that each of its three edges is notched or serrated with minute forward-pointing bristles.   So much does nature avoid an unbroken line that even this slender leaf is serrated, though, to my surprise, neither Gray nor Bigelow mentions it.   Loudon, however, says, " Scabrous and inconspicuously serrated in the margin ; spreading in summer, but in winter contracted, and lying close to the branches." Fine and smooth as it looks, it is serrated, after all. This is its concealed wildness, by which it connects with the wilder oaks.

Sept. 26, 1840. The day, for the most part, is heroic only when it breaks.

Every author writes in the faith that his book is to be the final resting-place, and sets up his fixtures as for a more than Oriental permanence; but it is only a caravansary, which we soon leave without ceremony. We read on his sign only refreshment for man and beast, and a drawn hand directs to Ispahan or Bagdad.

Sept. 26, 1852. Dreamed of purity last night. The thoughts seemed not to originate with me, but I was invested, my thought was tinged by another's thought. It was not I that originated, but I that entertained the thought. P. M. To Ministerial Swamp. The small cottony leaves of fragrant everlasting in the fields for some time, protected, as it were, by a little web of cotton against frost and snow; a little dense web of cotton spun over it, entangled in it, as if to restrain it from rising higher.

The increasing scarlet and yellow tints around the meadows and river remind me of the opening of a vast flower bud. They are the petals of its corolla, which are of the width of the valleys. It is the flower of autumn, whose expanding bud just begins to blush. As yet, however, in the forest there are very few changes of foliage.

The *Polygonum articulatum,* giving a rosy tinge to Jenny's desert, is very interesting now, with its slender dense racemes of rose-tinted flowers, apparently without leaves, rising cleanly out of the sand. It looks warm and brave, a foot or more high, and mingled with deciduous blue curls. It is much divided into many-spreading, slender-racemed branches, with inconspicuous linear leaves, reminding me, both by its form and its colors, of a peach orchard in blossom, especially when the sunlight falls on it ; minute rose-tinted flowers that brave the frosts, and advance the summer into fall, warming with their color sandy hillsides and deserts, like the glow of evening reflected on the sand ; apparently all flower and no leaf. Rising apparently with clean bare stems from the sand, it spreads out into this graceful head of slender rosy racemes, wisp-like. This little desert of less than an acre blushes with it.

The tree fern is in fruit now, with its delicate tendril-like fruit, climbing three or four feet over the asters, golden-rods, etc., on the edge of the swamp. The large ferns are yellow or brown now. Larks, like robins, fly in flocks. Succory in bloom; . . . it bears the frost well, though we have not had much.

Sept. 26, 1854. It is a warm and very pleasant afternoon. I walk along the river-side in

Merrick's pasture. Some single red maples are very splendid now; the whole tree bright scarlet against the cold green pines, while very few trees are changed, is a most remarkable object in the landscape, seen a mile off. It is too fair to be believed, especially seen against the light. Some are a reddish or else greenish yellow, others with red or yellow cheeks. I suspect that the yellow maples had not scarlet blossoms.

Sept. 26, 1857. P. M. Up river to Clamshell. These are warm, serene, bright autumn afternoons. I see far off the various-colored gowns of cranberry pickers against the green of the meadow. The river stands a little way over the grass again, and the summer is over. The pickerel weed is brown, and I see muskrat houses. I see a large black cricket on the river, a rod from shore, and a fish is leaping at it. As long as the fish leaps it is motionless, as if dead; but as soon as it feels my paddle under it, it is lively enough. I sit on Clamshell bank and look over the meadows. Hundreds of crickets have fallen into a sandy gully, and now are incessantly striving to creep or leap up again on the sliding sand, out of this dusty road into those bare solitudes which they inhabit; such their business this September afternoon.

I watch a marsh hawk circling low along the edge of the meadow, looking for a 'frog, and now at last it alights to rest on a tussock.

Coming home, the sun is intolerably warm on my left cheek. I perceive it is because the heat of the reflected sun, which is as bright as the real one, is added to that of the real one, for when I cover the reflection with my hand the heat is less intense.

That cricket seemed to know that if he lay quietly spread out on the surface, either the fishes would not suspect him to be an insect, or, if they tried to swallow him, would not be able. What blundering fellows these crickets are, both large and small! They are not only tumbling into the river all along shore, but into this sandy gully, to escape from which is a Sisyphus labor. I have not sat there many minutes, watching two foraging crickets which have decided to climb up two tall and slender weeds almost bare of branches, as a man shins up a liberty pole sometimes, when I find that one has climbed to the summit of my knee. They are incessantly running about on the sunny bank. Their still larger cousins, the mole crickets, are creaking loudly and incessantly all along the shore. Others have eaten themselves cavernous apartments, sitting-room and pantry at once, in windfall apples.

Speaking to Rice of that cricket's escape, he said that he once, with several others, saw a small striped snake swim across a piece of water about half a rod wide to a half-grown bull-frog which sat on the opposite shore, and attempt to seize him, but he found that he had caught a Tartar, for the bull-frog, seeing him coming, was not afraid of him, but at once seized his head in his mouth and closed his jaws upon it, and he thus held the snake a considerable time before the latter was able, by struggling, to get away. When that cricket felt my oar he leaped without the least hesitation, or perhaps consideration, trusting to fall in a pleasanter place. He was evidently trusting to drift against some weed which should afford him a *point d'appui.*

Sept. 26, 1858. I observe that the seeds of the *Panicum sanguinale* and *filiforme* are perhaps half fallen, evidently affected by the late frosts as chestnuts, etc., will be by later ones ; and now is the time, too, when flocks of sparrows begin to scour over the weedy fields, especially in the morning. I fancy they are attracted to some extent by this thin harvest of panic seed. The spikes of *Panicum crus-galli* also are partially bare. Evidently the small graminivorous birds abound more after these seeds are ripe. The seeds of the pigweed are yet apparently quite green. May be they are somewhat peculiar for hanging on all winter.

Sept. 26, 1859. To Clamshell by boat. The *Solanum Dulcamara* berries are another kind which grows in drooping clusters. I do not know any clusters more graceful and beautiful than these drooping cymes of scarlet or translucent, cherry-colored elliptical berries, with steel-blue or lead-colored (?) purple pedicels (not peduncles) like the leaves on the tips of the branches. No berries, I think, are so well spaced and agreeably arranged in their drooping cymes, somewhat hexagonally, like a honeycomb. Then what a variety of color! The peduncle and its branches are green, the pedicels and sepals only that rare steel-blue purple, and the berries a clear, translucent cherry-red. They hang more gracefully over the river's brim than any pendant in a lady's ear. Yet they are considered poisonous; not to look at, surely. Is it not a reproach that so much that is beautiful is poisonous to us? But why should they not be poisonous? Would it not be bad taste to eat these berries which are ready to feed another sense?

Sept. 27, 1852. P. M. To C. Smith's Hill. The flashing clearness of the atmosphere. More light appears to be reflected from the earth, less absorbed.

At Saw Mill Brook many finely cut and flat ferns are faded whitish and very handsome, as if pressed; very delicate.

The touch-me-not seed vessels go off like pistols, shoot their seeds off like bullets. They explode in my hat.

The arum berries are now in perfection, —
cone-shaped spikes one and a half inches long,
of scarlet or vermilion-colored, irregular, somewhat pear-shaped berries springing from a purplish core. They are exactly the color of bright
sealing-wax, on club-shaped peduncles. The
changed leaves are delicately white, especially
beneath. Here and there lies prostrate on the
damp leaves or ground this conspicuous red
spike. The medeola berries are common now,
and the large red berries of the panicled Solomon's seal.

It must have been a turtle-dove that eyed me
so near, turned its head sidewise to me for a
fair view, looking with a St. Vitus twitching of
its neck, as if to recover its balance on an un-
stable perch. That is their way.

From Smith's Hill I looked toward the mountain line. Who can believe that the mountain
peak which he beholds fifty miles off in the
horizon, rising far and faintly blue above an intermediate range, while he stands on his trivial
native hills or in the dusty highway, can be the
same as that which he looked up at once near at
hand from a gorge in the midst of primitive
woods ! For a part of two days we traveled
across lots, loitering by the way, through primitive woods and swamps, over the highest peak
of the Peterboro' Hills to Monadnock, by ways

from which all landlords and stage-drivers endeavored to dissuade us.   It was not a month
ago.   But now that I look across the globe in
an instant to that dim Monadnock peak, and
these familiar fields and copse-woods appear to
occupy the greater part of the interval, I cannot
realize that Joe Evely's house still stands there
at the base of the mountain, and that I made
the long tramp through the woods with invigor-
ating scents before I got to it.   I cannot realize that on the tops of those cool blue ridges
are berries in abundance still, bluer than themselves, as if they borrowed their blueness from
their locality.   From the mountains we do not
discern our native hills, but from our native hills
we look out easily to the far blue mountain which
seems to preside over them.   As I look north-
westward to that summit from a Concord cornfield, how little can I realize all the life that is
passing between me and it, the retired up-country
farmhouses, the lonely mills, wooded vales, wild
rocky pastures, new clearings on stark mountain sides, and rivers murmuring through primitive woods.   I see the very peak, — there can be
no mistake, — but how much I do not see that is
between me and it!   In this way we see stars.
What is it but a faint blue cloud, a mist that
may vanish!   But what is it, on the other hand,
to one who has traveled to it day after day, has

threaded the forest and climbed the hills that are between this and that, has tasted the raspberries and the blueberries that grow on it and the springs that gush from it, has been wearied with climbing its rocky sides, felt the coolness of its summit, and been lost in the clouds there.

When I could sit in a cold chamber, muffled in a cloak, each evening till Thanksgiving time, warmed by my own thoughts, the world was not so much with me.

Sept. 27, 1855. Yesterday I traced the note of what I have falsely thought the *Rana palustris*, or cricket frog, to its true source. As usual it sounded loud and incessant above all ordinary crickets, and led me at once to a bare and soft sandy shore. After long looking and listening, with my head directly over the spot from which the sound still came at intervals, as I had often done before, I concluded, as no creature was visible, that it must issue from the mud, or rather slimy sand. I noticed that the shore near the water was upheaved and cracked as by a small mole track, and, laying it open with my hand, I found a mole cricket, *Gryllotalpa breviformis.* Harris says their burrows " usually terminate beneath a stone or clod of turf." They live on the roots of grass and other vegetables, and in Europe the corresponding species does a great

deal of harm. They " avoid the light of day,
and are active chiefly during the night ; " have
their burrows " in moist and soft ground, particularly about ponds." " There   are   no   house
crickets in America."   Among crickets, " the
males only are musical."   The " shrilling " is
produced by shuffling their wing coverts together lengthwise.   The French call crickets
cri-cri.   Most of them die on the approach of
winter, but a few survive under stones.

See furrows made by many clams now moving
into deep water.

Some single red maples now fairly make a
show along the meadow.   I see a blaze of red
reflected from the troubled water.

Sept. 27, 1856.   The bluebird family revisit
their box and warble as iu spring.

P. M.   To Clamshell by boat.   It is a very
fine afternoon to be on the water, somewhat In-
dian-summer-like.   I do not know what constitutes the peculiarity and charm of this weather ;
the broad water so smooth notwithstanding the
slight wind, as if owing to some oiliness the wind
slid over without rippling it.   There is a slight
coolness in the air, yet the sun is occasionally
very warm.   I am tempted to say that the air
is singularly clear, yet I see it is quite hazy.
Perhaps there is that transparency it is said to
possess when full of moisture, before or after

rain. Through this I see the trees beginning to put on their October colors, and the creak of the mole cricket sounds late along the shore.

The *Aster multiflorus* may be easily confounded with the *Aster tradescanti*. Like it, it whitens the roadside in some places. It has purplish disks, but a less straggling top than the *tradescanti*.

Sept. 27, 1857. How out of all proportion to the value of an idea, when you come to one, in Hindoo literature for instance, is the historical fact about it, the when, where, etc., it was actually expressed, and what precisely it might signify to a sect of worshipers! Anything that is called history of India or of the world is impertinent beside any real poetry or inspired thought which is dateless.

White birches have fairly begun to yellow, and blackberry vines here and there in sunny places look like a streak of blood in the grass. I sit on the hillside at Miles's Swamp. A woodbine, investing the leading stem of an elm in the swamp quite to its top, is seen as an erect, slender red column through the thin and yellowing foliage of the elm. As I sit there, I see the shadow of a hawk flying above and behind me. I think I see more hawks nowadays. Perhaps it is both because the young are grown, and their food, the small birds, are flying in flocks and **are abundant.** I need only sit still a few minutes on any spot which overlooks the river meadows before I see some black circling mote beating along the meadow's edge, now lost for a moment as it turns edgewise in a peculiar light, now reappearing farther or nearer.

It is most natural, *i. e.*, most in accordance with the natural phenomena, to suppose that North America was discovered from the northern part of the eastern continent, for a study of the range of plants, birds, and quadrupeds points to a connection on that side. Many birds are common to the northern parts of both continents. Even the passenger pigeon has flown across there ; and some European plants have been detected on the extreme northeastern coast and islands, which do not extend inland. Men in their migrations obey the same law.

Sept. 27, 1860. Sawing up my raft by river. Monroe's tame ducks sail along and feed near me, as I am working there. Looking up, I see a little dipper, about one half their size, in the middle of the river, evidently attracted by these tame ducks as to a place of security. I sit down and watch it. The tame ducks have paddled four or five rods down stream along the shore. They soon detect the dipper three or four rods off, and betray alarm by a twittering note, especially when it dives, as it does continually. At last, when it is two or three rods off, and approaching them by diving, they all rush to the shore and come out upon it in their fear; but the dipper shows itself close to the shore, and when they enter the water again joins them within two feet, still diving from time to time, and threatening to come up in their midst. They return up stream more or less alarmed, and pursued in this wise by the dipper, who does not know what to make of their fears. It is thus toled along to within twenty feet of where I sit, and I can watch it at my leisure. It has a dark bill, and considerable white on the sides of the head or neck with black between, no tufts, and no observable white on back or tail. When at last disturbed by me, it suddenly sinks low (all its body) in the water without diving. Thus it can float at various heights. So, on the 30th, I saw one suddenly dash along the surface from the meadow ten rods before me to the middle of the river, and then dive, and though I watched fifteen minutes and examined the tufts of grass, I could see no more of it.

Sept. 28, 1840. The world thinks it knows only what it comes in contact with, and whose repelling points give it a configuration to the senses; a hard crust aids its distinct knowledge. But what we truly know has no points of repulsion, and consequently no objective form, being surveyed from within. We are acquainted with the soul and its phenomena as a bird with the air in which it floats. Distinction is superficial and formal merely. We touch objects as the earth we stand on, but the soul as the air we breathe. We know the world superficially, but the soul centrally. In the one case our surfaces meet, in the other our centres coincide.

Sept. 28, 1851. Hugh Miller, in his " Old Red Sandstone," speaking of " the consistency of style which obtains among the ichthyolites of this formation " and the " microscopic beauty of these ancient fishes," says : " The artist who sculptured the cherry-stone consigned it to a cabinet, and placed a microscope beside it ; the microscopic beauty of these ancient fishes was consigned to the twilight depths of a primeval ocean. There is a feeling which at times grows upon the painter and the statuary, as if the perception and love of the beautiful had been sublimed into a kind of moral sense. Art comes to be pursued for its own sake : the exquisite conception in the mind or the elegant and elaborate model becomes all in all to the worker, and the dread of criticism or the appetite for praise almost nothing ; and thus, through the influence of a power somewhat akin to conscience, but whose province is not the just and the good, but the fair, the refined, the exquisite, have works, prosecuted in solitude, and never intended for the world, been found fraught with loveliness." The hesitation with which this is said, to say nothing of its simplicity, betrays a latent infidelity, more fatal far than that of the "Vestiges of Creation" which in another work this author endeavors to correct. He describes that as an exception which is in fact the rule. The supposed want of harmony between "the perception and love of the beautiful" and a delicate moral sense betrays what kind of beauty the writer has been conversant with. He speaks of his work becoming all in all to the worker in rising above the dread of criticism and the appetite of praise, as if these were the very rare exceptions in a great artist's life, and not the very definition of it.

2 P. M. To Conantum. For a week or ten days I have ceased to look for new flowers or carry my Botany in my pocket. The fall dandelion is now very fresh and abundant, in its prime.

This swamp [the spruce swamp in Conant's Grove] contains beautiful specimens of the side-saddle flower, *Sarracenia purpurea*, better called pitcher plant. The leaves ray out around the dry scape and flower, which still remain, resting on rich uneven beds of a coarse reddish moss, through which the small-flowered andromeda puts up, presenting altogether a most rich and luxuriant appearance to the eye. Though the moss is comparatively dry, I cannot walk without upsetting the numerous pitchers, which are now full of water, and so wetting my feet. I once accidentally sat down on such a bed of pitcher plants, and found an uncommonly wet seat where I expected a dry one. These leaves are of various colors, from plain green to a rich striped yellow or deep red. No plants are more richly painted and streaked than the inside of the broad lips of these. Old Josselyn called this "hollow-leaved lavender." I think we have no other plant so singular and remarkable.

Here was a large hornets' nest which, when I went to take, first knocking on it to see if anybody was at home, out came the whole swarm upon me, lively enough. I do not know why they should linger longer than their fellows whom I saw the other day, unless because the swamp is warmer. They were all within, but not working.

What honest, homely, earth-loving, unaspiring houses people used to live in ! — that on Conantum, for instance, so low you can put your hand on the eaves behind. There are few whose pride could stoop to enter such a house to-day. And then the broad chimney, built for comfort, not for beauty, with no coping of bricks to catch the eye, no alto or basso relievo.

Sept. 28, 1852. P. M. To the Boulder Field. I find the hood-leaved violet quite abundant in a meadow, and the pedata in the Boulder Field. Those now seen, all but the blanda, palmata, and pubescens, blooming again. Bluebirds, robins, etc., are heard again in the air. This is the commencement, then, of the second spring. Violets, *Potentilla Canadensis*, lambkill, wild rose, yellow lily, etc., begin again.

A windy day. What have these high and roaring winds to do with the fall? No doubt they speak plainly enough to the sap that is in these trees, and perchance check its upward flow.

Ah, if I could put into words that music which I hear; that music which can bring tears to the eyes of marble statues, to which the very muscles of men are obedient!

Sept. 28, 1858. P. M. To Great Fields via Gentian Lane. The gentian (*Andrewsii*) now generally in prime, on low, moist, shady banks. Its transcendent blue shows best in the shade and suggests coolness; contrasts there with the fresh green; a splendid blue, light in the shade, turning to purple with age. They are particularly abundant under the north side of the willow row in Merrick's pasture. I count fifteen in a single cluster there, and afterward twenty in Gentian Lane near Flint's Bridge, and there were other clusters below; bluer than the bluest sky, they lurk in the moist and shady recesses of the banks.

Sept. 28, 1859. In proportion as a man has a poor ear for music, or loses his ear for it, he is obliged to go far for it, or fetch it from far, or pay a great price for such as he *can* hear. Operas and the like only affect him. It is like the difference between a young and healthy appetite and the appetite of an epicure, an appetite for a sweet crust and for a mock-turtle soup.

As the lion is said to lie in a thicket or in tall reeds and grass by day, slumbering, and sally out at night, just so with the cat. She will ensconce herself for the day in the grass or weeds in some out-of-the-way nook near the house, and arouse herself toward night.

Sept. 29, 1840. Wisdom is a sort of mongrel between Instinct and Prudence, which, however, inclining to the side of the father, will finally assert its pure blood again, as the white race at length prevails over the black. It is minister plenipotentiary from earth to heaven, but occasionally Instinct, like a born celestial, comes to earth and adjusts the controversy.

All fair action in man is the product of enthusiasm. There is enthusiasm in the sunset. The shell on the shore takes new layers and new tints from year to year with such rapture as the bard writes his poem. There is a thrill in the spring when it buds and blossoms. There is a happiness in the summer, a contentedness in the autumn, a patient repose in the winter. All the birds and blossoms and fruits are the product of enthusiasm. Nature does nothing in the prose mood, though she acts sometimes grimly, with poetic fury, as in earthquakes, etc., and at other times humorously.

Sept. 29, 1851. The intense brilliancy of the red - ripe maples scattered here and there in the midst of the green oaks and hickories on the hilly shore of Walden is quite charming. They are unexpectedly and incredibly brilliant, especially on the western shore and close to the water's edge, where, alternating with yellow birches and poplars and green oaks, they remind me of a line of soldiers, redcoats and riflemen in green mixed together.

The pine is one of the richest of trees, to my eye. It stands like a great moss, a luxuriant mildew, the pumpkin pine, which the earth produces without effort.

Sept. 29, 1853. The witch-hazel at Lee's Cliff, in a favorable situation, has but begun to blossom, has not been long out, so that I think it must be later than the gentian. Its leaves are yellowed. Bluets [Houstonia] still. Lambkill blossoms again.

Sept. 29, 1854. When I look at the stars,

nothing which the astronomers have said attaches to them, they are so simple and remote. Their knowledge is felt to be all terrestrial, and to concern the earth alone. This suggests that the same is the case with every object, however familiar ; our so-called knowledge of it is equally vulgar and remote. One might say that all views through a telescope or microscope were purely visionary, for it is only by his eye, and not by any other sense, not by the whole man, that the beholder is there where he is presumed to be. It is a disruptive mode of viewing so far as the beholder is concerned.

Sept. 29, 1856. P. M. To Grape Cliff. I can hardly clamber along this cliff without getting my clothes covered with desmodium ticks, these especially, the rotundifolium and paniculatum. Though you were running for your life, they would have time to catch and cling to your clothes, often the whole row of pods of the *Desmodium paniculatum,* like a piece of saw-blade with three teeth. They will even cling to your hand as you go by. They cling like babes to a mother's breast, by instinct. Instead of being caught ourselves and detained by bird-lime, we are compelled to catch these seeds and carry them with us. These almost invisible nets, as it were, are spread for us, and whole coveys of desmodium and bidens seeds steal transporta-

tion out of us. I have found myself often covered, as it were, with an imbricated coat of the
brown desmodium seeds or a bristling *chevaux-
de-frise* of beggar ticks, and had to spend a
quarter of an hour or more picking them off in
some convenient spot; and so they get just what
they wanted, deposited in another place. How
surely the *desmodium* growing on some rough
cliff-side, or the *bidens* on the edge of a pool,
prophesy the coming of the traveler, brute or
human, that will transport their seeds on his
coat!

Dr. Reynolds told me the other day of a Canada lynx (?) killed in Andover, in a swamp,
some years ago, when he was teaching school in
Tewksbury, thought to be one of a pair, the
other being killed or seen in Derry. Its large
track was seen in the snow in Tewksbury, and
traced to Andover and back. They saw where
it had leaped thirty feet, and where it devoured
rabbits. It was on a tree when shot.

Sept. 29, 1859. *Juniper repens* berries are
quite green yet. I see some of last year's dark
purple ones at the base of the branchlets. There
is a very large specimen on the side of Fair
Haven Hill, above Cardinal shore. It is very
handsome this bright afternoon, especially if you
stand on the lower and sunny side, on account
of the various ways in which its surging flakes

and leaflets, green or silvery, reflect the light.
It is as if we were giants and looked down on
an evergreen forest from whose flaky surface
the light is variously reflected.   Though so
low, it is so dense and rigid that neither men
nor cows think of wading through it.   We got
a bird's-eye view of this evergreen forest, as of
a hawk sailing over, looking into its inapproach-
able clefts and recesses, reflecting a green or
else a cheerful silvery light.

Having just dug my potatoes in the garden,
which did not turn out very well, I took a basket and trowel and went forth to dig my wild
potatoes, or ground nuts, by the railroad fence.
I dug up the tubers of some half a dozen plants,
and found an unexpected yield.   One string
weighed a little more than three quarters of a
pound.   There were thirteen that I should have
put with the large potatoes this year, if they
had been the common kind.   The biggest was
two and three quarters inches long, and seven
inches in circumference the smallest way.   Five
would have been called good-sized potatoes.   It
is but a slender vine, now killed by the frost,
and not promising such a yield ; but deep in the
soil, here sand, five or six inches, or sometimes
a foot, you come to the string of brown and
commonly knobby nuts.   The cuticle of the
tuber is more or less cracked longitudinally,

forming meridional furrows, and the root or shoot bears a large proportion to the tuber. In case of a famine I should soon resort to these roots. If they increased in size, on being cultivated, as much as the common potato, they would become monstrous.

Sept. 30, 1851. The white ash has got its autumnal mulberry hue. What is the autumnal tint of the black ash? The former contrasts strongly with the other shade trees on the village street, the elms and buttonwoods, at this season, looking almost black at the first glance. The different characters of the trees appear better now, when their leaves, so to speak, are ripe, than at any other season; than in the winter, for instance, when they are little remarkable, and almost uniformly gray or brown, or in the spring and summer, when they are undistinguishably green. Now, a red maple, an ash, a white birch, a *Populus grandidentata*, etc., is distinguished almost as far as it is visible. It is with leaves as with fruits and woods, animals and men : when they are mature, their different characters appear.

Sept. 30, 1852. 10 A. M. To Fair Haven Pond, bee-hunting, — Pratt, Rice, Hastings, and myself in a wagon. A fine, clear day after the coolest night and severest frost we have had. Our apparatus was first a simple round tin box, about four and a half inches in diameter and one and a half inches deep, containing a piece of empty honeycomb of its own size and form, filling it within one third of an inch of the top; then a wooden box, about two and a half inches square, with a glass window occupying two thirds of the upper side under a slide, with a couple of narrow slits in the wood, each side of the glass, to admit air, but too narrow for the bees to pass, the whole resting on a circular bottom a little larger than the lid of the tin box, with a sliding door in it. We were earnest to go this week, before the flowers were gone, and we feared the frosty night might make the bees slow to come forth. . . . After eating our lunch we set out on our return [having been unsuccessful thus far]. By the roadside at Walden, on the sunny hillside sloping to the pond, we saw a large mass of golden-rod and aster, several rods square and comparatively fresh. Getting out of our wagon, we found it to be resounding with the hum of bees. It was about one o'clock. Here were far more flowers than we had seen elsewhere, and bees in great numbers, both bumble-bees and honey-bees, as well as butterflies, wasps, and flies. So pouring a mixture of honey and water into the empty comb in the tin box, and holding the lid of the tin box in one hand and the wooden box with the slides shut in the other, we proceeded to catch the honey-bees by shutting them in suddenly between the lid of the tin box and the large circular bottom of the wooden one, cutting off the flower stem with the edge of the lid at the same time. Then holding the lid still against the wooden box, we drew the slide in the bottom, and also the slide covering the window at the top, that the light might attract the bee to pass up into the wooden box. As soon as he had done so, and was buzzing against the glass, the lower side was closed, and more bees were caught in the same way. Then placing the open tin box close under the wooden one, the slide was drawn again, and the upper slide closed, making it dark, and in about a minute they went to feeding, as was ascertained by raising slightly the wooden box. Then the latter was wholly removed, and they were left feeding or sucking up the honey in broad daylight. In from two to three minutes one had loaded himself and commenced leaving the box. He would buzz round it back and forth a foot or more, and then sometimes, perhaps, finding that he was too heavily loaded, alight to empty himself or clear his feet. Then, starting once more, he would circle round irregularly at first, in a small circle, only a foot or two in diameter, as if to examine the premises, that he might

know them again, till at length, rising higher
and higher, and circling wider and wider, and
swifter and swifter, till his orbit was ten or
twelve feet in diameter, and as much from the
ground, though its centre might be moved to
one side (all this as if to ascertain the course to
his nest), in a minute or less from his first starting, he darted off in a bee line, a waving or sinu-
ous line right and left, toward his nest ; that is,
as far as I could see him, which might be eight
or ten rods, looking against the sky. You had
to follow his whole career very attentively indeed, to see when and where he went off at a
tangent. It was very difficult to follow him,
especially if you looked against a wood or the
hill, and you had to lie low to fetch him against
the sky. You must operate in an open place,
not in a wood. We sent forth as many as a
dozen bees, which flew in about three directions,
but all toward the village, or where we knew
there were hives. They did not fly almost
straight, as I had heard, but within three or four
feet of the same course, for half a dozen rods, or
as far as we could see. Those belonging to one
hive all had to digress to get round an apple-
tree. As none flew in the right direction for us,
we did not attempt to line them. In less than
half an hour the first returned to the box, which
was lying on a woodpile. Not one of the bees

in the surrounding flowers had discovered it. So they came back one after another, loaded themselves and departed. But now they went off with very little preliminary circling, as if assured of their course. We were furnished with little boxes of red, blue, green, yellow, and white paint in dry powder, and with a stick we sprinkled a little of the red powder on the back of one while he was feeding, gave him a little dab, and it settled down amid the fuzz of his back, and gave him a distinct red jacket. He went off like most of them toward some hives about three quarters of a mile distant, and we observed, by the watch, the time of his departure. In just twenty-two minutes red jacket came back, with enough of the powder still on his back to mark him plainly. He may have gone more than three quarters of a mile. At any rate, he had a head wind to contend with while laden. They fly swiftly and surely to their nests, never resting by the way, and I was surprised, though I had been informed of it, at the distance to which the village bees go for flowers. The rambler in the most remote woods and pastures little thinks that the bees which are humming so industriously on the rare wild flowers he is plucking for the herbarium in some out-of-the-way nook, are, like himself, ramblers from the village, perhaps from his own yard, come to get their honey for his hives. All the honey-bees we saw were on the blue-stemmed golden-rod, *Solidago cæsia,* which lasts long and which emitted a sweet, agreeable fragrance, not on the asters. I feel the richer for this experience. It taught me that even the insects in my path are not loafers, but have their special errands, not merely and vaguely in this world, but in this hour each is about his business. If there are any sweet flowers still lingering on the hillsides, it is known to the bees, both of the forest and the village. The botanist should make interest with the bees if he would know when the flowers open and when they close. Those above named were the only common and prevailing flowers on which to look for them. Our red jacket had performed the voyage in safety. No bird had picked him up. Are the kingbirds gone? Now is the time to hunt bees and take them up, when their combs are full of honey, and before the flowers are so scarce that they begin to consume the honey they have stored. Forty pounds of honey was the most our company had got hereabouts. We also caught and sent forth a bumble-bee which manœuvred like the others, though we thought he took time to eat some before he loaded himself, and then he was so overloaded and bedaubed that he had to alight after he had started, and it took him several minutes to clear himself. It is not in vain that the flowers bloom, and bloom late, too, in favored spots. To us they are a culture and a luxury, but to bees meat and drink. The tiny bee which we thought lived far away there in a flower-bell, in that remote vale, is a great voyager, and anon he rises up over the top of the wood, and sets sail with his sweet cargo straight for his distant haven. How well they know the woods and fields, and the haunt of every flower! The flowers are widely dispersed, perhaps because the sweet which they collect from the atmosphere is rare and also widely dispersed, and the bees are enabled to travel far to find it, a precious burden which the heavens bear and deposit on the earth.

Sept. 30, 1858. A large flock of grackles amid the willows by the river-side, or chiefly concealed low in the button bushes beneath them, though quite near me. There they keep up their spluttering notes, though somewhat less loud, I fancy, than in spring. These are the first I have seen, and now for some time I think the redwings have been gone. These are the first arrivers from the north, where they breed.

I observe the peculiar steel-bluish purple of the night-shade, *i. e.*, the tips of the twigs, while all beneath is green, dotted with bright berries over the water. Perhaps this is the most sin-

gular among the autumnal tints. It is almost
black in some lights, distinctly steel-blue in the
shade, contrasting with the green beneath; but
seen against the sun, it is a rich purple, its veins
full of fire. The form of the leaf is peculiar.

The pearly everlasting is an interesting white
at present. Though the stem and leaves are
still green, it is dry and unwithering like an
artificial flower; its white flexuous stem and
branches, too, like wire wound with cotton.
Neither is there any scent to betray it. Its
amaranthine quality is instead of high color.
Its very brown centre now affects me as a
fresh and original color. It monopolizes small
circles in the midst of sweet fern, perchance, on
a dry hillside.

In our late walk on the Cape [Ann], we
entered Gloucester each time in the dark at
mid-evening, traveling partly across lots till we
fell into the road, and as we were simply seeking a bed, inquiring the way of villagers whom
we could not see. The town seemed far more
home-like to us than when we made our way
out of it in the morning. It was comparatively
still, and the inhabitants were sensibly or poetically employed, too. Then we went straight
to our chamber, and saw the moonlight reflected
from the smooth harbor and lighting up the
fishing-vessels, as if it had been the harbor of

Venice. By day we went remarking on the peculiar angles of the beveled roofs, of which there is a remarkable variety there. There are also many large square three-story houses, with short windows in the upper story, as if the third story were as good as a gig for respectability. When entering the town by moonlight, we could not always tell whether the road skirted the back yards or the front yards of the houses, and the houses did not so impertinently stare after the traveler and watch his coming as by day. Walking early in the day and approaching the rocky shore from the north, the shadows of the cliffs were very distinct and grateful, and our spirits were buoyant. Though we walked all day, it seemed the days were not long enough to get tired in. Some villages we went through or by, without communicating with any inhabitant, but saw them as quietly and distantly as in a picture.

Oct. 1, 1851. 5 P. M. Just put a fugitive slave, who has taken the name of Henry Williams, into the cars for Canada. He escaped from Stafford County, Virginia, to Boston last October. Has been in Shadrack's place at the Cornhill Coffee House ; had been corresponding through an agent with his master, who is his father, about buying himself, his master asking $600, but he having been able to raise but $500; heard that there were writs out for two Williamses, fugitives, and was informed by his fellow-servants and employer that Auger-hole Burns and others of the police had called for him when he was out. Accordingly he fled to Concord last night on foot, bringing a letter to our family from Mr. Lovejoy, of Cambridge, and another which Garrison had formerly given him on another occasion. He lodged with us and waited in the house till funds were collected with which to forward him. Intended to dispatch him at noon through to Burlington, but when I went to buy his ticket saw one at the station who looked and behaved so much like a Boston policeman that I did not venture that time. He was an intelligent and very well behaved man, a mulatto; said he could guide himself by many other stars than the north star, knowing their rising and setting. They steered for the north star even when it appeared to have got round to the south. They frequently followed the telegraph when there was no railroad.

Oct. 1, 1856. Examined an *Asclepias Cornuti* pod, already opening. As they dry, the pods crack open by the seam along their convex or outer side, revealing the seeds with their silky parachutes, closely packed in an imbricated manner, already right side up, to the number in one instance of 134, as I counted, and again

270.   As they lie, they resemble somewhat a round plump fish, with the silk ends exposed at the tail.   Children call them fishes.   The silk is divided once or twice by the raised partition of the spongy core around which they are arranged.   At the top of some more open and drier is already a little clump of loosened seeds and down two or three inches in diameter, held by the converging tips of the down, like meridians, and just ready to float away when the wind rises.

I do not perceive the poetic and dramatic capabilities of an anecdote or story which is told me, its significance, till some time afterwards. One of the qualities of a pregnant fact is that it does not surprise us, and we only perceive afterwards how interesting it is, and then must know all the particulars.   We do not enjoy poetry fully unless we know it to be poetry.

Oct. 1, 1858.   Let a full-grown but young cock stand near you.   How full of life he is from the tip of his bill through his trembling wattles and comb and his bright eye to the extremity of his clean toes !   How alert and restless, listening to every sound and watching every motion ! How various his notes, from the finest and shrillest alarum, as a hawk sails over, surpassing the most accomplished violinist on the short strings, to a hoarse and terrene voice or cluck !   He has a word for every occasion ; for the dog that rushes past, and Partlet cackling in the barn. And then, how, elevating himself and flapping his wings, he gathers impetus and air, and launches forth that world - renowned and ear - piercing strain ; not a vulgar note of defiance, but the mere effervescence of life, like the bursting of bubbles in a wine vat. Is any gem so bright as his eye ?

The cat sleeps on her head! What does that portend ? It is more alarming than a dozen comets. How long prejudice survives! The big-bodied fisherman asks me doubtingly about the comet seen these nights in the northwest — if there is any danger to be apprehended from that side. I would fain suggest that only he is dangerous to himself.

Oct. 1, 1860. Remarkable frost and ice this morning; quite a wintry prospect. The leaves of trees stiff and white at 7 A. M. I hear it was 21° + this morning early. I do not remember such cold at this season. One man tells me he regretted that he had not taken his mittens with him when he went to his morning's work, mowing in a meadow, and when he went to a spring, at 11 A. M., found the dipper with two inches of ice in it frozen solid.

Oct. 2, 1851. P. M. Some of the white pines on Fair Haven Hill have just reached the acme of their fall ; others have almost entirely shed their leaves. The same is the state of the pitch pines.

Oct. 2, 1852. The beggar ticks, bidens, now adhere to my clothes. I also find the desmodium sooner thus — as a magnet discovers the steel filings in a heap of ashes — than if I used my eyes alone.

How much more beautiful the lakes now, like Fair Haven, surrounded by the autumn-tinted woods and hills, as in an ornamental frame !

Some maples in sprout lands are of a delicate, clear, unspotted red inclining to crimson, surpassing most flowers. I would fain pluck the whole tree and carry it home for a nosegay.

Oct. 2, 1856. Succory still, with its cool blue, here and there, and *Hieracium Canadense* still quite fresh, with its pretty, broad, strapshaped rays, broadest at the end, alternately long and short, with five very regular sharp teeth in the end of each. The scarlet leaves and stem of the rhexia, some time out of flower, make almost as bright a patch in the meadow now as the flowers did. Its seed vessels are perfect little cream pitchers of graceful form.

The prinos berries are in their prime, seven sixteenths of an inch in diameter. They are scarlet, somewhat lighter than the arum berries. They are now very fresh and bright, and what

adds to their effect is the perfect freshness and
greenness of the leaves amid which they are
seen. *Gerardia purpurea* still. *Solidago speciosa* completely out, though not a flower was
out September 27th, or five days ago ; say three
or four days. Now and then I see a *Hypericum
Canadense* flower still. The leaves of this and
the angalosam are turned crimson.

I am amused to see four little Irish boys, only
five or six years old, getting a horse in a pasture, for their father apparently, who is at work
in a neighboring field. They have, all in a row,
got hold of a very long halter, and are leading
him. All wish to have a hand in it. It is surprising that he obeys such small specimens of
humanity, but he seems to be very docile, a real
family horse. At length, by dint of pulling
and shouting, they get him into a run down a
hill, and though he moves very deliberately,
scarcely faster than a walk, all but the one at
the end of the line soon run to right and left,
without having looked behind, expecting him to
be upon them. They stop at last at the bars,
which are down, and then the family puppy,
a brown pointer (?), about two thirds grown,
comes bounding to join them and assist. He is
as youthful and about as knowing as any of
them. The horse marches gravely behind, obeying the faint tug at the halter, or honestly stands

still from time to time, as if not aware that they are pulling at all, though they are all together straining every nerve to start him. It is interesting to behold the faithful beast, the oldest and wisest of the company, thus implicitly obeying the lead of the youngest and weakest.

Corydalis still fresh.

Oct. 2, 1857. Generally speaking, it is only the lower edge of the woods that now shows the bright autumnal tints, while the superstructure is green, the birches, very young oaks and hickories, huckleberry bushes, blueberries, etc., that stand around the edges, though here and there some taller maple flames upward amid the masses of green, or some other riper and mellower tree.

The chief incidents of Minott's life must be more distinct and interesting now than immediately after they occurred, for he has recalled and related them so often that they are stereotyped in his mind. Never having traveled far from his hillside, he does not suspect himself, but tells his stories with fidelity and gusto to the minutest details, as Herodotus does in his histories.

Oct. 3, 1840. No man has imagined what private discourse his members have with surrounding nature, or how much the tenor of that intercourse affects his own health and sickness. While the head goes star-gazing, the legs are not necessarily astronomers, too, but are acquiring independent experience in lower strata of nature. How much do they feel which they do not impart! How much rumor dies between the knees and the ears! Surely instinct was this experience. I am no more a freeman of my members than of universal nature. After all, the body takes care of itself. It eats, drinks, sleeps, digests, grows, dies, and the best economy is to let it alone in all these.

Why need I travel to seek a site, and consult the points of the compass? My eyes are south windows, and out of these I command a southern prospect. The eye does the least drudgery of any of the senses. It oftenest escapes to a higher employment. The rest serve and escort and defend it. I attach some superiority, even priority, to this sense. It is the oldest servant in the soul's household; it images what it imagines, it ideates what it idealizes. Through it idolatry crept in, which is a kind of religion. If any joy or grief is to be expressed, the eye is the swift runner that carries the news. In circumspection, double, in fidelity, single, it serves truth always, and carries no false news. Of five castes, it is the Brahmin. It converses with the heavens. How man serves this sense more than any other! When he builds a house, he does not forget to put a window in the wall. We see truth. We are children of light. Our destiny is dark. No other sense has so much to do with the future. The body of science will not be complete till every sense has thus ruled our thought and language and action in its turn.

Oct. 3, 1852. P. M. To Flint's Pond. I hear a hylodes (?) from time to time. Hear the loud laughing of a loon on the pond from time to time, apparently alone in the middle. A wild sound, heard far, and suited to the wildest lake.

Seen from Heywood's Peak at Walden, the shore is now more beautifully painted. The most prominent trees are the red maples and the yellowish aspens.

The pine fall or change has commenced, and the trees are mottled green and yellowish.

Oct. 3, 1853. *Viola lanceolata* in Moore's Swamp.

Oct. 3, 1857. How much more agreeable to sit in the midst of old furniture like Minott's clock and secretary and looking-glass, which have come down from other generations, than amid that which was just brought from the cabinetmaker's, and smells of varnish, like a coffin! To sit under the face of an old clock that has been ticking one hundred and fifty years, — there is something mortal, not to say immortal, about it; a clock that began to tick when Massachusetts was a province.

Oct. 3, 1858.   How many men have a fatal excess of manner! There was one came to our house the other evening, and behaved very simply and well till the moment he was passing out the door. He then suddenly put on the airs of a well-bred man, and consciously described some arc of beauty or other with his head or hand. It was but a slight flourish, but it has put me on the alert.

It is interesting to consider how that *crotalaria* spreads itself, sure to find out the most suitable soil. One year I find it on the Great Fields, and think it rare. The next I find it in a new and unexpected place. It flits about like a flock of sparrows from field to field.

Standing on the railroad, I look across the pond to Pine Hill, where the outside trees, and the shrubs scattered generally through the wood, glow yellow and scarlet through the green, like fires just kindled at the base of the trees, a general conflagration just fairly under way, soon to envelop every tree. The hillside forest is all aglow along its edge, and in all its cracks and fissures, and soon the flames will leap upwards to the tops of the tallest trees.

I hear out towards the middle, or a dozen rods from me, the plashing made apparently by the shiners; for they look and shine like them, leaping in schools on the surface. Many lift themselves quite out for a foot or two, but most rise only part way out, twenty black points at once. There are several schools indulging in this sport from time to time, as they swim slowly along. This I ascertain by paddling out to them. Perhaps they leap and dance in the water just as gnats dance in the air at present. I have seen it before in the fall. Is it peculiar to this season ?

The large leaves of some black oak sprouts are dark purple, almost blackish above, but greenish beneath.

Oct. 3, 1859. P. M. To Bateman's Pond ; back by the hog pasture and old Carlisle road.

Some faces that I see are so gross that they affect me like a part of the person improperly exposed, and it seems to me that they might be covered, and, if necessary, some other and perhaps better looking part of the person be exposed.

Looking from the hog pasture over the valley of Spencer Brook westward, we see the smoke rising from a huge chimney above a gray roof and the woods at a distance, where some family is preparing its evening meal. There are few more agreeable sights than this to the pedestrian traveler. No cloud is fairer to him than that little bluish one which arises from the chimney. It suggests all of domestic felicity beneath.

There we imagine that life is lived of which we have only dreamed. In our minds we clothe each unseen inhabitant with all the success, all the serenity, we can conceive of. If old, we imagine him serene ; if young, hopeful. We have only to see a gray roof with its plume of smoke curling up, to have this faith. There we suspect no coarse haste or bustle, but serene labors which proceed at the same pace with the declining day. There is no hireling in the barn nor in the kitchen. Why are distant valleys, why lakes, why mountains in the horizon, ever fair to us? Because we imagine for a moment that they may be the home of man, and that man's life may be in harmony with them. The sky and clouds and earth itself, with their beauty, forever preach to us, saying, Such an abode we offer you, to such a life we encourage you. Here is not haggard poverty and harassing debt ; here is not intemperance, moroseness, meanness, or vulgarity. Men go about sketching, painting landscapes, or writing verses which celebrate man's opportunities. To go into an actual farmer's family at evening, see the tired laborers come in from their day's work thinking of their wages, the sluttish help in the kitchen and sink-room, the indifferent stolidity and patient misery which only the spirits of the youngest children rise above, suggests one train of thought ; it suggests

another to look down on that roof from a distance, on an October evening, when its smoke is
ascending peacefully to join the kindred clouds
above. We are ever busy hiring house and
lands, and peopling them in our imaginations.
There is no beauty in the sky, but in the eye
that sees it. Health, high spirits, serenity, are
the great landscape painters. Turners, Claudes,
Rembrandts, are nothing to them. We never
see any . beauty but as the garment of some
virtue. Consider the infinite promise of a man,
so that the sight of his roof at a distance suggests an idyl or a pastoral, or of his grave, an
Elegy in a Country Churchyard. How all poets
have idealized the farmer's life! What graceful
figures and unworldly characters they have assigned to them! Serene as the sky, emulating
nature with their calm and peaceful lives.

Oct. 4, 1840. It is vastly easier to discover
than to see when the cover is off.

Oct. 4, 1851. Minott was telling me to-day
that he used to know a man in Lincoln who had
no floor to his barn, but waited till the ground
froze, then swept it clean in the barn and
threshed his grain on it. He also used to see
men threshing their buckwheat in the field where
it grew, having just taken off the surface down
to a hard pan. He used the word *gavel* to describe a parcel of stalks cast on the ground to

dry.   His are good old English words, and I am
always sure to find them in the dictionary,
though I never heard them before in my life.   I
was admiring his cornstalks disposed about the
barn, to-day, over or astride the braces and the
timbers, of such a fresh, clean, and handsome
green, retaining their strength and nutritive
properties, so unlike the gross and careless hus-
bandry of speculating, money-making farmers,
who suffer their stalks to remain out till they
are dry and dingy and black as chips.   Minott
is perhaps the most poetical farmer, the one who
most realizes to me the poetry of the farmer's
life, that I know.   He does nothing with haste
and drudgery, but everything as if he loved it.
He makes the most of his labor, and takes infinite satisfaction in every part of it.   He is not
looking forward to the sale of his crops, but he
is paid by the constant satisfaction which his
labor yields him.   He has not too much land to
trouble him, too much work to do, no hired man
nor boy, but simply to amuse himself and live.
He cares not so much to raise a large crop as to
do his work well.   He knows every pin and nail
in his barn.   If any part of it is to be floored,
he lets no hired man rob him of that amusement,
but he goes slowly to the woods, and at his
leisure selects a pitch-pine tree, cuts it, and
hauls it or gets it hauled to the mill; and so he

knows the history of his barn floor. Farming is an amusement which has lasted him longer than gunning or fishing. He is never in a hurry to get his garden planted, and yet it is always planted soon enough, and none in the town is kept so beàutifully clean. He always prophesies a failure of the crops, and yet is satisfied with what he gets. His barn floor is fastened down with oak pins, and he prefers them to iron spikes, which he says will rust and give way. He handles and amuses himself with every ear of his corn crop as much as a child with his playthings, and so his small crop goes a great way. He might well cry if it were carried to market. The seed of weeds is no longer in his soil. He loves to walk in a swamp in windy weather, and hear the wind groan through the pines. He indulges in no luxury of food, or dress, or furniture, yet he is not penurious, but merely simple. If his sister dies before him, he may have to go to the almshouse in his old age, yet he is not poor, for he does not want riches. With never failing rheumatism and trembling hands, he seems yet to enjoy perennial health. Though he never reads a book since he finished the " Naval Monument," he speaks the best of English.

Oct. 4, 1858. Just at the edge of evening, I saw on the sidewalk something bright like fire,

as if molten lead were scattered along, and then
I wondered if a drunkard's spittle were luminous, and proceeded to poke it on to a leaf with
a stick. It was rotten wood. I found that it
came from the bottom of some old fence posts
which had just been dug up near by; and there
glowed for a foot or two, being quite rotten and
soft. It suggested that a lamp-post might be
more luminous at bottom than at top. I cut
out a handful and carried it about. It was a
very pale brown, some almost white, in the
light, quite soft and flaky ; and as I withdrew it
gradually from the light, it began to glow with
a distinctly blue fire in its recesses, becoming
more universal and whiter as the darkness increased. Carried toward a candle, its light is
quite blue. A man whom I met in the street
was able to tell the time by his watch, holding
it over what was in my hand. The posts were
oak, probably white. Mr. M——, the mason,
told me that he heard his dog barking the other
night, and going out found that it was at the
bottom of an old post he had dug up during
the day, which was all aglow.

See B—— a-fishing notwithstanding the wind.
A man runs down, fails, loses self-respect, and
goes a-fishing, though he were never on the river
before. Yet methinks his misfortune is good
fortune, and he is the more mellow and humane.

Perhaps he begins to perceive more clearly that the object of life is something else than acquiring property, and he really stands in a truer relation to his fellow-men than when he commanded a false respect from them. There he stands at length, perchance better employed than ever, holding communion with nature and himself, and coming to understand his real position and relation to men in the world. It is better than a poor debtors' prison, better than most successful money-getting.

The hickories on the northwest side of this hill are in the prime of their color, of a rich orange ; some with green intimately mixed, handsomer than those that are wholly changed. The outmost parts and edges of the foliage are orange ; the recesses green, as if the outmost parts, being turned toward the sunny fire, were first baked by it.

Oct. 4, 1859. When I have made a visit where my expectations are not met, I feel as if I owed my hosts an apology for troubling them so. If I am disappointed, I find that I have no right to visit them.

I have always found that what are called the best of manners are the worst, for they are simply the shell without the meat. They cover no life at all. They are the universal slave-holders who treat men as things. Nobody holds you more cheap than the man of manners. They are marks by the help of which the wearers ignore you, and remain concealed themselves.

All men sympathize by their lower natures, few only by the higher. The appetites of the mistress are commonly the same as those of her servant, but her society is commonly more select. The help may have some of the tenderloin, but she must eat it in the kitchen.

p. m. To Conantum. How interesting now, by wall-sides and on open springy hillsides, the large straggling tufts of the Dicksonia fern above the leaf-strewn green sward, the cold, fall-green sward! They are unusually preserved about the Corner Spring, considering the earliness of this year. Long, handsome, lanceolate green fronds pointing in every direction, recurved and full of fruit, intermixed with yellowish and sere brown and shriveled ones, the whole clump perchance strewn with fallen and withered maple leaves, and overtopped by now withered and unnoticed osmundas. Their lingering greenness is so much the more noticeable now that the leaves generally have changed. They affect us as if they were evergreen, such persistent life and greenness in the midst of decay. No matter how much they are strewn with withered leaves, moist and green they spire above them, not fearing the frosts, fragile as they are. Their greenness is so much the more interesting, because so many have already fallen, and we know that the first severer frost will cut off them too. In the summer greenness is cheap, now it is a thing comparatively rare, and is the emblem of life to us.

It is only when we forget all our learning that we begin to know. I do not get nearer by a hair's breadth to any natural object, so long as I presume that I have an introduction to it from some learned man. To conceive of it with a total apprehension, I must for the thousandth time approach it as something totally strange. If you would make acquaintance with the ferns, you must forget your botany. Not a single scientific term or distinction is the least to the purpose. You would fain perceive something, and you must approach the object totally unprejudiced. You must be aware that no thing is what you have taken it to be. In what book is this world and its beauty described? Who has plotted the steps toward the discovery of beauty? You must be in a different state from common. Your greatest success will be simply to perceive that such things are, and you will have no communication to make to the Royal Society. If it were required to know the position of the fruit dots or the character of the indusium, nothing could be easier than to ascertain it; but if

it is required that you be affected by ferns, that
they amount to anything, signify anything, to
you, that they be another sacred scripture and
revelation to you, helping to redeem your life,
this end is not so easily accomplished.

I see and hear probably flocks of grackles
with their split and shuffling note, but no redwings for a long time ; chipbirds (but without
chestnut crowns ; is that the case with the
young ?), baywings on the walls and fences,
and the yellow-browed sparrow. Hear the pine
warblers in the pines, about the needles, and
see them on the ground and on rocks, with a
yellow ring round the eye, reddish legs, and a
slight whitish bar on the wings. Going over
the large hillside stubble field west of Holden
wood, I start up a large flock of shore larks,
hear their *sveet sveet* and *sveet sveet sveet*, and
see their tails dark beneath. They are very
wary, and run in the stubble, for the most part
invisible, while one or two appear to act the
sentinel at some rock, peeping out behind it, perhaps, and give their note of alarm, when away
goes the whole flock. Such a flock circled back
and forth several times over my head, just like
ducks reconnoitring before they alight. If you
look with a glass, you are surprised to see how
alert the spies are. These larks have dusky bills
and legs.

The birds seem to delight in these first fine days of the fall, in the warm hazy light, — robins, bluebirds (in families on the almost bare elms), phœbes, and probably purple finches.   I hear half-strains from many of them, as the song sparrow, bluebird, etc., and the sweet *phe-be* of the chickadee.   Now the year itself begins to be ripe, ripened by the frost like a persimmon.

The maiden-hair fern at Conantum is apparently unhurt by frost as yet.

Oct. 5, 1840.   A part of me, which has reposed in silence all day, goes abroad at night like the owl, and has its day.   At night we recline and nestle, and infold ourselves in our being.   Each night I go home to rest.   Each night I am gathered to my fathers.   The soul departs out of the body, and sleeps in God, a divine slumber.   As she withdraws herself, the limbs droop and the eyelids fall, and Nature reclaims her clay again.   Man has always regarded the night as ambrosial or divine.   The air is then peopled, fairies come out.

Oct. 5, 1851.   I observe that the woodchuck has two or more holes a rod or two apart : one, or the front door, where the excavated sand is heaped up ; another not so easily discovered, very small, without any sand about it, by which he emerges, smaller directly at the surface than beneath, on the principle by which a well is dug, making as small a hole as possible at the surface, to prevent caving.

Still, purplish asters, late golden-rods, fragrant life-everlasting, purple gerardia, great bidens, etc.

I hear the red-winged blackbirds by the riverside again, as if it were a new spring. They seem to have come to bid farewell. The birds appear to depart with the coming of the frosts which kill the vegetation, and directly or indirectly the insects on which they feed. The American bittern, *Ardea minor*, flew across the river, trailing his legs in the water, scared up by us. This, according to Peabody, is the boomer [stake-driver]. In their sluggish flight, they can hardly keep their legs up. I wonder if they can soar.

8 p. m. To Cliffs. Moon three quarters full. The nights now are very still, for there is hardly any noise of birds or insects. The whippoorwill is not heard, nor the mosquito; only the occasional lisping of some sparrow. As I go through the woods, I perceive a sweet dry scent from the under woods like that of the fragrant life-everlasting. I suppose it is that. I frequently see a light on the ground within thick and dark woods, where all around is in shadow, and hasten forward, expecting to find some decayed and phosphorescent stump, but find it to

be some clear moonlight that falls through a crevice in the leaves.

The fairies are a quiet, gentle folk, invented plainly to inhabit the moonlight. As moonlight is to sunlight, so are the fairies to men.

Oct. 5, 1852. I was told at Bunker Hill Monument to-day that Mr. Savage saw the White Mountains several times while working on the monument. It required very clear weather in the northwest, and a storm clearing up here.

Oct. 5, 1853. The howling of the wind about the house just before a storm to-night sounds extremely like a loon on the pond. How fit!

Oct. 5, 1856. P. M. To Hill and over the pastures westward. In the huckleberry pasture, by the fence of old barn boards, I notice many little pale-brown, dome-shaped puffballs puckered to a centre beneath. When you pinch them, a smoke-like, brown, snuff-colored dust rises from the orifice at their top, just like smoke from a chimney. It is so fine and light that it rises into the air, and is wafted away like smoke from a chimney. They are low Oriental domes or mosques, sometimes crowded together in nests, like a collection of humble cottages on the moor; for there is suggested some humble hearth beneath, from which this smoke comes up, as it were the homes of slugs and crickets.

They please me not a little by their resemblance
to rude, dome-shaped, turf-built cottages on the
plain, where some humble but everlasting life is
lived.   I imagine a hearth and pot, and some
snug but humble family passing its Sunday evening beneath each one.   I locate there at once all
that is simple and admirable in human life.
There is no virtue which these roofs exclude.
I imagine with what contentment and faith I
could come home to them at evening.   On one
I find a slug feeding, with a little hole beneath
him ; this is a different species, the white pigeon-
egg kind, with rough, crystallized surface.   A
cricket has eaten out the whole inside of another in which he is housed.   This before they
are turned to dust.

It is well to find your employment and amusement in simple and homely things.   These wear
best and yield most.   I think I would rather
watch the motions of these cows in their pasture
for a day, which I now see all headed one way
and slowly advancing, watch them and project
their course carefully on a chart, and report
all their behavior faithfully, than wander to
Europe or Asia, and watch other motions there ;
for it is only ourselves that we report in either
case, and perchance we shall report a more restless, worthless self in the latter case than the
former.

Oct. 5, 1857. There is not now that profusion, and consequent confusion, of events
which belongs to a summer walk. There are
few flowers, birds, insects, or fruits now, and
hence what does occur affects us as more simple and significant, as the cawing of a crow or
the scream of a jay. The latter seems to scream
more fitly and with more freedom through the
vacancies occasioned by fallen maple leaves.

I hear the alarum of a small red squirrel, and
see him running by fits and starts along a chestnut bough toward me. His head looks dispro-
portionally large for his body, like a bull-dog's,
perhaps because he has his chaps full of nuts.
He chirrups and vibrates his tail, holds himself
in, and scratches along a foot as if it was a
mile. He finds noise and activity for both of
us. It is evident that all this ado does not
proceed from fear. There is at the bottom,
no doubt, an excess of inquisitiveness and cau-
tion, but the greater part is make-believe, and
a love of the marvelous. He can hardly keep
it up till I am gone, however, but takes out his
nut and tastes it in the midst of his agitation.
" See there, see there," says he. " Who 's that ?
Oh, dear, what shall I do ? " and makes believe
run off, but does not get along an inch, lets
it all pass off by flashes through his tail, while
he clings to the bark as if he were holding in

a race-horse. He gets down the trunk at last upon a projecting knob, head downward, within a rod of you, and chirrups and chatters louder than ever, trying to work himself into a fright. The hind part of his body is urging the forward part along, snapping the tail over it like a whip-lash, but the fore part mostly clings fast to the bark with desperate energy. Squirr, " to throw with a jerk," seems to have quite as much to do with the name as the Greek " skia," " oura," shadow and tail.

Oct. 5, 1858. In the evening I am glad to find that my phosphorescent wood of last night still glows somewhat, but I improve it much by putting it in water. The little chips which remain in the water or sink to the bottom are like so many stars in the sky.

The comet makes a great show these nights. Its tail is at least as long as the whole of the Great Dipper, to whose handle, till within a night or two, it reached in a great curve, and we plainly see stars through it.

Oct. 6, 1840. The revolution of the seasons is a great and steady flow, a graceful, peaceful motion, like the swell on lakes and seas. Nowhere does any rigidity grow upon nature, no muscles harden, no bones protrude, but she is supple-jointed now and always. No rubbish accumulates from day to day, but still does fresh-

ness predominate on her cheek, and cleanliness
in her attire. The dust settles on the fences
and the rocks and the pastures by the roadside,
but still the sward is just as green, nay greener,
for all that. The morning air is clear even at
this day. It is not begrimed with all the dust
that has been raised. The dew makes all clean
again. Nature keeps her besom always wagging.
She has no lumber-room, no dust-hole, in her
house. No man was ever yet too nice to walk
in her woods and fields. His religion allows
the Arab to cleanse his body with sand, when
water is not at hand.

Oct. 6, 1851. ⋅ 7.30 P. M. To Fair Haven
Pond by boat, the moon four fifths full ; not a
cloud in the sky. The water is perfectly still,
and the air almost so, the former gleaming like
oil in the moonlight, and the moon's disk reflected in it. When we started, saw some fishermen kindling their fire for spearing, by the river-
side. It was a lurid, reddish blaze, contrasting
with the white light of the moon, with a dense
volume of black smoke from the burning pitch-
pine roots, rolling upward in the form of an inverted pyramid. The blaze was reflected in the
water almost as distinct as the substance. It
looked like tarring a ship on the shore of Styx
or Cocytus ; for it is dark notwithstanding the
moon, and there is no sound but the crackling

of the fire. The fishermen can be seen only near at hand, though their fire is visible far away, and then they appear as dusky, fuliginous figures, half enveloped in smoke, seen only by their enlightened sides. Like devils they look, clad in old clothes to defend themselves from the fogs, one standing up forward holding the spear ready to dart, while the smoke and flames are blown in his face, the other paddling the boat slowly and silently along close to the shore with almost imperceptible motion. . . .

Now the fishermen's fire left behind becomes a star. As surely as the sunlight falling through an irregular chink makes a round figure on the opposite wall, so the blaze at a distance appears a star. Such is the effect of the atmosphere. The bright sheen of the moon is constantly traveling with us, and is seen at the same angle in front on the surface of the pads, and the reflection of its disk on the rippled water by our boat-side appears like bright gold pieces falling on the river's counter.

Oct. 6, 1857. I have just read Ruskin's "Modern Painters." I am disappointed in not finding it a more out-of-door book, for I had heard that such was its character. But its title might have warned me. He does not describe nature as nature, but as Turner painted her. Although the work betrays that he has given close attention to nature, it appears to have been with an artist's and critic's design. How much is written about nature as somebody has portrayed her, how little about nature as she is and chiefly concerns us; *i. e.*, how much prose, how little poetry !

Oct. 7, 1851. By boat to Corner Spring. A very still, warm, bright, clear afternoon. Our boat so small and low that we are close to the water. The muskrats all the way are now building their houses ; about two thirds done. They are of an oval form, composed of mouthfuls of pontederia leaf stems, now dead, the capillaceous roots or leaves of the water marigold and other capillaceous-leaved water-plants, flagroot, a plant which looks like a cock's tail or a peacock's feather in form, the *Potamogeton Robbinsii*, clamshells, etc. ; sometimes rising from amidst the dead pontederia stems or resting on the button bushes or the willows. The mouthfuls are disposed in layers successively smaller, forming a somewhat conical mound. Seen at this stage, these houses show some art and a good deal of labor. We pulled one to pieces to examine the inside. There was a small cavity which might hold two or three full-grown muskrats, just above the level of the water, quite wet and of course dark and narrow, communicating immediately with a gallery under water. There were a few pieces of the white root of some water-plant, perhaps a pontederia or lily, in it. There they dwell in close contiguity to the water itself, always in a wet apartment, in a wet coat never changed, with immeasurable water in the cellar, through which is the only exit. They have reduced life to a lower scale than Diogenes. Certainly they do not fear cold, ague, or consumption. Think of bringing up a family in such a place, worse than a Broad Street cellar! But probably these are not their breeding-places. The muskrat and the fresh-water mussel are very native to our river. The Indian, their human *confrère*, has departed. This is a settler whom our lowlands and our bogs do not hurt. How long has the muskrat dined on mussels? The river mud itself will have the ague as soon as he. What occasion has he for a dentist? Their unfinished, rapidly rising nests look now like truncated cones. They seem to be all building at once in different parts of the river, and to have advanced equally far.

Saw the *Ardea minor* walking along the shore like a hen with long green legs. Its penciled throat is so like the reeds and other shore plants amid which it holds its head erect to watch the passer that it is difficult to discern it. You can get very near it, for it is unwilling to fly, preferring to hide amid the weeds.

Oct. 7, 1852.   P. M.   To Great Meadows.   I find no fringed gentians.   Perhaps the autumnal tints are as bright and interesting now as they will be.   Now is the time to behold the maple swamps, one mass of red and yellow, all on fire ; these and the blood-red huckleberries are the most conspicuous, and then in the village the warm brownish-yellow elms, and there and elsewhere the dark red ashes.   I notice the *Viola ovata*, houstonia, *Ranunculus repens*, caducous polygala, small, scratchgrass polygonum, autumnal dandelion very abundant, small bushy white aster, a few golden-rods, *Polygonum hydropiperoides*, the unknown, flowerless bidens, soapwort gentian, now turned dark purple, yarrow, the white erigeron, red clover, and hedge-mustard.

The muskrats have begun to erect their cabins. Saw one done.   Do they build them in the night ?

Hear and see larks, bluebirds, robins, and song sparrows.   Also see painted tortoises and shad frogs.

I sit on Poplar Hill.   It is a warm, Indian-summerish afternoon.   The sun comes out of clouds, and lights up and warms the whole scene. It is perfect autumn.   I see a hundred smokes rising through the yellow elm tops in the village, where the villagers are preparing for tea.   It is the mellowing year.   The sunshine harmonizes with the imbrowned and fiery foliage.

Oct. 7, 1857. Halfway up Fair Haven Hill, I am surprised for the thousandth time by the beauty of the landscape, and sit down by the orchard wall to behold it at my leisure. It is always incredibly fair, but ordinarily we are mere objects in it, and not witnesses of it. I see through the bright October air a valley, some two miles across, extending southwest and northeast, with a broad, yellow meadow tinged with brown at the bottom, and a blue river winding slowly through it northward, with a regular edging of low bushes of the same color with the meadow. Skirting the meadow are straggling lines, and occasionally large masses, one quarter of a mile wide, of brilliant scarlet and yellow and crimson trees, backed by green forests and green and russet fields and hills, and on the hills around shoot up a million scarlet and orange and yellow and crimson fires. Here and there amid the trees, often beneath the largest and most graceful of them, are white or gray houses. Beyond stretches a forest, wreath upon wreath, and between each two wreaths I know lies a similar vale, and far beyond all, on the verge of the horizon, rise half a dozen dark blue mountain summits. Large birds of a brilliant blue and white plumage are darting and screaming amid the glowing foliage a quarter of a mile below, while smaller bluebirds are warbling faintly but sweetly around me.   Such is the dwelling-place of man ; but go to a caucus in the village to-night, or to a church to-morrow, and see if there is anything said to suggest that the inhabitants of these houses know what manner of world they live in.   It chanced that I heard just then the tolling of a distant funeral bell.   Its serious sound was more in harmony with that scenery than any ordinary bustle would have been.   It suggested that man must die to his present life before he can appreciate his opportunities and the beauty of the abode that is appointed him.

I do not know how to entertain those who cannot take long walks.   The first thing that suggests itself is to get a horse to draw them, and that brings me at once into contact with the stables and dirty harness, and I do not get over my ride for a long time.   I give up my forenoon to them, and get along pretty well, the very elasticity of the air and promise of the day abetting me ; but they are as heavy as dumplings by mid-afternoon.   If they can't walk, why won't they take an honest nap in the afternoon and let me go?   But when two o'clock comes, they alarm me by an evident disposition to sit.   In the midst of the most glorious Indian summer afternoon, there they sit, breaking your chairs and wearing out the house, with their backs to the light, taking no note of the lapse of time.

As I sat on the high bank at the east end of Walden this afternoon at five o'clock, I saw by a peculiar intention of the eye, a very striking, sub-aqueous rainbow-like phenomenon. A passer-by might have noticed the reflections of those bright-tinted shrubs along the high shore on the sunny side, but unless on the alert for such effects he would have failed to perceive the full beauty of the phenomenon. Those brilliant shrubs, from three to a dozen feet in height, were all reflected, dimly so far as the details of leaves, etc., were concerned, but brightly as to color, and of course in the order in which they stood, scarlet, yellow, green, etc.; but there being a slight ripple on the surface, these reflections were not true to the height of their substances, only as to color, breadth of base, and order, but were extended downward with mathematical per- pendicularity three or four times too far for the height of the substances, forming sharp pyramids of the several colors gradually reduced to mere dusky points. The effect of this prolongation was a very agreeable softening and blending of the colors, especially when a small bush of one bright tint stood directly before another of a contrary and equally bright tint. It was just as if you were to brush firmly aside with your hand or a brush a fresh hue of paint or so many lumps of friable colored powders. There was accord-

ingly a sort of belt, as wide as the height of the
hill, extending downward along the whole north
or sunny side of the pond, composed of exceedingly short and narrow inverted pyramids of the
most brilliant colors intermixed. I have seen
similar inverted pyramids in the old drawings of
tattooing about the waists of the aborigines of
this country. Walden, like an Indian maiden,
wears this broad, rainbow-like belt of brilliant-
colored points or cones round her waist in October. The colors seem to be reflected and re-
reflected from ripple to ripple, losing brightness
each time by the softest possible gradation, and
tapering towards the beholder.

Oct. 7, 1860. Remarking to old Mr. ———
the other day on the abundance of the apples,
"Yes," says he, "and fair as dollars, too."
That 's the kind of beauty they see in apples.

Many people have a foolish way of talking
about small things, and apologize for themselves
or another as having attended to such, having
neglected their ordinary business, and amused
or instructed themselves by attending to small
things, when, if the truth were known, their ordinary business was the small thing, and almost
their whole lives were misspent.

Oct. 8, 1851. 2 P. M. To the Marlboro' road.
Picked up an Indian gouge on Dennis's Hill.
Some white oak acorns in the path by a wood-

side I found to be unexpectedly sweet and palatable, the bitterness being scarcely perceptible.
To my taste they are quite as good as chestnuts.
No wonder the first men lived on acorns. Such
as these are no mean food, as they are represented to be. Their sweetness is like the sweetness of bread. The whole world is sweeter to
me for having discovered such palatableness in
this neglected nut. I am related again to the
first men. What can be handsomer, wear better
to the eye, than the color of the acorn, like the
leaves on which it falls, polished or varnished.
I should be at least equally pleased, if I were
to find that the grass tasted sweet and nutri-
tious. It increases the number of my friends,
it diminishes the number of my foes. How
easily, at this season, I could feed myself in the
woods ! There is mast for me too, as well as for
the pigeon and the squirrels, — this Dodonean
fruit. The sweet-acorn tree is famous and well
known to the boys. There can be no question
respecting the wholesomeness of this diet.

The jointed polygonum in the Marlboro' road
is an interesting flower, it is so late, so bright a
red, though inobvious from its minuteness, without leaves, above the sand like sorrel, mixed
with other minute flowers.

An arrow - head at the desert. Filled my
pockets with acorns. Found another gouge on

Dennis's Hill. To have found two Indian gouges and tasted sweet acorns, is it not enough for one afternoon ?

A warm night like this at this season produces its effect on the village. The boys are heard in the street now at nine o'clock, in greater force and with more noise than usual, and my neighbor has got out his flute.

The moon is full. The tops of the woods in the horizon, seen above the fog, look exactly like long, low, black clouds, the fog being the color of the sky.

Oct. 8, 1857. Walking through the Lee farm swamp, a dozen or more rods from the river, I found a large box trap closed. I opened it and found in it the remains of a gray rabbit, skin, bones, and mould closely fitting the right-angled corner of one side. It was wholly inoffensive, as so much vegetable mould, and must have been dead some years. None of the furniture of the trap remained, only the box itself ; the stick which held the bait, the string, etc., were all gone. The box had the appearance of having been floated off in an upright position by a freshet. It had been a rabbit's living tomb. He had gradually starved to death in it. What a tragedy to have occurred within a box in one of our quiet swamps ! The trapper lost his box, the rabbit its life. The box had not

been gnawed.   After days and nights of moan-
ing and struggle, heard for a few rods through
the swamp, increasing weakness and emaciation
and delirium, the rabbit breathed its last.   They
tell you of opening the tomb and finding, by
the contortions of the body, that it was buried
alive.   This was such a case.   Let the trapping
boy dream of the dead rabbit in its ark, as it
sailed, like a small meeting house with its rude
spire, slowly, with a grand and solemn motion,
far amid the alders.

Oct. 9, 1850.   I am always exhilarated, as
were the early voyagers, by the sight of sassafras, Laurus sassafras.   The green leaves
bruised have the fragrance of lemons and a
thousand spices.   To the same order belong
cinnamon, cassia, camphor.

The seed vessel of the sweetbrier is a very
beautiful, glossy, elliptical fruit.   This shrub,
what with the fragrance of its leaves, its blossom, and its fruit, is thrice crowned.

Oct. 9, 1851.   Heard two screech owls in
the night.

Boiled a quart of acorns for breakfast, but
found them not so palatable as the raw, having
acquired a bitterish taste, perchance from being
boiled with the shells and skins.   Yet one would
soon get accustomed to this.

2 P. M.   To Conantum.   I hear the green

locust again on the alders of the causeway, but he is turned straw color. The warm weather has revived them.

All the acorns on the same tree are not equally sweet. They appear to dry sweet.

I see half a dozen snakes in this walk, green and striped, one very young striped snake. They appear to be out enjoying the sun, and to make the most of the last warm days of the year.

The hill and plain on the opposite side of the river are covered with the warm deep red leaves of shrub oak. On Lee's hillside by the pond, the red leaves of some pitch pines are almost of a golden yellow hue seen in the sunlight, a rich autumnal look. The green are, as it were, set in the yellow.

The witch hazel here is in full blossom on this magical hillside, while its broad yellow leaves are falling. Some bushes are completely bare of leaves, and leather-colored they strew the ground. It is an extremely interesting plant, October and November child, and yet reminds me of the very earliest spring. Its blossoms smell like the spring, like the willow catkins. By their color as well as fragrance they belong to the saffron dawn of the year, suggesting amid all these signs of autumn, falling leaves, and frost, that the life of nature by which she eternally flourishes is untouched. It stands here in the shadow on the side of the hill, while the sunlight from over the top of the hill lights up its topmost sprays and yellow blossoms. Its spray, so jointed and angular, is not to be mistaken for any other. I lie on my back with joy under its boughs. While its leaves fall, its blossoms spring. The autumn, then, is indeed a spring. All the year is a spring. I see two blackbirds high overhead going south, but I am going in my thoughts with these hazel blossoms. It is a fairy place. This is a part of the immortality of the soul. When I was thinking that it bloomed too late for bees or other insects to extract honey from its flowers, that perchance they yielded no honey, I saw a bee upon it. How important, then, to the bees this late blossoming plant.

A large sassafras tree behind Lee's, two feet in diameter at the ground.

There is a thick bed of leaves in the road under Hubbard's elms. This reminds me of Cato, as if the ancients made more use of nature than we. He says, " Stramenta si deerunt, frondem iligneam legito ; eam substernito ovibus bubusque." If litter is wanting, gather the leaves of the holm oak, and strew them under your sheep and oxen. In another place he says, " Circum vias ulmos serito et partim populos, uti frondem ovibus et bubus habeas."

There is little or no use made by us of the leaves of trees, not even for beds, unless it be sometimes to rake them up in the woods, and cast them into hogpens and compost heaps.

Oct. 9, 1857. It has come to this, that the lover of art is one, and the lover of nature another, though true art is but the expression of our love of nature. It is monstrous when one cares but little about trees, and much about Corinthian columns ; yet this is exceedingly common.

Oct. 9, 1858. I watch two marsh hawks which rise from the woods before me as I sit on the cliff, at first plunging at each other, gradually lifting themselves, as they come round in their gyrations, higher and higher, and floating toward the southeast. Slender dark motes they are at last, but every time they come round eastward, I see the light of the westering sun reflected from the under sides of their wings.

Oct. 9, 1860. Up Assabet. I now see one small red maple which is all a pure yellow within, and a bright red or scarlet on its outer surface and prominences. It is a remarkably distinct painting of scarlet on a yellow ground. It is an indescribably beautiful contrast of scarlet and yellow. Another is yellow and green where this was scarlet and yellow, and in this case, the bright and liquid green, now getting to be rare, is by contrast as charming a color as the scarlet.

I wonder that the very cows and the dogs in the street do not manifest a recognition of the bright tints about and above them. I saw a terrier dog glance up and down the painted street before he turned in at his master's gate, and I wondered what he thought of these lit trees, if they did not touch his philosophy or spirits, but I fear he had only his common doggish thoughts after all. He trotted down the yard as if it were a matter of course, or else as if he deserved it all.

For two or more nights past we have had remarkable glittering golden sunsets as I came home from the post-office, it being cold and cloudy just above the horizon. There was the most intensely bright golden light at the west end of the street extending under the elms, and the very dust a quarter of a mile off was like gold dust. I wondered how a child could stand quietly in that light, as if it had been a furnace.

This haste to kill a bird or quadruped, and make a skeleton of it, which many young men and some old men exhibit, reminds me of the fable of the man who killed the hen that laid golden eggs, and so got no more gold. It is a perfectly parallel case. Such is the knowledge you get from anatomy as compared with that you may get from the living creature. Every fowl lays golden eggs for him who can find them, or can detect alloy and base metal.

Oct. 10, 1851. The air this morning is full of bluebirds, and again it is spring. There are many things to indicate the renewing of spring at this season, the blossoming of spring flowers, not to mention the witch-hazel, the notes of spring birds, the springing of grain and grass and other plants.

Ah, I yearn toward thee, my friend, but I have not confidence in thee. We do not believe in the same God. I am not thou, thou art not I. We trust each other to-day, but we distrust to-morrow. Even when I meet thee unexpectedly, I part from thee with disappointment. Though I enjoy thee more than other men, I am more disappointed with thee than with others. I know a noble man; what is it hinders me from knowing him better? I know not how it is that our distrust, our hate, is stronger than our love. Here I have been on what the world would call friendly terms with one fourteen years, have pleased my imagination sometimes with loving him, and yet our hate is stronger than our love. Why are we related thus unsatisfactorily to each other? We are almost a sore to one another. Ever and anon will come the thought to mar our love, that change the theme but a hair's breadth, and we shall be tragically strange to one another. We do not know what hinders us from coming

together, but when I consider what my friend's
relations and acquaintances are, what his tastes
and habits, then the difference between us gets
named.   I see that all these friends and acquaintances and tastes and habits are indeed
my friend's self.

The witch-hazel loves a hillside with or without wood or shrubs.   It is always pleasant to
come upon it unexpectedly as you are threading
the woods in such places.   Methinks I attribute to it some elfish quality apart from its fame.
I love to behold its gray speckled stems.   The
leaf first green, then yellow for a short season ;
then, when it touches the ground, tawny leather-
color.   As I stood amid the witch-hazels near
Flint's Pond, a flock of a dozen chickadees came
flitting and singing about me with great ado, a
most cheering and enlivening sound, with incessant *day - day - day*, and a fine wiry strain, between whiles, flitting ever nearer and nearer inquisitively, till the boldest was within five feet
of me ; then suddenly, their curiosity sated, they
flitted by degrees farther away, disappeared, and
I heard with regret their retreating *day - day-
days.*

Oct. 10, 1857.   This is the end of the sixth
day of glorious weather, which I am tempted to
call the finest in the year, so bright and serene
the air, such a sheen from the earth, so brilliant

the foliage, so pleasantly warm (except perhaps
this day, which is cooler), too warm for a thick
coat, yet not sultry nor oppressive, so ripe the
season and our thoughts. Certainly these are
the most *brilliant* days in the year, ushered
in perhaps by a frosty morning, as this. As
a dewy morning in summer, compared with a
parched and sultry, languid one, so a frosty
morning at this season compared with a merely
dry or foggy one. These days you may say the
year is ripened like a fruit by frost, and puts on
the brilliant tints of maturity, but not yet the
color of decay. It is not sere and withered as
in November.

Oct. 10, 1858. The simplest and most lumpish fungus has a peculiar interest for us, compared with a mere mass of earth, because it is
so obviously organic and related to ourselves,
however remote. It is the expression of an idea,
growth according to a law, matter not dormant,
not raw, but inspired, appropriated by spirit. If
I take up a handful of earth, however separately
interesting the particles may be, their relation to
one another appears to be that of mere juxtapo-
sition generally. I might have thrown them together thus. But the humblest fungus betrays a
life akin to my own. It is a successful poem in
its kind. There is suggested something superior
to any particle of matter in the idea or mind
which uses and arranges the particles.

I find the fringed gentian abundantly open at three and at four P. M. (in fact it must be all the afternoon), open to catch the cool October sun and air in its low position. Such a dark blue! surpassing that of the male bluebird's back.

I see dumb-bells in the minister's study, and some of their dumbness gets into his sermons. Some travelers carry them round the world in their carpet bags. Can he be said to travel who requires still this exercise? A party of school children had a picnic in the Easterbrook country the other day, and they carried bags of beans for their gymnasium, to exercise with there. I cannot be interested in these extremely artificial amusements. The traveler is no longer a wayfarer with his staff and pack and dusty coat. He is not a pilgrim, but he travels in a saloon, and carries dumb-bells to exercise with in the intervals of his journey.

Oct. 11, 1840. It is always easy to infringe the law, but the Bedouin of the desert finds it impossible to resist public opinion.

Oct. 11, 1852. The chestnut leaves already rustle with a great noise as you walk through the woods, lying light, firm and crisp. Now the chestnuts are rattling out. The burrs are gaping and showing the plump nuts. They fill the ruts in the road and are abundant amid the fallen leaves in the midst of the wood. The jays scream and the red squirrels scold while you are clubbing and shaking the trees. Now it is true autumn, and all things are crisp and ripe.

I observed the other day that those insects whose ripple I could see from the peak were water bugs. I could detect the progress of a water bug over the smooth surface in almost any part of the pond, for they furrow the water slightly, making a conspicuous ripple, bounded by two diverging lines, but the skaters slide over it without producing a perceptible ripple. In this clear air and with this glassy surface, the motion of every water bug, here and there amid the skaters, was perceptible.

Oct. 11, 1859. The note of the chickadee heard now in cooler weather above many fallen leaves, has a new significance.

There was a very severe frost this morning; ground stiffened, probably a chestnut-opening frost, a season ripeness, opener of the burrs that contain the Indian Summer. Such is the cold of early or mid October. The leaves and weeds had a stiff, hoary appearance.

Oct. 11, 1860. Pears are a less poetic though more aristocratic fruit than apples. They have neither the beauty nor the fragrance of apples, but their excellence is in their flavor, which speaks to a grosser sense, they are *glout-mor-*

ceaux; hence while children dream of apples, judges, ex-judges, and honorables are connoisseurs of pears, and discourse of them at length between sessions. How much more attention they get from the proprietor. The hired man gathers the apples and barrels them. The proprietor plucks the pears at odd hours for a pastime. They are spread on the floor of the best room, they are a gift to the most distinguished guest. They are named after emperors, kings, queens, dukes, and duchesses. I fear I shall have to wait till we get to pears with American names, which a republican can swallow.

Oct. 12, 1840. The springs of life flow in ceaseless. tides down below, and hence this greenness everywhere on the surface. But they are as yet untapped; only here and there men have sunk a well.

Oct. 12, 1851. I love very well this cloudy afternoon, so sober and favorable to reflection, after so many bright ones. What if the clouds shut out the heavens, provided they concentrate my thoughts and make a more celestial heaven below! I hear the crickets plainer. I wander less in my thoughts, am less dissipated, am aware how shallow was the current of my thoughts before. Deep streams are dark, as if there were a cloud in their sky; shallow ones are bright and sparkling, reflecting the sun from their bottoms. The very wind on my cheek seems more fraught with meaning.

I seem to be more constantly merged in nature, my intellectual life is more obedient to nature than formerly, but perchance less obedient to spirit. I have less memorable seasons. I exact less of myself. I am getting used to my meanness, getting to accept my low estate. Oh, if I could be discontented with myself! if I could feel anguish at each descent!

P. M. To Cliffs. I hear Lincoln bell tolling for church. At first I thought of the telegraph harp. Heard at a distance, the sound of a bell acquires a certain vibratory hum, as it were from the air through which it passes, like a harp. All music is a harp music at length, as if the air were full of vibrating strings. It is not the mere sound of the bell, but the humming in the air that enchants me, just as the azure tint which much air or distance imparts, delights the eye. It is not so much the object, as the object clothed with an azure veil. All sound heard at a great distance thus tends to produce the same music, vibrating the strings of the universal lyre. There comes to me a melody which the air has strained, which has conversed with every leaf and needle of the woods. It is by no means the sound of the bell as heard near at hand, and which at this distance I can plainly distinguish, but its vibrating echoes, that portion of the sound which the elements take up and modulate, a sound which is very much modified, sifted, and refined before it reaches my ear. The echo is to some extent an independent sound, and therein is the magic and charm of it. It is not merely a repetition of my voice, but it is in some measure the voice of the wood.

Oct. 12, 1852. I am struck by the simplicity of light in the atmosphere in the autumn, as if the earth absorbed none, and out of this profusion of dazzling light came the autumnal tints. Can it be because there is less vapor?

The delicacy of the stratification in the white sand by the railroad, where they have been getting out sand for the brickyards, the delicate stratification of this great globe, like the leaves of the choicest volume just shut on a lady's table! The piled up history! I am struck by the slow and delicate process by which the globe was formed.

What an ample share of the light of heaven each pond and lake on the surface of the globe enjoys! No woods are so dark and deep but it is light above the pond. Its window or skylight is as broad as its surface. It lies out, patent to the sky. From the mountain top you may not be able to see out, because of the woods, but on the lake you are bathed in light.

Oct. 12, 1857. The elm, I think, can be distinguished farther than any other tree, and however faintly seen in the distant horizon, its little dark dome, which the thickness of my nail will conceal, apparently not so big as the prominence on an orange, suggests ever the same quiet, rural and domestic life passing beneath it. It is like the vignette to an unseen idyllic poem. Though the little prominence appears so dark here, I know that it is now a rich brownish or yellow canopy of rustling leaves, whose harvest time has already come, sending down its showers from time to time. Homestead telegraphs to homestead through these distant elms seen from the hilltops. I fancy I hear the house dog bark, and lowing of the cows asking admittance to their yard beneath it. The tea-table is spread. The master and the hired men in their shirt-sleeves, with the mistress, have just sat down.

Oct. 12, 1858. I have heard of judges accidentally met at an evening party, discussing the efficacy of laws and courts, and deciding that with the aid of the jury system substantial justice was done. But taking those cases in which honest men refrain from going to law, together with those in which men honest and dishonest do go to law, I think the law is really a humbug, and a benefit principally to the lawyers. This town has made a law recently against cattle going at large, and assigned a penalty of five dollars. I am troubled by an Irish neighbor's cow and horse, and have threatened to have them put in the pound. But a lawyer tells me these town laws are hard to put through, there are so many quibbles. He never knew the complainant to get his case, if the defendant had a mind to contend. However, the cattle were kept out several days, till a Sunday came, and then they were all in my grounds again, as I heard, but all my neighbors tell me that I cannot have them impounded on that day. Indeed, I observe that very many of my neighbors do for this reason regularly turn their cattle loose on Sundays. The judges may discuss the question of the courts and law over their nuts and raisins, and mumble for the decision that " substantial justice is done," but I must believe they mean that they really get paid a " substantial " salary.

Oct. 13, 1840. The only prayer for a brave man is to be a-doing. This is the prayer that is heard. Why ask God for a respite when he has not given it? Has he not done his work, and made man equal to his occasions, but he must needs have recourse to him again? God cannot give us any other than self-help.

The workers in stone polish only their chimney ornaments. But their pyramids are roughly done. There is a soberness in a rough aspect, in unhewn granite, which addresses a depth in us, but the polished surface only hits the ball of the eye.

The draft of my stove sounds like the dashing of waves on the shore, and the lid sings like the wind in the shrouds. The steady roar of the surf on the beach is as incessant in my ear as in the shell on the mantelpiece. I see vessels stranded, and gulls flying, and fishermen running to and fro on the beach.

Oct. 13, 1851. The alert and energetic man leads a more intellectual life in winter than in summer. In summer the animal and vegetable in him flourish more, as in a torrid zone; he lives in his senses mainly. In winter cold reason, not warm passion, has sway; he lives in thought and reflection. If he has passed a merely sensual summer, he passes his winter in a torpid state like some reptiles and other animals. Man depends more on himself, his own resources, in winter, less on what is outward. Insects disappear for the most part, and those animals which depend upon them, but the nobler animals abide with man the severity of winter. He migrates into his mind, to perpetual summer, and to the healthy man the winter of his discontent never comes.

Oct. 13, 1852. P. M. To Cliffs. Fair Haven Pond never, I think, looks so handsome as at this season. It is a sufficiently clear and warm, a rather Indian summer day, and they are gathering the apples in the orchard. The warmth is required now, and we welcome and appreciate it all. The shrub-oak plain is a deep red with grayish, withered, apparently white-oak leaves intermixed. The chickadee takes heart too, and sings above these warm rocks. Birches, hickories, aspens, etc., are like innumerable small flames on the hillsides about the pond, which is now most beautifully framed with the autumn-tinted woods and hills. The water or lake, from however distant a point seen, is always the centre of the landscape. Fair Haven lies more open, and can be seen from more distant points than any other of our ponds. The air is singularly fine-grained, the sward looks short and firm. The mountains are more distinct from the rest of the earth and slightly impurpled, seeming to lie up more. How peaceful great nature! There is no disturbing sound, but far amid the western hills there rises a pure, white smoke in constant volumes.

Oct. 13, 1852. To Poplar Hill. Maple fires are burnt out generally, and look smoky in the swamps. When my eyes were resting on those smoke-like bare trees, it did not at first occur to me why the landscape was not as brilliant as a few days ago. The outside trees in the swamps lose their leaves first.

I see a pretty large flock of tree sparrows, very lively and tame, pursuing each other and drifting along a bushy fence and ditch like driving snow. Two pursuing each other would curl upward like a breaker in the air, and drop into the hedge again. This has been the ninth of these wonderful days, and one of the warmest. I am obliged to sit with my window wide open all the evening as well as all day. It is the earlier Indian summer.

Oct. 13, 1859. The shad bush is leafing again by the sunny swamp side. It is like a youthful or poetic thought in old age. Several times I have been cheered by this sight when surveying in former years. The chickadee seems to lisp a sweeter note at the sight of it. I would not fear the winter more than the shad bush, which puts forth fresh and tender leaves on its approach. In the fall I will take this for my coat of arms. It seems to detain the sun that expands it. These twigs are so full of life that they can hardly contain themselves. They ignore winter. They anticipate spring. What faith! Away in some sheltered recess of the swamp you find where these leaves have expanded. In my latter years let me have some shad-bush thoughts.

I perceive the peculiar scent of witch hazel in bloom for several rods around, which at first I refer to the decaying leaves.

British naturalists very generally apologize to the reader for having devoted their attention to natural history to the neglect of some important duty.

I remember seeing in an old work a plate of a fungus which grew in a wine-cellar and got its name from that circumstance. It is related in " Chambers' Journal " that Sir Joseph Banks, having ordered a cask of wine to be placed in a cellar in order to improve it, " at the end of three years he directed his butler to ascertain the state of the wine, when on attempting to open the cellar door, he could not effect it in consequence of some powerful obstacle. The door was consequently cut down, when the cellar was found to be completely filled with a fungus production so firm that it was necessary to use an axe for its removal. This appeared to have grown from, or to have been nourished by the decomposing particles of the wine, the cask being empty and carried up to the ceiling, where it was supported by the fungus." Perhaps it was well that the fungus instead of Sir Joseph Banks drank up the wine. The life of a wine-bibber is like that of a fungus.

Oct. 13, 1860. The scientific differs from the poetic or lively description somewhat as the photographs which we become so weary of viewing differ from paintings and sketches, though

the comparison is too favorable to science. All
science is only a makeshift, a means to an end
which is never attained. After all, the truest
description and that by which another living
man can most readily recognize a flower, is the
unmeasured and eloquent one which the sight of
it inspires. No scientific description will supply
the want of this, though you should count and
measure and analyze every atom which seems to
compose it. Surely poetry and eloquence are a
more universal language than that Latin which
is confessedly dead. In science I should say all
description is postponed till we know the whole,
and then science itself will be cast aside. But
unconsidered expressions of delight which any
natural object draws from us are something
complete and final in themselves, since all nature
is to be regarded as it concerns man, and who
knows how near to absolute truth such unconscious affirmations may come. Which are the
truest, the sublime conceptions of Hebrew prophets and seers, or the guarded statements of
modern geologists which we must modify or un-
learn so fast? A scientific description is such
as you would get, if you should send out the
scholars of the polytechnic school with all sorts
of metres made and patented to take the measure
for you of any natural object. In a sense, you
have got nothing new thus, for every object that

we see mechanically is mechanically daguerreotyped on our eyes, but a true description growing
out of the conception and appreciation of it is
itself a new fact, never to be daguerreotyped,
indicating the highest quality of the object, its
relation to man. The one description interests
those chiefly who have not seen the thing, the
other chiefly interests those who have seen it
and are most familiar with it, and brings it
home to the reader. We like to read a good
description of nothing so well as of that which
we already know the best, as our friend or ourselves even.

Gerard has not only heard of and seen and
raised a plant, but smelled and tasted it, applied
all his senses to it. You are not distracted from
the thing to the system or arrangement. In the
true natural order, the order or system is not
insisted on. Each object is first, and each last.
That which presents itself to us this moment,
occupies the whole of the present, and rests on
the very topmost point of the sphere, under the
zenith. The species and individuals of all the
natural kingdoms ask our attention and admira-
tion in a round robin. We make straight lines,
putting a captain at the head and a lieutenant at
the tail, with sergeants and corporals all along
the line, and a flourish of trumpets at the beginning, where nature has made curves to which

belong their own sphere music. It is indispensable for us to square her circles, and we offer our rewards to him who will do it. The best observer describes the most familiar object with a zest and vividness of imagery as if he saw it for the first time, the novelty consisting not in the strangeness of the object, but in the new and clearer perception of it.

Oct. 14, 1851. Down the railroad before sunrise. A freight train in the Deep Cut. When the vapor from the engine rose above the woods, the level rays of the rising sun falling on it presented the same redness, morning red inclining to saffron, which the clouds in the western horizon do.

There was but little wind this morning, yet I heard the telegraph harp. It does not require a strong wind to wake its strings. It depends more on its direction and the tension of the wire apparently. A gentle but steady breeze will often call forth its finest strains, when a strong but unsteady gale, blowing at the wrong angle withal, will fail to elicit any melodious sound.

In the psychological world, there are phenomena analogous to what zoölogists call *alternate reproduction*, in which it requires several generations unlike each other to evolve the perfect animal. Some men's lives are but an aspiration, a yearning toward a higher state, and they

are wholly misapprehended until they are referred to or traced through all their metamor-
phoses. We cannot pronounce upon a man's
intellectual and moral state until we foresee
what metamorphosis it is preparing him for.

Oct. 14, 1856. Any flowers seen now may be
called late ones. I see perfectly fresh succory,
not to speak of yarrow, a *Viola ovata,* some *Polygala sanguinea,* autumnal dandelion, tansy, etc.

Oct. 14, 1857. P. M. To White Pond. Another, the tenth or eleventh of these memorable
days. This afternoon it is warmer even than
yesterday. I am glad to reach the shade of
Hubbard's Grove. The coolness is refreshing.
It is indeed a golden autumn. All kinds of
crudities have a chance to get ripe this year.
Was there ever such an autumn? And yet
there was never such a panic and hard times
in the commercial world. The merchants and
banks are failing all the country over, but not
the sand banks, solid and warm, and streaked
with bloody blackberry vines. You may run on
them as much as you please, even as the crickets
do, and find their account in it. They are the
stockholders in these banks, and I hear them
creaking their content. You may see them on
change in any warmer hour. In these banks,
too, and such as these, are my funds deposited,
funds of health and enjoyment. Invest in these

country banks. Let your capital be simplicity and contentment. I do not suspect the solvency of these banks. I know who is the president and cashier.

I take these walks to every point of the compass, and it is always harvest time with me. I am always gathering my crop from these woods and fields and waters, and no man is in my way, or interferes with me. My crop is not their crop. To-day I see them getting in their beans and corn, and they are a spectacle to me, but are soon out of my sight. I go abroad over the land each day to get the best I can find, and that is never carted off, even to the last day of November.

Sat in the old pasture beyond the Corner Spring woods to look at that pine wood now at the height of its change, pitch and white. Their change produces a very singular and pleasing effect. They are regularly parti-colored. The last year's leaves about a foot beneath the extremities of the twigs on all sides, now changed and ready to fall, have their period of brightness as well as broader leaves. They are a clear yellow, contrasting with the fresh and liquid green of the terminal plumes, or this year's leaves. These quite distinct colors are regularly and equally distributed over the whole tree. You have the warmth of the yellow and

the coolness of the green. So it should be with
our own maturity, not yellow to the very extremity of our shoots, but youthful and untried green
ever putting forth afresh at the extremities,
foretelling a maturity as yet unknown. The
ripe leaves fall to the ground, and become nutriment for the green ones which still aspire to
heaven. In the fall of the leaf there is no fruit,
there is no true maturity, neither in our science
and wisdom.

Oct. 14, 1859. To and around Flint's Pond
with Blake. A fine Indian-summer day. We
sit on the rock on Pine Hill overlooking Walden. There is a thick haze almost concealing
the mountains. There is wind enough to raise
waves on the pond and make it bluer. What
strikes me in the scenery here now is the contrast
of the universally blue water with the brilliant
tinted woods around it. The tints generally
may be about at their height. The earth appears like a great inverted shield painted yellow
and red, or with imbricated scales of those colors, and a blue navel in the middle where the
pond lies, with a distant circumference of whitish haze. The nearer woods where chestnuts
grow are a mass of warm glowing yellow, but on
other sides the red and yellow are intermixed.

I hear a man laughed at because he went to
Europe twice in search of an imaginary wife

who he thought was there, though he had never seen nor heard of her. But the majority have gone further while they stayed in America, have actually allied themselves to one whom they thought their wife, and found out their mistake too late to mend it. It would be cruel to laugh at them.

Oct. 15, 1840. Men see God in the ripple, but not in miles of still water. Of all the two thousand miles that the St. Lawrence flows, pilgrims go only to Niagara.

Oct. 15, 1851. 8.30 A. M. Up the river in a boat to Pelham's Pond with W. E. C. The muskrat houses appear now, for the most part, to be finished, though some are still rising. They line the river all the way. Some are as big as small haycocks. There is a wind, and the sky is full of flitting clouds, so that sky and water are quite unlike what they were that warm, bright, transparent day when I last sailed on the river and the surface was of such oily smoothness. You could not now study the river bottom for the black waves and the streaks of foam. It is pleasant to hear the sound of the waves, and feel the surging of the boat, inspiriting, as if you were bound on adventures. It is delightful to be tossed about in such a harmless storm, and see the waves look so angry and black. We see objects on shore, trees, etc.,

much better from the boat. From a low and
novel point of view, it brings them against the
sky, and what is low on the meadow is conspicuous as well as the hills. In this cool sunlight,
Fair Haven Hill shows to advantage. Every
rock and shrub and protuberance has justice
done it, the sun shining at an angle on the hills
and giving each a shadow. The hills have a
hard and distinct outline, and I see into their
very texture. On Fair Haven I see the sunlit
light green grass in the hollows where the snow
makes pools of water sometimes, and the sunlit
russet slopes. Cut three white-pine boughs opposite Fair Haven, and set them up in the bow
of our boat for a sail. It was pleasant to hear
the water begin to ripple under the prow, telling
of our easy progress, and thus without a tack
we made the south side of Fair Haven. Then
we threw our sails overboard, and the moment
after mistook them for green bushes or weeds
which had sprung from the bottom unusually
far from shore. Then to hear the wind sough
in your sail, that is to be a sailor and hear a
land sound. . . . On the return . . . the sun
sets when we are off Israel Rice's. A few golden
coppery clouds glow intensely like fishes in some
molten metal of the sky, then the small scattered
clouds grow blue-black above, or one half, and
reddish or pink the other half, and after a short

twilight the night sets in. The reflections of the stars in the water are dim and elongated like the zodiacal light, straight down into the depths. We row across Fair Haven in the thickening twilight and far below it, steadily and without speaking. As the night draws on her veil, the shores retreat, we only keep in the middle of this low stream of light, we know not whether we float in the air or in the lower regions. It is pleasant not to get home till after dark, to steer by the lights of the villagers.

The lamps in the houses twinkle now like stars ; they shine doubly bright. We rowed about twenty-four miles going and coming. In a straight line it would be fifteen and a half.

Oct. 15, 1852. 9 A. M. The first snow is falling (after not very cool weather) in large flakes, filling the air and obscuring the distant woods‧and houses, as if the inhabitants above were emptying their pillow-cases. Like a mist it divides the uneven landscape at a little distance into ridges and vales. The ground begins to whiten and our thoughts to prepare for winter. White-weed. The Canada snapdragon is one of the latest flowers noticed, a few buds being still left to blossom at the top of its spike or raceme. The snow lasted but half an hour.

How Father Le Jeune (?) pestered the poor Indians with his God at every turn (they must have thought it his one idea), only getting their attention when they required some external aid to save them from starving. Then indeed they were good Christians.

Oct. 15, 1858. If you stand fronting a hill-side covered with a variety of young oaks, the brightest scarlet ones — uniformly deep, dark scarlet — will be the scarlet oaks. The next most uniformly reddish, a peculiar dull crimson (or salmon ?), are the white oaks. Then the large-leaved and variously tinted red oaks, scarlet, yellow, and green, and finally the yellowish and half-decayed brown leaves of the black oak.

Oct. 15, 1859. The chickadees sing as if at home. Theirs is an honest, heartfelt melody. Shall not the voice of man express as much content as the note of a bird ?

Oct. 16, 1857. P. M. Up Assabet. I stop a while at Cheney's shore to hear an incessant musical twittering from a large flock of young goldfinches which have dull yellow, drab and black plumage. Young birds can hardly restrain themselves, and, if they did not leave us, might perchance burst forth into song in the later Indian-summer days. Am surprised to find an abundance of witch hazel now at the height of its change. The tallest bushes are bare, though in bloom ; but the lowest are full of leaves, many of them green, but chiefly clear and handsome yellow of various shades, from a pale lemon in the shade or within the bush, to a darker and warmer yellow without. Some have even a hue of crimson ; some are green with bright yellow along the veins. This reminds me that plants exposed turn early, or not at all, while the same species in the shade of the woods at a much later date assume very pure and delicate tints.

A great part of the pine needles have just fallen. See the pale brown carpet of them under this pine ; how light it lies up on the grass, and that great rock, and the wall, resting thick on its top and its shelves, and on the bushes and underwood. The needles are not yet flat and reddish, but a more delicate pale brown, and lie up light on joggle - sticks, just dropped. The ground is nearly concealed by them. How beautifully they die, making cheerfully their annual contribution to the soil. They fall to rise again ; as if they knew that it was not one annual deposit alone that made this rich mould in which pine-trees grow. They live in the soil whose fertility and bulk they increase, and in the forests that spring from it.

Oct. 16, 1859. P. M. Paddle to Puffer's, and thence walk to Ledum Swamp and Conantward. A cold, clear Novemberish day. When I get to Willow Bay, I see the new muskrat houses erected, conspicuous on the now nearly leafless shores. For thirty years I have annually observed, about this time or earlier, the freshly erected winter lodges of the muskrat along the river-side, reminding us that, if we have no gypsies, we have a more indigenous race of puny, quadrupedal men maintaining their ground in our midst still. This may not be an annual phenomenon to you, but it has an important place in my Kalendar. So surely as the sun appears to be in Libra or Scorpio, I see the conical winter lodges of the muskrat rising above the withered pontederia and flags. There will be some reference to it by way of parable or otherwise in *my* New Testament. Surely it is a defect in our Bible that it is not truly ours, but a Hebrew Bible. The most pertinent illustrations for us are to be drawn not from Egypt or Babylonia, but from New England. Natural objects and phenomena are the original symbols or types which express our thoughts and feelings. Yet American scholars, having little or no root in the soil, commonly strive with all their might to confine themselves to the imported symbols alone. All the true growth and experience, the living speech, they would fain reject as " Americanisms." It is the old error which the church, the state, the school, ever commit, choosing darkness rather than light, holding fast to the old and to tradition. When I really know that our river pursues a serpentine course to the Merrimack, shall I continue to describe it by referring to some other river, no older than itself, which is like it, and call it a meander? It is no more meandering than the Meander is musketaquiding.

This clear, cold, Novemberish light is inspiriting. Some twigs which are bare, and weeds, begin to glitter with hoary light. The very edge or outline of a tawny or russet hill has this hoary light on it. Your thoughts sparkle like the water surface and the downy twigs. From the shore you look back on the silver-plated river.

Every rain exposes new arrow-heads. We stop at Clamshell, and dabble for a moment in the relics of a departed race.

When we emerged from the pleasant footpath through the birches at Witherel Glade, the glittering white tufts of the *Andropogon scoparius* lit up by the sun were affectingly fair and cheering to behold. How cheerful these cold, but bright, white waving tufts! They reflect all the sun's light without a particle of his heat, as yellow rays. A thousand such tufts now catch up the sun, and send to us its light, but not heat. Light without heat is getting to be the prevailing phenomenon of the day now.

This cold refines and condenses us. Our

spirits are strong, like that pint of cider in the middle of a frozen barrel.

The cool, placid, silver-plated waters at even coolly await the frost. The muskrat is steadily adding to his winter lodge. There is no need of adding a peculiar instinct telling him how high to build his cabin. He has had a longer experience in this river valley than we.

I love to get out of cultivated fields, where I walk on an imported sod or English grass, and walk on the fine sedge of woodland hollows, on an American sward. In the former case my thoughts are heavy and lumpish, as if I fed on turnips. In the other, I nibble ground nuts.

Oct. 17, 1840. In the presence of my friend I am ashamed of my fingers and toes. I have no feature so fair as my love for him. There is a more than maiden modesty between us. I find myself more simple and sincere than in my most private moment to myself. I am literally true *with a witness*. We should sooner blot out the sun than disturb friendship.

Oct. 17, 1850. I observed to-day the small blueberry bushes by the pathside, now blood-red, full of white blossoms, as in the spring. The blossoms of spring contrast strangely with the leaves of autumn. The former seemed to have expanded from sympathy with the maturity of the leaves.

Oct. 17, 1856.   Many fringed gentians quite fresh yet, though most are faded and withered. I suspect that their very early and sudden fading and withering has nothing or little to do with frost after all, for why should so many fresh ones succeed still ?

As I stood looking, I heard a smart *tche-day-day-day* close to my ear, and looking up saw four or five chickadees which had come to scrape acquaintance with me, hopping amid the alders within three or four feet of me.   I had heard them further off at first, and they had followed me along the hedge.   They *day-day*'d, and lisped their faint notes alternately, and then, as if to make me think they had some other errand than to peer at me, they pecked the dead twigs, the little top-heavy, black-crowned, volatile fellows.

Oct. 17, 1857.   What a new beauty the blue of the river acquires seen at a distance in the midst of the variously tinted woods, great masses of gray, yellow, etc.!   It appears as color which ordinarily it does not, elysian.

The trainers are out with their band of music, and I find my account in it, though I have not subscribed for it.   I am walking with a hill between me and the soldiers.   I think perhaps it will be worth while to keep within hearing of their strains this afternoon.   Yet I hesitate.   I am wont to find music unprofitable, a luxury. It is surprising, however, that so few habitually intoxicate themselves with music, so many with alcohol. I think, perchance, I may risk it, it will whet my senses so, it will reveal a glory where none was seen before. No doubt these strains do sometimes suggest to Abner, walking behind in his red-streaked pants, an ideal which he had lost sight of or never perceived. It is remarkable that our institutions can stand before music, it is so revolutionary.

Oct. 17, 1858. I think the reflections are never purer and more distinct than now at the season of the fall of the leaf, just before the cool twilight has come, when the air has a finer grain, just as our mental reflections are more distinct at this season of the year when the evenings grow cool and lengthen, and our winter evenings with their brighter fires may be said to begin. One reason why I associate perfect reflections from still water with this and a later season may be that now by the fall of the leaves so much more light is let in to the water. The river reflects more light, therefore, in this twilight of the year, as it were, an afterglow.

Oct. 17, 1859. What I put into my pocket, whether berry or apple, generally has to keep company with an arrow-head or two. I hear the latter chinking against a key as I walk. These

are the perennial crop of Concord fields. If
they were sure it would pay, we should see
farmers raking the fields for them.

Oct. 17, 1860. While the man that killed
my lynx thinks, as do many others, that it came
out of a menagerie, and the naturalists call it
the Canada lynx, and at the White Mountains
they call it the Siberian lynx, in each case forgetting or ignoring the fact that it belongs here, I
call it the Concord lynx.

Oct. 18, 1840. The era of greatest change is
to the subject of it the condition of greatest in-
variableness. The longer the lever, the less perceptible its motion. It is the slowest pulsation
which is the most vital. I am independent of
the change I detect. My most essential progress
must be to me a state of absolute rest. So in
geology we are nearest to discovering the true
causes of the revolutions of the globe, when we
allow them to consist with a quiescent state of
the elements. We discover the causes of all
past change ·in the present invariable order of
the universe. The pulsations are so long that
in the interval there is almost a stagnation of
life. The first cause of the universe makes the
least noise. Its pulse has beat but once, is now
beating. The greatest appreciable revolutions
are the work of the light-footed air, the stealthy-
paced water, and the subterranean fire. The

wind makes the desert without a rustle. To every being, consequently, its own first cause is an invisible and inconceivable agent.

Some questions which are put to me are as if I should ask a bird what she will do when her nest is built, and her brood reared.

I cannot make a disclosure. You should see my secret. Let me open my doors never so wide, still within and behind them, where it is unopened, does the sun rise and set, and day and night alternate. No fruit will ripen on the common.

Oct. 18, 1855. How much beauty in decay! I pick up a white-oak leaf, dry and stiff, but yet mingled red and green, October-like, whose pulpy part some insect has eaten, beneath, exposing the delicate network of its veins. It is very beautiful held up to the light; such work as only an insect eye could perform. Yet, perchance, to the vegetable kingdom, such a revelation of ribs is as repulsive as the skeleton in the animal kingdom. In each case, it is some little gourmand working for another end, that reveals the wonders of nature. There are countless oak leaves in this condition now, and also with a submarginal line of network exposed.

Oct. 18, 1856. Rain all night and half this day. P. M. A-chestnutting, down turnpike and across to Britton's. It is a rich sight, that of

a large chestnut tree, with a dome-shaped top,
where the yellow leaves have been thinned out
(for most now strew the ground evenly as a carpet throughout the chestnut woods, and so save
some seed), all richly rough with great brown
burrs which are opened into several segments, so
as to show the wholesome-colored nuts peeping
forth, ready to fall on the slightest jar. The individual nuts are very interesting, and of various
forms, according to the season and the number
in a burr. They are a pretty fruit, thus com-
pactly stowed away in their bristly chest. Three
is the regular number, and there is no room to
spare. The two outside nuts have each one convex side without, and one flat side within. The
middle nut has two flat sides. Sometimes there
are several more in a burr, but this year the
burrs are small, and there are not commonly
more than two good nuts, very often only one,
the middle one, both sides of which will then be
convex, each bulging out into a thin, abortive,
mere reminiscence of a nut, all shell, beyond it.
The base of each nut, where it was joined to the
burr, is marked with an irregular dark figure on
a light ground, oblong or crescent-shaped, commonly like a spider or other insect with a dozen
legs, while the upper or small end tapers into a
little white woolly spire crowned with a star, and
the whole upper slopes of the nuts are covered

with the same hoary wool which reminds you of
the frosts on whose advent they peep forth.
Within this thick, prickly burr, the nuts are
about as safe, until they are quite mature, as a
porcupine behind its spines.   Yet I see where
the squirrels have gnawed through many closed
burrs, and left the pieces on the stumps.   There
are sometimes two meats within one chestnut
shell, divided transversely, and each covered by
its separate brown-ribbed skin, as if nature had
smuggled the seed of one more tree into this chest.

Men commonly exaggerate the theme.   Some
themes they think are significant, and others insignificant.   I feel that my life is very homely,
my pleasures very cheap; joy and sorrow, success and failure, grandeur and meanness, and
indeed most words in the English language, do
not mean for me what they do for my neighbors.
I see that they look with compassion on me, that
they think it is a mean and unfortunate destiny
which makes me walk in these fields and woods
so much, and sail on this river alone.   But so
long as I find here the only real elysium, I cannot hesitate in my choice.   My work is writing,
and I do not hesitate, though no subject is too
trivial for me, tried by the ordinary standards.
The theme is nothing, the life is everything.
All that interests the reader is the depth and
intensity of the life exerted.   We touch our

subject but by a point which has no breadth, but the pyramid of our experience, our interest in it, rests on us by a broader or narrower base ; that is, man is all in all, nature nothing but as she draws him out and reflects him. Give me simple, cheap, and homely themes.

Oct. 18, 1859. Why can we not oftener refresh one another with original thoughts? If the fragrance of the Dicksonia fern is so grateful and suggestive to us, how much more refreshing and encouraging, re-creating, would be fresh and fragrant thoughts communicated to us from a man's experience. I want none of his pity nor sympathy in the common sense, but that he should emit and communicate to me his essential fragrance, that he should not be forever repenting and going to church (when not otherwise sinning), but as it were going a-huckleberrying in the fields of thought, and enriching all the world with his visions and his joys.

Why flee so soon to the theatres, lecture-rooms, and museums of the city? If you will stay here awhile, I will promise you strange sights. You shall walk on water. All these brooks and rivers and ponds shall be your highway. You shall see the whole earth covered a foot or more deep with purest white crystals in which you slump or over which you glide, and all the trees and stubble glittering in icy armor.

Oct. 19, 1840. My friend dwells in the eastern horizon as rich as an eastern city there. There he sails all lonely under the edge of the sky ; but thoughts go out silently from me, and belay him, till at length he rides in my roadstead. But never does he fairly come to anchor in my harbor. Perhaps I afford no good anchorage. He seems to move in a burnished atmosphere, while I peer in upon him from surrounding spaces of Cimmerian darkness. His house is incandescent to my eye, while I have no house, but only a neighborhood to his.

Oct. 19, 1855. Talking with Bellew [?] this evening about Fourierism and communities, I said that I suspected any enterprise in which two were engaged together. But, said he, it is difficult to make a stick stand, unless you slant two or more against it. Oh, no, I answered, you may split its lower end into three, or drive it single into the ground, which is the best way, but men, when they start on a new enterprise, not only figuratively, but really, *pull up stakes.* When the sticks prop one another, none, or only one, stands erect.

Oct. 19, 1856. P. M. Conantum. Now and for some weeks is the time for flocks of sparrows of various kinds flitting from bush to bush and tree to tree (and both bushes and trees are thinly leaved or bare), and from one seared

meadow to another. They are mingled together
and their notes even, being faint, are, as well
as their colors and motions, much alike. The
sparrow youth are on the wing. They are still
further concealed by their resemblance in color
to the gray twigs and stems which are now beginning to be bare.

I have often noticed the inquisitiveness of
birds, as the other day of a sparrow, whose
motions I should not have supposed had any
reference to me, if I had not watched it from
first to last. I stood on the edge of a pine and
birch wood. It flitted from seven or eight rods
distant to a pine within a rod of me, where it
hopped about stealthily and chirped awhile, then
flew as many rods the other side, and hopped
about there awhile, then back to the pine again,
as near to me as it dared, and again to its first
position, very restless all the while. Generally
I should have supposed that there was more than
one bird, or that it was altogether accidental,
that the chipping of this sparrow had no reference to me, for I could see nothing peculiar
about it. But when I brought my glass to bear
on it, I found that it was almost steadily eyeing
me, and was all alive with excitement.

Oct. 19, 1858. A remarkably warm day.
74° + at 1 P. M. Ride to Sam Barrett's mill.
Am pleased again to see the cobweb drapery of

the mill. Each fine line, hanging in festoons from the timbers overhead, and on the sides, and on the discarded machinery lying about, is covered and greatly enlarged by a coating of meal, like the twigs under thin ridges of snow in winter. It is like the tassels and dimity in a lady's bed-chamber, and I pray that the cobwebs may not have been brushed away from the mill which I visit. It is as if I were aboard a man-of-war, and this were the fine rigging, the sails being taken in. All things in the mill wear this drapery, down to the miller's hat and coat. Barrett's apprentice, it seems, makes trays of black birch and of red maple in a dark room under the mill. I was pleased to see the work done here, a wooden tray is so handsome. You could count the circles of growth on the end of the tray, and the dark heart of the tree was seen at each end above, producing a semicircular ornament. It was a satisfaction to be reminded that we may so easily make our own trenchers as well as fill them. To see the tree reappear on the table instead of going to the fire or some equally coarse use is some compensation for having it cut down. I was the more pleased with the sight of these trays, because the tools used were so simple, as they were made by hand, not by machinery. They may make equally good pails with the hand-made ones, and cheaper as well as faster, at the pail factory, but that interests me less because the man is turned partly into a machine there himself. In the other case, the workman's relation to his work is more poetic. He also shows more dexterity and is more of a man. You come away from the great factory saddened, as if the chief end of man were to make pails; but in the case of the countryman who makes a few by hand rainy days, the relative importance of human life and of pails is preserved, and you come away thinking of the simple and helpful life of the man, and would fain go to making pails yourself. When labor is reduced to turning a crank, it is no longer amusing nor truly profitable. Let the business become very profitable in a pecuniary sense, and so be " driven," as the phrase is, and carried on on a large scale, and the man is sunk in it, while only the pail or tray floats; we are interested in it only in the same way as the proprietor or company is.

Oct. 20, 1840. My friend is the apology for my life. In him are the spaces which my orbit traverses.

There is no quarrel between the good and the bad, but only between the bad and the bad. In the former case there is inconsistency merely, in the latter a vicious consistency.

Men chord sometimes as the flute and the

pumpkin vine, a perfect chord, a harmony, but no melody. They are not of equal fineness of tone. For the most part I find that in another man and myself the keynote is not the same, so that there are no perfect chords in our gamuts. But if we do not chord by whole tones, nevertheless his sharps are sometimes my flats, and so we play some very difficult pieces together, though the sameness at last fatigues the ear. We never rest on a full natural note, but I sacrifice my naturalness, and he his. We play no tune through, only chromatic strains, or trill upon the same note till our ears ache.

Oct. 20, 1852. The clouds have lifted in the northwest, and I see the mountains in sunshine (all the more attractive from the cold I feel here), with a tinge of purple on them, — a cold, but memorable and glorious outline. This is an advantage of mountains in the horizon; they show you fair weather from the midst of foul. Many a man, when I tell him that I have been upon a mountain, asks if I took a glass with me. No doubt I could have seen further with a glass, and particular objects more distinctly; could have counted more meeting-houses; but this has nothing to do with the peculiar beauty and grandeur of the view which an elevated position affords. It was not to see a few particular objects as if they were near at hand, as I had been

accustomed to see them, that I ascended the
mountain, but to see an infinite variety far and
near, in their relation to each other, thus reduced to a single picture.   The facts of science
in comparison with poetry are wont to be as
vulgar as looking from a mountain with a telescope.   It is a counting of meeting-houses.

Oct. 20, 1854: Saw the sun rise from the
mountain top [Wachusett].   Soon after sunrise
I saw the pyramidal shadow of the mountain
reaching quite across the State, its apex resting
on the Green or Hoosac mountains, appearing
as a deep-blue section of a cone there.   It rapidly contracted, and its apex approached the
mountain itself.   When about three miles distant, the whole conical shadow was very distinct.
The shadow of the mountain makes some minutes' difference in the time of sunrise to the inhabitants of Hubbardston, a few miles west.

Oct. 20, 1855. · I have collected and split up
now quite a pile of driftwood, rails and riders
and stems and stumps of trees, perhaps one half
or three fourths of a tree.   It is more amusing
not only to collect this with my boat, and bring
it from the river on my back, but to split it also,
than it would be to speak to a farmer for a load
of wood, and to saw and split that.   Each stick
I deal with has a history, and I read it as I am
handling it, and last of all, I remember my ad-

ventures in getting it, while it is burning in the winter evening. That is the most interesting part of its history. When I am splitting it, I study the effects of water on it, and, if it is a stump, the curiously winding grain by which it separates into so many prongs, how to take advantage of its grain, and split it most easily. I find that a dry oak stump will· split most easily in the direction of its diameter, not at right angles with it, or along its circles of growth. I got out some good knees for a boat. Thus one half the value of my wood is enjoyed before it is housed, and the other half is equal to the whole value of an equal quantity of the wood which I buy.

Some of my acquaintances have been wondering why I took all this pains, bringing some nearly three miles by water, and have suggested various reasons for it. I tell them, in my despair of making them understand me, that it is a profound secret, which it has proved, yet I did hint that one reason was that I wanted to get it. I take some satisfaction in eating my food, as well as in being nourished by it. I feel well at dinner time, as well as after it. The world will never find out why you don't love to have your bed tucked up for you, why you will be so perverse. I enjoy more, drinking water at a clear spring, than out of a goblet at a gentleman's

table. I like best the bread which I have
baked, the garment which I have made, the
shelter I have constructed, the fuel I have gathered. It is always a recommendation to me to
know that a man has ever been poor, has been
regularly born into this world, knows the language. I require to be assured of certain philosophers that they have once been barefooted,
footsore, have eaten a crust because they had
nothing better, and know what sweetness resides
in it. I have met with some barren accomplished gentlemen who seemed to have been at
school all their lives, and never had a vacation
to live in. Oh, if they could only have been
stolen by the gypsies, and carried far beyond
the reach of their guardians! They had better
have died in their infancy, and been buried under the leaves, their lips besmeared with black-
berries, and cock robin for their sexton.

Oct. 20, 1856. I think that all spiders can
walk on water, for when last summer I knocked
one off my boat by chance, he ran swiftly back to
the boat and climbed up, as if more to avoid the
fishes than the water. This would account for
those long lines stretched low over the water
from one grass-stem to another. I see one of
them now, five or six feet long, and only three or
four inches above the surface. It is remarkable
that there is no perceptible sag to it, weak as
the line must be.

Oct. 20, 1857. P. M. To the Easterbrook country. I had gone but little way on the old Carlisle road when I saw Brooks Clark, who is now about eighty, and bent like a bow, hastening along the road, barefooted as usual, with an axe in his hand, in haste perhaps on account of the cold wind on his bare feet. When he got up to me, I saw that beside the axe in one hand, he had his shoes in the other, filled with knurly apples and a dead robin. He stopped and talked with me a few moments; said that we had had a noble autumn and might now expect some cold weather. I asked if he had found the robin dead. No, he said, he found it with its wing broken, and killed it. He also added that he had found some apples in the woods, and as he had not anything to carry them in, he put them in his shoes. They were queer looking trays to carry fruit in. How many he got in along toward the toes, I don't know. I noticed, too, that his pockets were stuffed with them. His old frock coat was hanging in strips about the skirts, as were his pantaloons about his naked feet. He appeared to have been out on a scout this gusty afternoon to see what he could find, as the youngest boy might. It pleased me to see this cheery old man, with such a feeble hold on life, bent almost double, thus enjoying the evening of his days. · Far be it from me

to call it avarice or penury, this childlike delight in finding something in the woods or fields,
and carrying it home in the October evening, as
a trophy to be added to his winter's stores. Oh,
no, he was happy to be nature's pensioner still,
and bird-like to pick up his living. Better his
robin than your turkey, his shoes full of apples
than your barrels full. They will be sweeter,
and suggest a better tale. He can afford to tell
how he got them, and I to listen. There is an
old wife, too, at home, to share them, and hear
how they were obtained; like an old squirrel
shuffling to his hole with a nut. Far less
pleasing to me the loaded wain, more suggestive
of avarice and of spiritual penury. This old
man's cheeriness was worth a thousand of the
church's sacraments and memento moris. It
was better than a prayerful mood. It proves
to me old age as tolerable, as happy, as infancy.
I was glad of an occasion to suspect that this
afternoon he had not been at *work*, but living
somewhat after my own fashion (though he did
not explain the axe), and been out to see what
nature had for him, and was now hastening
home to a burrow he knew of, where he could
warm his old feet. If he had been a young
man he would probably have thrown away his
apples, and put on his shoes for shame when he
saw me coming, but old age is manlier. It has

learned to live, makes fewer apologies, like infancy. This seems a very manly man. I have known him within a few years building stone wall by himself, barefooted.

What a wild and rich domain that Easterbrook country! Not a cultivated, hardly a cultivable field in it, and yet it delights all natural persons, and feeds more still. Such great rocky and moist tracts, which daunt the farmer, are reckoned as unimproved land, and therefore worth but little; but think of the miles of huckleberries, and of barberries, and of wild apples, so fair both in flower and fruit, resorted to by men and beasts, Clark, Brown, Melvin, and the robins. There are barberry bushes or clumps there, behind which I could actually pick two bushels of berries without being seen by you on the other side. They are not a quarter picked at last by all creatures together. I walk for two or three miles, and still the clumps of barberries, great sheaves with their wreaths of scarlet fruit, show themselves before me and on every side.

Oct. 21, 1852. To Second Division Brook and Ministerial Swamp. I find caddis - cases with worms in Second Division Brook; and what mean those little piles of yellow sand on dark-colored stones at the bottom of the swift-running water, kept together and in place by some kind of gluten, and looking as if sprinkled on the stones, one eighteenth of an inch in diameter? These caddis-worms build a little case around themselves, and sometimes attach a few dead leaves to disguise it, and then fasten it slightly to some swaying grass-stem or blade at the bottom in swift water, and these are their quarters till next spring. This reminds me that winter does not put his rude fingers in the bottom of the brooks. When you look into them, you see various dead leaves floating or resting on the bottom, and you do not suspect that some are the disguises which the caddis-worms have borrowed.

Oct. 21, 1857. I see many myrtle birds now about the house, this forenoon, on the advent of cooler weather. They keep flying up against the house and the window, and fluttering there as if they would come in, or alight on the woodpile or the pump. They would commonly be mistaken for sparrows, but show more white when they fly, beside the yellow on the rump and sides of breast, seen near to, and two white bars on the wings; chubby birds.

P. M. Up Assabet. Cool and windy. Those who have put it off thus long make haste now to collect what apples were left out, and dig their potatoes before the ground shall freeze hard. Now again as in the spring we begin to look for sheltered and sunny places where we may sit. I cannot go by a large dead swamp white-oak log this cool evening, but with no little exertion get it aboard, and some blackened swamp white-oak stumps whose earthy parts are all gone. As I am paddling home swiftly before the northwest wind, absorbed in my wooding, I see, this cool and grayish evening, that peculiar yellow light in the east, from the sun a little before setting. It has just come out beneath a great cold slate-colored cloud that occupies most of the western sky, as smaller ones the eastern, and now its rays, slanting over the hill in whose shadow I float, fall on the eastern trees and hills with a thin yellow light like a clear yellow wine ; but somehow it reminds me that now the hearth-side is getting to be a more comfortable place than out-of-doors. Before I get home the sun has set, and a cold white light in the west succeeded.

Is not the poet bound to write his own biography ? Is there any other work for him but a good journal ? We do not wish to know how his imaginary hero, but how he the actual hero, lived from day to day.

That big swamp white-oak limb or tree which I found prostrate in the swamp was longer than my boat, and tipped it considerably. One whole side, the upper, was covered with green hypnum,

and the other was partly white with fungi.
That green coat adhered when I split it. Immortal wood! that had begun to live again.
Others burn unfortunate trees that lose their
lives prematurely. These old stumps stand like
anchorites or yogees, putting off their earthly
garments, more and more sublimed from year
to year, ready to be translated, and then they
are ripe for my fire. I administer the last sac-
rament and purification. I find old pitch-pine
sticks which have lain in the mud at the bottom
of the river, nobody knows how long, and weigh
them up, almost as heavy as lead, float them
home, saw and split them. Their pitch, still fat
and yellow, has saved them for me, and they
burn like candles. I become a connoisseur in
wood, at last, take only the best.

Oct. 22, 1853. Yesterday toward night, gave
Sophia and mother a sail as far as the Battle-
ground. One-eyed John Goodwin, the fisherman, was loading into a handcart and conveying
home the piles of driftwood which of late he
had collected with his boat. It was a beautiful
evening, and a clear amber sunset lit up all
the eastern shores, and that man's employment,
so simple and direct (though he is regarded by
most as a vicious character), whose whole motive
was so easy to fathom, thus to obtain his winter's wood, charmed me unspeakably. So much

do we love actions that are simple. They are
all poetic. We, too, would fain be so employed,
in a way so unlike the artificial and complicated
pursuits of most men. Consider how the broker
collects his winter's wood, what sport he makes
of it, what is his boat and handcart. Postpon-
ing instant life, he makes haste to Boston in the
cars, and there deals in stocks, not quite relish-
ing his employment, and so earns the money
with which he buys his fuel. When by chance
I meet him about this indirect complicated business, I am not struck with 'the beauty of his
employment. It does not harmonize with the
amber sunset. How much more the former
consults his genius, — some genius, at any rate.
Now I should love to get my fuel so, have got
some of it so. But, though I am glad to have
it, I do not love to get it in any other way less
simple and direct. If I buy one necessary of
life, I cheat myself to some extent. I deprive
myself of the pleasure, the inexpressible joy
which is the unfailing reward of satisfying any
want of my nature simply and truly. No trade
is simple, but artificial and complex. It goes
against the grain, it postpones life. If the first
generation does not die of it, the third or fourth
does. In face of all statistics, I will never
believe that it is the descendants of tradesmen
who keep the state alive, but of simple yeomen

or laborers. This indeed statistics say of the city reinforced by the country. This simplicity it is and the vigor it imparts, that enables the vagabond, though he does get drunk and is sent to the house of correction so often, to hold up his head among men. " If I go to Boston every day and sell tape from morning till night," says the merchant (which we will admit is not a beautiful action), " some time or other I shall be able to buy the best of fuel without stint." Yes, but not the pleasure of picking it up by the river-side, which, I may say, is of even more value than the warmth it yields. It is to give no account of my employment to say that I cut wood to keep me from freezing, or cultivate beans to keep me from starving. Oh, no, the greatest value of these labors is received before the wood is teamed home, or the beans are harvested. Goodwin stands on the solid earth. For such as he, no political economies, with their profit and loss, supply and demand, need ever be written, for they will need to use no policy. As for the complex ways of living, I love them not, however much I practice them. In as many places as possible, I will get my feet down to the earth. There is no secret in Goodwin's trade more than in the sun's. He is a most constant fisherman. He must well know the taste of pickerel by this time. When I can remember to have seen him fishing almost daily for some time, if it rains, I am surprised on looking out to see him slowly wending his way to the river in his oilcloth coat, with his basket and pole. I saw him the other day fishing in the middle of the stream, the day after I had seen him fishing on the shore, while by a kind of magic I sailed by him. He said he was catching minnows for bait in the winter. When I was twenty rods off, he held up a pickerel that weighed two and a half pounds, which he had forgotten to show me before, and the next morning, as he afterwards told me, he caught one that weighed three pounds. If it is ever necessary to appoint a committee on fish ponds and pickerel, let him be one of them.

Oct. 22, 1857. P. M. To and round Flint's Pond. Crossing my old beanfield, I see the blue pond between the green pines in the field, and am reminded that we are almost reduced to the russet (*i. e.*, pale brown grass tinged with red blackberry vines) of such fields as this, the blue of water, the green of pines, and the dull reddish-brown of oak leaves. This sight of the blue water between the now perfectly green pines, seen over the light-brown pasture, is peculiarly Novemberish, though it may be like this in early spring.

Look from the high hill just before sundown,

over the pond. The mountains are a mere cold slate color. But what a perfect crescent of mountains we have in our northwest horizon. Do we ever give thanks for it? Even as pines and larches and hemlocks grow in communities in the wilderness, so it seems do mountains love society. Though there may be two or more ranges, one behind the other, and ten or twelve miles between them, yet, if the farthest are the highest, they are all seen as one group at this distance. I look up northwest to my mountains, as a farmer to his hill-lot or rocky pasture from his door. I drive no cattle to the Ipswich hills. I own no pasture for them there. My eyes it is alone that wander to those blue pastures which no drought affects. I am content to dwell here and see the sun go down behind my mountain fence.

Oct. 23, 1852. The milk weed (*Syriaca*) now rapidly discounting. The lanceolate pods having opened, the seeds spring out on the least jar, or when dried by the sun, and form a little fluctuating white silky mass or tuft, each held by a fine thread until a stronger puff of wind sets them free. It is pleasant to see the plant thus dispersing its seeds.

October has been the month of autumnal tints. The first of the month, the tints began to be more general, at which time the frosts began.

There were scattered bright tints long before, but not till then did the forest begin to be painted. By the end of the month, the leaves will either have fallen, or be seared and turned brown by the frosts, for the most part.

My friend is one who takes me for what I am. A stranger takes me for something else than what I am. We do not speak, we cannot communicate, till we find that we are recognized. The stranger supposes in our stead a third person whom we do not know, and we leave him to converse with that one. It is suicide for us to become abettors in misapprehending ourselves. Suspicion creates the stranger. I cannot abet any man in misapprehending myself.

What men call social virtues, good fellowship, is commonly but the virtue of pigs in a litter which lie close together to keep each other warm. It brings men together in crowds and mobs in bar-rooms and elsewhere, but it does not deserve the name of virtue.

Oct. 23, 1853. Many phenomena remind me that now is to some extent a second spring, not only the new springing and blossoming of flowers, but the peeping of the hylodes for some time, and the faint warbling of their spring notes, by many birds.

Oct. 23, 1855. Now is the time for chestnuts. A stone cast against the trees shakes them down in showers upon one's head and shoulders. But I cannot excuse myself for using the stone. It is not innocent, it is not just so to maltreat the tree that feeds us. I am not disturbed by considering that if I thus shorten its life, I shall not enjoy its fruit so long, but am prompted to a more innocent course by motives purely of humanity. I sympathize with the tree, yet I heaved a big stone against the trunk, like a robber, not too good to commit murder. I trust I shall never do it again. These gifts should be accepted not merely with gentleness, but with a certain humble gratitude. It is not a time of distress when a little haste and violence even might be pardoned. It is worse than boorish, it is criminal, to inflict an unnecessary injury on the tree that feeds or shades us. If you would learn the secrets of nature, you must practice more humanity than others. The thought that I was robbing myself by injuring the tree did not occur to me, but I was affected as if I had cast a rock at a sentient being, with a duller sense than my own, it is true, but yet a distant relative. Behold a man cutting down a tree to come at the fruit! What is the moral of such an act? Shall we begin, old men in crime ; would that we might grow innocent, at last, as the children of light.

Oct. 24, 1837. Every part of nature teaches that the passing away of one life is the making room for another. The oak dies down to the ground, leaving within its rind a rich virgin mould which will impart a vigorous life to an infant forest. The pine leaves a sandy and sterile soil, the harder woods, a strong and fruitful mould. So this constant abrasion and decay of our lives makes the soil of our future growth. The wood we now mature, when it becomes mould, determines the character of our second growth. If I grow pines and birches, my mould will not sustain oak, but pines and birches, or, perchance, weeds and brambles.

Oct. 24, 1857. P. M. To Smith's chestnut grove. I get a couple of quarts of chestnuts. I find my account in this long-continued monotonous labor of picking chestnuts all the afternoon, brushing the leaves aside without looking up, absorbed in that, and forgetting better things awhile. My eye is educated to discover anything on the ground. It is probably wholesomer to look at the ground much, than at the heavens. This occupation affords a certain broad pause, and opportunity to start again afterwards, turn over a new leaf.

Oct. 24, 1858. A northeast storm, though not much rain falls to-day, but a fine driving mizzle. This, as usual, brings the geese, and at 2.30 P. M. I see two flocks go over, faintly honking. A great many must go over to-day, and also alight in this neighborhood. This weather warns them of the approach of winter, and this wind speeds them on their way.

The brilliant autumnal colors are red and yellow, and the various tints and shades of these. Blue is reserved to be the color of the sky, but yellow and red are the colors of the earth-flower. Every fruit on ripening, and just before its fall, acquires a bright tint. So do the leaves ; so the sky before the end of the day, and the year near its setting. October is the red sunset sky, November the later twilight. Color stands for all ripeness and success. The noblest feature, the eye, is the fairest-colored, the jewel of the body.

Oct. 25, 1852. P. M. Down river to Ball's Hill in boat. Another perfect Indian-summer day. One of my oars makes a creaking sound like a block in a harbor, such a sound as would bring tears into an old sailor's eyes. It suggests to me adventure and seeking one's fortune. The water for some time has been clear of weeds mostly, and looks cool for fishes. We get into the lee of the hill near Abner Buttrick's (?) where is smooth water, and here it is very warm and sunny under the pitch pines. Some small husky white asters still survive. The autumnal tints grow gradually darker and duller, but not less rich to my eye. And now a hillside near the river exhibits the darkest crispy reds and browns of every hue, all agreeably blended. At the foot, next the meadow, stands a front rank of smoke-like maples, bare of leaves, intermixed with yellow birches. Higher up are red oaks, of various shades of dull red, with yellowish, perhaps black oaks, intermixed, and walnuts now brown, and near the hill-top or rising above the rest, a still yellow oak, and here and there amid the rest or in the foreground on the meadow, dull, ashy, salmon-colored white oaks, large and small, all these contrasting with the clear, liquid, sempiternal green of pines. The sheen on the water blinds my eyes. Mint is still green and wonderfully recreating to smell. I had put such things behind me. It is hard to remember lilies now.

The constitution of the Indian mind appears to be the very opposite of the white man's. He is acquainted with a different side of nature. He measures his life by winters, not summers. His year is not measured by the sun, but consists of a certain number of moons, and his moons are measured not by days, but by nights. He has taken hold of the dark side of nature, the white man of the bright side.

Oct. 25, 1857. I am amused to see that Varro tells us the Latin *e* represents the vowel sound in the bleat of a sheep (Bee); if he had referred instead to some word pronounced by the

Romans, we should not be the wiser, but we do not doubt that sheep bleat to-day as they did then.

Oct. 25, 1860. The thistles which I now see have their heads recurved, which at least saves their down somewhat from moisture. When I pull out the down, the seed is, for the most part, left in the receptacle (?) in regular order there, like the pricks in a thimble ; a slightly convex surface, the seeds set like cartridges in a circular cartridge box, in hollow cylinders, which look like circles crowded into more or less of a diamond, pentagonal, or hexagonal form. The perfectly dry and bristly involucre which hedges them round, so repulsive externally, is very neat and attractive within, as smooth and tender toward its charge as it is rough and prickly externally toward the foes that might do it injury. It is a hedge of imbricated, thin, and narrow leaflets, of a light brown color, beautifully glossy like silk, a most fit receptacle for the delicate, downy parachutes of the seed. The little seeds are kept dry under this unsuspected silky or satiny ceiling, whose old, weather-worn, and rough outside alone we see, like a mossy roof. I know of no object more unsightly to a careless glance than an empty thistle - head, yet if you examine it closely, it may remind you of the silk - lined cradle in which a prince was rocked.. That which seemed a mere brown and worn-out relic of the summer, sinking into the earth by the roadside, turns out to be a precious casket.

Oct. 26, 1851.   I awoke this morning to infinite regret.   In my dream I had been riding, but the horses bit each other, and occasioned endless trouble and anxiety, and it was my employment to hold their heads apart.   Next I sailed over the sea in a small vessel such as the Northmen used, as it were, to the Bay of Fundy, and thence overland I sailed still, over the shallows about the sources of rivers toward the deeper channel of a stream which emptied into the gulf beyond.   Again I was in my own small pleasure boat, learning to sail on the sea, and I raised my sail before my anchor, which I dragged far into the sea.   I saw the buttons which had come off the coats of drowned men, and suddenly I saw my dog, when I knew not that I had one, standing in the sea up to his chin to warm his legs, which had been wet, and which the cool wind had numbed.   Then I was walking in a meadow where the dry season permitted me to walk further than usual.   Then I met Mr. Alcott and we fell to quoting and referring to grand and pleasing couplets and single lines which we had read in time past, and I quoted one which in my waking hours I have no knowledge of, but in my dream it was familiar enough. I only know that those I quoted expressed regret, and were like the following, though they were not these, viz. : —

"The short parenthesis of life was sweet,"
"The remembrance of youth is a sigh," etc.

Then again the instant I awoke, methought I was a musical instrument from which I heard a strain die out, — a bugle, a clarionet, or a flute. My body was the organ and channel of melody, as a flute is of the music that is breathed through it. My flesh sounded and vibrated still to the strain, and my nerves were the chords of the lyre. I awoke, therefore, to an infinite regret, to find myself not the thoroughfare of glorious and world-stirring inspirations, but a scuttle full of dirt, such a thoroughfare only as the street and the kennel, where perchance the wind may sometimes draw forth a strain of music from a straw.

I can partly account for this. Last evening I was reading Laing's account of the Northmen, and though I did not write in my journal, I remember feeling a fertile regret, and deriving even an inexpressible satisfaction as it were from my ability to feel regret, which made that evening richer than those which had preceded it. I heard the last strain or flourish, as I woke, played on my body as the instrument. Such I knew I had been and might be again, and my regret arose from the consciousness how little like a musical instrument my body was now.

Oct. 26, 1852. Walden and Cliffs. P. M. It is cool to-day and windier. The water is rippled considerably. As I stand in the boat, the farther off the water, the bluer it is. Looking straight down, it is a dark green. Hence apparently the celestial blueness of those distant river reaches, when the water is agitated so that the surfaces of the waves reflect the sky at the right angle. It is a darker blue than that of the sky itself. When I look down on the pond from the peak, it is far less blue.

The blue-stemmed and white golden-rod apparently survive till winter, push up and blossom anew.

At this season we seek warm, sunny lees and hillsides, as that under the pitch pines by Walden shore, where we cuddle and warm ourselves in the sun, as by a fire, where we may get some of its reflected as well as direct heat.

Coming by Haden's I see that, the sun setting, its rays, which yet find some vapor to lodge on in the clear cold air, impart a purple tinge to the mountains in the northwest. I think it is only in cold weather that I see this.

Oct. 26, 1853. I well remember the time this year when I first heard the dreaming of the toads. I was laying out house lots on Little River in Haverhill. We had had some raw, cold, and wet weather, but this day was remarkably warm and pleasant, and I had thrown off my overcoat. I was going home to dinner past a shallow pool, green with springing grass, when it occurred to me that I heard the dreaming of the toad. It rung through and filled all the air, though I had not heard it once, before. I turned my companion's attention to it, but he did not appear to perceive it as a new sound in the air. Loud and prevailing as it is, most men do not notice it at all. It is to them perchance a sort of simmering or seething of all nature. It affects their thoughts, though they are not conscious of hearing it. How watchful we must be to keep the crystal well that we are made, clear. Often we are so jarred by chagrins in dealing with the world that we cannot reflect.

Everything beautiful impresses us as sufficient to itself. Many men who have had much intercourse with the world, and not borne the trial well, affect me as all resistance, all burr and rind, without any gentle man or tender and innocent core left.

It is surprising how any reminiscence of a different season of the year affects us. When I meet with any such in my journal, it affects me as poetry, and I appreciate that other season

and that particular phenomenon more than at
the time.   The world so seen is all one spring,
and full of beauty.   You only need to make a
faithful record of an average summer day's experience and summer mood, and read it in the
winter, and it will carry you back to more than
that summer day alone could show.   Only the
rarest flower, the purest melody of the season,
thus comes down to us.

When, after feeling dissatisfied with my life,
I aspire to something better, am more scrupu-
lous, more reserved and continent, as if expecting somewhat, suddenly I find myself full of life
as a nut of meat, even overflowing with a quiet,
genial mirthfulness.   I think to myself, I must
attend to my diet.   I must get up earlier and
take a morning walk.   I must have done with
business, and devote myself to my muse.   So I
dam up my stream, and my waters gather to a
head.   I am freighted with thought.

Oct. 26, 1855.   P. M.   To Conantum.   I examine some frost weed.   It is still quite alive,
indeed just out of bloom, the leaves now a purplish brown, and its bark at the ground is quite
tight and entire.   Pulling it up, I find bright
pink shoots to have put forth, half an inch long,
and starting even at the surface of the sod.   Is
not this, as well as its second blossoming, somewhat peculiar to this plant? and may it not be

that when at last the cold is severe, the sap is
frozen and bursts the bark, and the breath of the
dying plant is frozen about it? I see a red
squirrel dash out from the wall, snatch an apple
from amid many on the ground, and, running
swiftly up the tree with it, proceed to eat it,
sitting on a smooth dead limb with its back to
the wind, and its tail curled close over its back.
It allows me to approach within eight feet. It
holds the apple between its two fore paws, and
scoops out the pulp mainly with its lower inci-
sors, making a saucer-like cavity, high and thin
at the edge, where it bites off the skin and lets
it drop. It keeps its jaws moving very briskly,
from time to time turning the apple round and
round with its paws, as it eats, like a wheel in a
plane at right angles with its body. It holds it
up and twirls it with ease. Suddenly it pauses,
having taken alarm at something, then drops
the remainder of the apple in the hollow of a
bough, and glides off in short snatches, uttering
a faint, sharp, bird-like note.

I sometimes think I must go off to some wilderness, where I can have a better opportunity
to play life, can find more suitable materials to
build my house with, and enjoy the pleasure of
collecting my fuel in the forest.

I have more taste for the wild sports of hunting, fishing, wigwam building, and collecting

wood wherever you find it, than for butchering, farming, carpentry, working in a factory or going to a wood market.

Oct. 26, 1857.   P. M.   Round by Puffer's via Clamshell.   A driving east or northeast storm. I can see through the stormy mist only a mile. The river is getting partly over the meadows at last, and my spirits rise with it.   Methinks this rise of the waters must affect every thought and deed in the town.   It qualifies my sentence and life.   I trust there will appear in this journal some flow, some gradual filling of the springs and raising of the streams, that the accumulating grists may be ground.   A storm is a new and in some respects more active life in nature. Larger migratory birds make their appearance. They at least sympathize with the movements of the watery element and the winds.   I see two great fishhawks (*possibly* blue herons) slowly beating northeast against the storm, — by what a curious tie circling ever near each other and in the same direction, as if you might expect the very motes in the air to be paired, two long undulating wings conveying a feathered body through the misty atmosphere and thus inseparably associated with another planet of the same species.   I can just glimpse their undulating lives.   Damon and Pythias they must be.   The waves beneath, which are of kindred form, are

still more social, multitudinous, ἀνήριθμον. Where
is my mate, beating against the storm with me ?
They fly according to the valley of the river,
northeast or southwest. I start up snipes also
at Clamshell meadow. This weather sets the
migratory birds in motion, and also makes
them bolder. These regular phenomena of the
seasons get at last to be (they were, at first,
of course) simply and plainly phenomena or
phases of my life. The seasons and all their
changes are in me. I see not a dead eel or
floating snake, or a gull, but it sounds my life,
and is like a line or accent in its poem. Almost
I believe the Concord would not rise and over-
flow its banks again, were I not here. After a
while I learn what my moods and seasons are. I
would have nothing subtracted, I can imagine
nothing added. My moods are thus periodical,
not two days in the year alike : the perfect cor-
respondence of nature with man, so that he is at
home in her !

Many sparrows are flitting past amid the
birches and sallows. They are chiefly *Fringilla
hiemalis.* How often they may be seen thus
flitting along in a straggling manner from bush
to bush, so that the hedgerow will be all alive
with them, each uttering a faint chip from time
to time, bewildering you so that you know not if
the greater part are gone by, or still to come.

One rests but a moment in the tree before you and is gone again. You wonder if they know whither they are bound, and how their leader is appointed. Those sparrows, too, are thoughts I have ; they come and go, they flit by quickly on their migrations, uttering only a faint chip, I know not whither or why, exactly. One will not rest on its twig for me to scrutinize it. The whole copse will be alive with my rambling thoughts, bewildering me by their very multitude, but they will be all gone directly without leaving me a feather.

My loftiest thought is somewhat like an eagle that suddenly comes into the field of view, suggesting great things and thrilling the beholder, as if it were bound hitherward with a message for me. But it comes no nearer, circles and soars away, disappointing me, till it is lost behind a cliff or a cloud.

Spring is brown ; summer, green ; autumn, yellow ; winter, white ; November, gray.

Oct. 27, 1851. This morning I awoke and found it snowing and the ground covered with snow, quite unexpectedly, for last night it was rainy and not cold. The strong northwest wind blows the damp snow along almost horizontally. The birds fly about as if seeking shelter. The cold numbs my fingers this morning. Winter, with its inwardness, is upon us. A man is constrained to sit down and to think.

The obstacles which the heart meets with are like granite blocks, which one alone cannot move. She who was as the morning light to me, is now neither the morning star nor the evening star. We meet but to find each other further asunder, and the oftener we meet, the more rapid the divergence. So a star of the first magnitude pales in the heavens, not from any fault in the observer's eye, nor from any fault in itself, perchance, but because its progress in its own system has put a greater distance between.

The night is oracular. What have been the intimations of the night? I ask. How have you passed the night? Good night!

My friend will be bold to conjecture. He will guess bravely at the significance of my words.

The *Ardea minor* still with us. Saw a woodcock or snipe (?) feeding, probing the mud with its long bill, under the railroad bridge, within two feet of me. For a long time I could not scare it far away. What a disproportionate length of bill!

Oct. 27, 1853. I love to be reminded of that universal and eternal spring when the minute, crimson-starred female flowers of the hazel are peeping forth on the hillsides, when nature revives in all her pores.

Some less obvious and commonly unobserved signs of the progress of the seasons interest me most, like the loose dangling catkins of the hop-hornbeam, or of the black or yellow birch. I can recall distinctly to my mind the image of these things, and that time in which they flourished is glorious, as if it were before the fall of man. I see all nature for the time under this aspect. These features are particularly prominent; as if the first object I saw on approaching this planet in the spring was the catkins of the hop hornbeam on the hillsides. As I sailed by, I saw the yellowish waving sprays.

Oct. 27, 1857. P. M. Up river. The third day of steady rain. Wind northeast. I go up the river as far as Hillard's second grove in order to share the general commotion and excitement of the elements, wind and waves and rain. A half dozen boats at the landing were full, and the waves beating over them. It was hard getting out, hauling up, and emptying mine. It was a rod and a half from the water's edge. Now look out for your rails and other fencing stuff and loose lumber, lest it be floated off. I sailed swiftly, standing up, and tipping my boat to make it keel on its side, though at first it was hard to keep off a lee shore. It was exciting to feel myself tossed by the dark waves, and hear them surge about me. The reign of water now begins, and how it gambols and revels; waves are its leaves, foam its blossoms. How they run and leap in great droves, deriving new excitement from each other; schools of porpoises and blackfish are only more animated waves, and have acquired the gait and gambols of the sea itself.

I hear that Sammy Hoar saw geese go over to-day. The fall, strictly speaking, is approaching an end in this probably annual northeast storm. Thus the summer winds up its accounts. The Indians, it is said, did not look for winter till the springs were full. The ducks and other fowl, reminded of the lateness, go by. The few remaining leaves come fluttering down. The snow-fleas, as to-day, are washed out of the bark of meadow trees, and cover the surface of the flood. The winter's wood is bargained for and being hauled. There is not much more for the farmer to do in the fields. This storm reminds men to put things on a winter footing.

The real facts of a poet's life would be of more value to us than any work of his art. I mean that the very scheme and form of his poetry, so called, is adopted at a sacrifice of vital truth and poetry. Shakespeare has left us his fancies and imaginings, but the truth of his life, with its becoming circumstances, we know nothing about. The writer is reported, the liver not at all. Shakespeare's house! how hollow it is! No man can conceive of Shakespeare in that house. We want the basis of fact, of

an actual life, to complete our Shakespeare as
much as a statue wants its pedestal. A poet's
life, with this broad actual basis, would be as
superior to Shakespeare's, as a lichen, with its
base or thallus, is superior, in the order of being,
to a fungus.

The Littleton giant brought us a load of coal
within the week. He appears deformed and
weakly, though actually well-formed. He does
not nearly stand up straight. His knees knock
together. They touch when he is standing most
upright, and so reduce his height at least three
inches. He is also very round-shouldered and
stooping, probably from the habit of crouching
to conceal his height. He wears a low hat for
the same purpose. The tallest man looks like a
boy beside him. He has a seat to his wagon
made on purpose for him. He habitually stops
before all doors. You wonder what his horses
think of him, that a strange horse is not afraid
of him. His voice is deep and full, but mild,
for he is quite modest and retiring, really a
worthy man, 't is said. Pity he could not have
been undertaken by a committee in season, and
put through like the boy Safford, been well developed bodily and mentally, taught to hold up
his head, and not mind people's eyes or remarks.
It is remarkable that the giants have never cor-
respondingly great hearts.

Oct. 27, 1858. Who will attempt to describe in words the difference in tint between two neighboring leaves on the same tree [in autumn] or of two thousand ? for by so many the eye is addressed in a glance. In describing the richly spotted leaves, for instance, how often we find ourselves using ineffectually words which indicate faintly our good intentions, giving them in our despair a terminal twist toward our mark, such as reddish, yellowish, purplish, etc. We cannot make a hue of words, for they are not to be compounded like colors, and hence we are obliged to use such ineffectual expressions as reddish-brown, etc. They need to be ground together.

Oct. 28, 1853. For a year or two past, my publisher, falsely so called, has been writing from time to time, to ask what disposition should be made of the copies of " A Week on the Concord and Merrimack Rivers " still on hand, and at last suggesting that he had use for the room they occupied in his cellar. So I had them all sent to me here, and they have arrived to-day by express, filling the man's wagon, 706 copies out of an edition of 1000, which I bought of Munroe four years ago, and have been ever since paying for and have not quite paid for yet. The wares are sent to me at last, and I have an opportunity to examine my purchase. They are something more substantial than fame, as

my back knows, which has borne them up two
flights of stairs to a place similar to that to
which they trace their origin.   Of the remaining 290 and odd, 75 were given away, the rest
sold.   I have now a library of nearly 900 volumes, over 700 of which I wrote myself.   Is
it not well that the author should behold the
fruits of his labor ?   My works are piled up on
one side of my chamber half as high as my head,
my opera omnia.   This was authorship, these are
the works of my brain.   There was just one
piece of good luck in the venture.   The un-
bound were tied up by the printer four years
ago in stout paper wrappers, and inscribed : —

> H. D. Thoreau,
> Concord River,
> 50 cops.

so Munroe had only to cross out " River " and
write " Mass.," and deliver them to the express-
man at once.   I can see now what I write for,
the result of my labors.   Nevertheless in spite
of this result, sitting beside the inert mass of my
works, I take up my pen to-night to record what
thought or experience I may have had, with as
much satisfaction as ever.   Indeed I believe
that the result is more inspiring and better for
me than if a thousand had bought my wares.
It affects my privacy less and leaves me freer.

   Oct. 28, 1855.   By boat to Leaning Hemlocks. As I paddle under the hemlock bank this shady afternoon, about three o'clock, I see a screech-owl sitting on the edge of a hollow hemlock stump about three feet high, at the base of a large hemlock. It sits with its head down, eying me with its eyes partly open, about twenty feet off. When it hears me move, it turns its head toward me, perhaps one eye partly open, with its great, gleaming, golden iris. You see two whitish triangular lines above the eye, meeting at the bill, with a sharp reddish-brown triangle between, and a narrow curved line of black under each eye. At this distance and in this light, you see only a black spot where the eye is, and the question is whether the eyes are open or not. It sits on the lee side of the tree this raw and windy day. You would say this was a bird without a neck. Its short bill, which rests upon its breast, scarcely projects at all, but in a state of rest the whole upper part of the bird from the wings is rounded off smoothly, except the horns, which stand up conspicuously or are slanted back. After watching it ten minutes from the boat, I landed two rods above, and, stealing up quietly behind the hemlock, though from the windward, I looked carefully round it, and to my surprise, saw the owl still sitting there ; so I sprang round quickly with my arm outstretched, and caught it in my hand. It was so surprised that it offered no resistance at first, only glared at me in mute astonishment with eyes as big as saucers. But erelong it began to snap its bill, making quite a noise, and as I rolled it up in my handkerchief and put it in my pocket, it bit my finger slightly. I soon took it out of my pocket, and tying the handkerchief, left it on the bottom of the boat. So I carried it home, and made a small cage in which to keep it for a night. When I took it up, it clung so tightly to my hand as to sink its claws into my fingers and bring blood. When alarmed or provoked most, it snaps its bill and hisses. It puffs up its feathers to nearly twice its usual size, stretches out its neck, and with wide-open eyes stares this way and that, moving its head slowly and undulatingly from side to side with a curious motion. While I write this evening, I see there is ground for much superstition in it. It looks out on me from a dusky corner of its box with its great solemn eyes, perfectly still. I was surprised to find that I could imitate its note, as I remember it, by a guttural whimpering. A remarkably squat figure, being very broad in proportion to its length, with a short tail, and very cat - like in the face with its horns and great eyes. Remarkably large feet and talons, legs thickly clothed to the talons with whitish down. It would lower its head, stretch out its neck, and, bending it from side to side, peer at you with laughable circumspection ; from side to side, as if to catch or absorb into its eyes every ray of light, strain at you with complacent yet earnest scrutiny, raising and lowering its head, and moving it from side to side in a slow and regular manner, at the same time snapping its bill smartly perhaps and faintly hissing and puffing itself up more and more, cat-like, turtle-like, both in hissing and swelling. The slowness and gravity, not to say solemnity of this motion are striking. There is plainly no jesting in this case. General color of the owl a rather pale and perhaps slightly reddish brown, the feathers centred with black. Perches with two claws above, and two below the perch. He has a slight body covered with a mass of soft and light-lying feathers, his head muffled in a great hood. He must be quite comfortable in winter. Dropped a pellet of fur and bones (?) in his cage. He sat not really moping, but trying to sleep in a corner of his box all day, yet with one or both eyes slightly open all the while. I never once caught him with his eyes shut. Ordinarily he stood rather than sat on his perch.

Oct. 29. Up Assabet. Carried my owl to the hill again ; had to shake him out of the box, for he did not go of his own accord. (He had learned to alight on his perch, and it was surprising how lightly and noiselessly he would hop upon it.) There he stood on the grass, at first bewildered, with his horns pricked up and looking toward me. In this strong light, the pupils of his eyes suddenly contracted and the iris expanded, till they were two great brazen orbs with a central spot merely. His attitude expressed astonishment more than anything else. I was obliged to toss him up a little that he might feel his wings, and then he flapped away low and heavily to a hickory on a hillside twenty rods off. I had let him out on the plain just east of the hill. Thither I followed and tried to start him again. He was now on the qui vive, yet would not start. He erected his head, showing some neck narrower than the round head above. His eyes were broad brazen rings around bullets of black. His horns stood quite an inch high, as not before. As I moved around him, he turned his head always toward me till he looked *directly* behind himself, as he sat crosswise on a bough. He behaved as if bewildered and dazzled, gathering all the light he could, and even straining his great eyes to make me out, but not inclining to fly. I had to lift him again with a stick to make him fly, and then he only rose to a higher perch, where at last he seemed to seek the shelter of a thicker cluster of sere leaves, partly crouching there. He never appeared so much alarmed as surprised and astonished. At the bottom of the hollow [stump?] on the edge of which he sat when I first saw him yesterday, eighteen inches beneath him, was a very soft bed of the fine green moss, hypnum, which grows on the bank close by, probably his own bed. It had been recently put there.

I have got a load of great hard-wood stumps.

For sympathy with my neighbors, I might about as well live in China. They are to me barbarians, with their committee-works and gregariousness.

Oct. 28, 1857. As I sat at the wall corner, high on Conantum, the sky generally covered with continuous, cheerless-looking slate-colored clouds, except in the west, I saw through the hollows of the clouds here and there the blue appearing, and all at once a low-slanted glade of sunlight from one of heaven's west windows behind me fell on the bare gray maples, lighting them up with an incredibly intense and pure white light; then, going out there, it lit up some white birch stems south of the pond, then the gray rocks and the pale reddish young oaks of the lower cliffs, then the very pale brown meadow grass, and at last the brilliant white breasts of two ducks tossing on the agitated

surface far off on the pond, which I had not detected before.   It was but a transient ray, and
there was no sunshine afterward, but the intensity of the light was surprising and impressive,
a halo, a glory in which only the just deserved
to live.   It was as if the air, purified by the
long storm, reflected these few rays from side
to side with a complete illumination, like a perfectly polished mirror, while the effect was
greatly enhanced by the contrast with the dull,
dark clouds and the sombre earth.   As if nature did not dare at once to let in the full blaze
of the sun to this combustible atmosphere.   It
was a serene Elysian light, in which the deeds I
have dreamed of, but not realized, might have
been performed.   No perfectly fair weather
ever offered such an arena for noble deeds.   It
was such a light as we behold but dwell not in.
Late in the year, at the eleventh hour, we have
visions of the life we might have lived.   In
each case, every recess was filled and lit up by
the pure white light.   The maples were Potter's,
far down stream, but I dreamed I walked like
a liberated spirit in the maze; the withered
meadow grass was as soft and glorious as paradise.   And then it was remarkable that the
light-giver should have revealed to me for all
life the heaving white breasts of those two
ducks within this glade of light.   It was extin-

guished and relit as it traveled. Tell me precisely the value and significance of these transient gleams which come sometimes at the end of the day before the final dispersion of the clouds at the close of a storm ; too late to be of any service to the works of man for the day, and though the whole night after may be overcast. Is not this a language to be heard and understood? There is in the brown and gray earth and rocks, and the withered leaves and bare twigs at this season a purity more correspondent to the light itself than summer offers.

I look up and see a male marsh-hawk, with his clean-cut wings, that has just skimmed past over my head, not at all disturbed, only tilting his body a little, now twenty rods off, with a demi-semi-quaver of his wings. He is a very neat flyer. I do not often see the marsh-hawk thus. What a regular figure this fellow makes with his broad tail and broad wings ! Does he perceive me, that he rises higher and circles to one - side? He goes round now one full circle without a flap, tilting his wing a little. Then flaps three or four times, and rises higher. Now he comes on like a billow, screaming, steady as a planet in its orbit, with his head bent down, but on second thought that small sprout land seems worthy of a longer scrutiny, and he gives one circle backward over it. His

scream is something like the whinnying of a
horse, if it is not rather a *split squeal.* It is a
hoarse, tremulous breathing forth of his winged
energy. But why is it so regularly repeated
at that height? Is it not to scare his prey,
that he may see by its motion where it is, or
to inform its mate or companion of its where-
abouts? Now he crosses the at present broad
river steadily, desiring to have one or two rabbits at least to swing about him. What majesty
there is in this small bird's flight!

Oct. 28, 1858. How handsome the great
red-oak acorns now. I stand under the tree on
Emerson's lot. They are still falling. I heard
one fall into the water as I approached, and
thought a muskrat had plunged. They strew
the ground and the bottom of the river thickly,
and while I stand here, I hear one strike the
boughs with force, as it comes down and drops
into the water. The part that was covered by
the cup is whitish woolly. How munificent is
nature to create this profusion of wild fruit, as
it were merely to gratify our eyes. Though in-
edible, they stand by me longer than the fruits
which I eat. If they had been plums or chestnuts I should have eaten them on the spot, and
probably forgotten them. They would have
afforded me only a momentary gratification, but,
being acorns, I remember and, as it were, feed

on them still. They are untasted fruits, forever
in store for me. I know not of their flavor
as yet. That is postponed to some unimagined
winter evening. These which we admire, but
do not eat, are nuts of the gods. When time is
no more we shall crack them. I cannot help
liking them better than horse chestnuts, not
only because they are of a much handsomer form
but because they are indigenous. What pale
plump fellows they are! They can afford not
to be useful to me, not to know me or be known
by me. They go their way, I go mine, and it
turns out that sometimes I go after them.

Oct. 28, 1859. Walnuts commonly fall, and
the black walnuts at Smith's are at least
one half fallen. They are of the form and size
of a small lemon, and, what is singular, have a
rich nutmeg fragrance. They are turning dark
brown. Gray says it is rare in the eastern, but
very common in the western states. Is it indigenous in Massachusetts? Emerson says it is,
but rare. If so, it is much the most remarkable
nut we have.

Oct. 29, 1837. A curious incident happened
a few weeks ago which I think it worth while
to record. John and I had been searching for
Indian relics, and been successful enough to
find two arrow-heads and a pestle, when, of a
Sunday evening, with our heads full of the past

and its remains, we strolled to the mouth of Swamp Bridge Brook. As we neared the brow of the hill forming the bank of the river, inspired by my theme, I broke forth into an extravagant eulogy of the savage times, using most violent gesticulations by way of illustration. " There on Nawshawtuck," said I, " was their lodge, the rendezvous of the tribe, and yonder on Clamshell Hill, their feasting ground. This was no doubt a favorite haunt; here on this brow was an eligible lookout-post. How often have they stood on this very spot, at this very hour, when the sun was sinking behind yonder woods, and gilding with his last rays the waters of the Musketaquid, and pondered the day's success and the morrow's prospects, or communed with the spirits of their fathers gone before them to the land of the shades! Here," I exclaimed, " stood Tahatowan, and there," to complete the period, " is Tahatowan's arrow-head." We instantly proceeded to sit down on the spot I had pointed to, and I, to carry out the joke, to lay bare an ordinary stone which my whim had selected, when lo! the first I laid hands on, the grubbing stone that was to be, proved a most perfect arrow-head, as sharp as if just from the hands of the Indian fabricator.

Oct. 29, 1857. There are some things of

which I cannot at once tell, whether I have
dreamed them or they are real, as if they were
just perchance establishing or else losing a real
basis in my world. This is especially the case
in the early morning hours, when there is a
gradual transition from dreams to waking
thoughts, from illusions to actualities. Such
early morning thoughts as I speak of occupy a
debatable ground between dreams and waking
thoughts ; they are a sort of permanent dream
in my mind. At least, until we have for some
time changed our position from prostrate to
erect, and faced or commenced some of the
duties of the day, we cannot tell what we have
dreamed from what we have actually experienced. This morning, for instance, for the
twentieth time, at least, I thought of that mountain in the easterly part of the town, where no
high hill actually is, which once or twice I had
ascended, and often allowed my thoughts alone to
climb. I now contemplate it as a familiar thought
which I have surely had for many years from
time to time, but whether anything could have
reminded me of it in the middle of yesterday,
whether I ever remembered it before in broad
daylight, I doubt. I can now eke out the vision
I had of it this morning with my old and yes-
terday-forgotten dreams. My way up used to
be through a dark and unfrequented ' wood at

its base.   (I cannot now tell exactly, it was so long ago, under what circumstances I first ascended, only that I shuddered, as I went along, and have an indistinct remembrance of having been out one night alone.)   Then I steadily ascended along a rock ridge, half clad with stunted trees, where wild beasts haunted, till I lost myself quite in the upper air and clouds, seeming to pass an imaginary line which separates a hill, mere earth heaped up, from a mountain, into a superterranean grandeur and sublimity.   What distinguishes that summit above the earthy line, is that it is unhandseled, awful, grand.   It can never become familiar.   You are lost the moment you set foot there.   You know no path, but wander, thrilled, over the bare and pathless rock, as if it were solidified air and cloud.   That rocky, misty summit, secreted in the cloud, was far more thrillingly awful and sublime than the crater of a volcano spouting fire.

This is a matter we can partly understand. The perfect mountain height is already thoroughly purified.   It is as if you trod with awe the face of a god turned up, unwillingly, but helplessly, yielding to the law of gravity.   In dreams I am shown this height from time to time, and I seem to have asked my fellow once to climb there with me, and yet I am constrained to believe that I never actually ascended it.

Now first I recall that it rises in my mind where lies the burying hill. You might go through that gate to enter the dark wood. Perchance it was the grave, but that hill and its graves are so concealed and obliterated by the awful mountain that I never thought of them as underlying it. My old way down was different, and indeed this was another way up, though I never so ascended. I came out, as I descended, from the belt of wood, breathing the thicker air, into a familiar pasture, and along down by a wall. Often as I go along the low side of this pasture, I let my thoughts ascend toward the mount, gradually entering the stunted wood (nature subdued) and the thinner air. Ever there are two ways up, one through the dark wood, the other through the sunny pasture. That is, I reach and discover the mountain only through the dark wood, but I see to my surprise, when I look off between the mists from its summit, how it is ever adjacent to my native fields, nay, imminent over them, and accessible through a sunny pasture. Why is it that in the lives of men we hear more of the dark wood than of the sunny pasture? Though the pleasure of ascending the mountain is largely mixed with awe, my thoughts are purified and sublimed by it, as if I had been translated.

We see mankind generally, who toil to acquire wealth, or perhaps inherit it, or acquire it by other accident, having recourse for relaxation after excessive toil, or as a mere relief from idle ennui, to artificial amusements, rarely elevating, often debasing. I think men are commonly mistaken with regard to amusements. Every one who deserves to be regarded as higher than the brute may be supposed to have an earnest purpose, to accomplish which is the object of his existence, and this is at once his work and his supreme pleasure, and for diversion and relaxation, for suggestion and education and strength, there is offered the never-failing amusement of getting a living, — never-failing, I mean, when temperately indulged in. I know of no such amusement, so wholesome, and in every sense profitable, for instance, as to spend an hour or two in a day, picking berries or other fruits which will be food for the winter, or collecting driftwood from the river for fuel, or cultivating the few beans or potatoes which I want. Theatres and operas, which intoxicate for a season, are as nothing compared with these pursuits. And so it is with all the true arts of life. Farming and building and manufacturing and sailing are the greatest and wholesomest amusements that were ever invented, for God invented them, and I suppose that the farmers and mechanics know it, only I think they indulge to excess generally, and so what was meant for a joy becomes the sweat of the brow. Gambling, horseracing, loafing, and rowdyism generally after all tempt but few. The mass are tempted by those other amusements, of farming, etc. By these various pursuits your experience becomes singularly complete and rounded. Their novelty and significance are remarkable. Such is the path by which we climb to the height of our being. Compare the poetry which such simple pursuits have inspired with the unreadable volumes which have been written about art. I find when I have been building a fence or surveying a farm, or even collecting simples, that these were the true path to perception and enjoyment. My being seems to have put forth new roots, and to be more strongly planted. This is the true way to crack the nut of happiness. If as a poet or naturalist you wish to explore a given neighborhood, go and live in it, that is, get your living in it. Fish in its streams, hunt in its forests, gather fuel from its water, its woods, cultivate the ground, and pluck the wild fruits, etc., etc. This will be the surest and speediest way to those perceptions you covet. No amusement has worn better than farming. It tempts men just as strongly to-day as in the day of Cincinnatus. Healthily and properly pursued, it is not a whit more grave than huckleberrying, and if it takes airs on itself as superior, there is something wrong about it. I have aspired to practice in succession all the honest arts of life that I may gather all the fruits. But if you are intemperate, if you toil to raise an unnecessary amount, even the large crop of wheat becomes as a small crop of chaff. If our living were once honestly got, then it would be time to invent other amusements.

After reading Ruskin on the love of nature, I think, "Drink deep, or taste not the Pierian spring!" He there, to my surprise, expresses the common infidelity of his age and race. He has not implicitly surrendered himself to nature. And what does he substitute for her? I do not know, unless it be the Church of England, questioning whether that relation to nature was of so much value after all. It is sour grapes! He does not speak to the condition of foxes that have more spring in the legs. The love of nature and fullest perception of the revelation which she is to man, is not compatible with belief in the peculiar revelation of the Bible which Ruskin entertains.

Oct. 29, 1858. The cat comes stealthily creeping towards some prey amid the withered flowers in the garden, which being disturbed by my approach, she runs low toward it, with an unusual glare or superficial light in her eye,

ignoring her oldest acquaintance, as wild as her
remotest ancestor, and presently I see the first
tree sparrow hopping there. I hear them also
amid the alders by the river singing sweetly, but
with a few notes.

English plants have English habits here.
They are not yet acclimated. They are early or
late, as if ours were an English spring or autumn,
and no doubt in course of time a change will be
produced in their constitutions similar to that
which is observed in the English man here.

Oct. 30, 1858. I see that Prichard's mountain
ash (European) has lately put forth new leaves
when all the old have fallen. They are four or
five inches long. But the American has not
started. It knows better.

Oct. 31, 1850. This has been the most perfect afternoon of the year. The air quite warm
enough, perfectly still and dry and clear, and
not a cloud in the sky. Scarcely the song of a
cricket is heard to disturb the stillness.

Our Indian summer, I am tempted to say, is
the finest season of the year. Here has been
such a day as I think Italy never sees.

A fair afternoon, a celestial afternoon, cannot
occur but we mar our pleasure by reproaching
ourselves that we do not make all our days
beautiful. The thought of what I am, of my
pitiful conduct, deters me from receiving what

joy. I might from the glorious days that visit me. After the era of youth is passed, the knowledge of ourselves is an alloy that spoils our satisfactions. I am wont to think that I could spend my days contentedly in any retired country house that I see, for I see it to advantage now and without incumbrance. I have not yet imported my humdrum thoughts, my prosaic habits, into it to mar the landscape. What is this beauty in the landscape but a certain fertility in me? I look in vain to see it realized but in my own life. If I could wholly cease to be ashamed of myself, I think all my days would be fair.

Oct. 31, 1853. P. M. By boat with Sophia to my grapes laid down in front of Fair Haven. It is a beautiful, warm, and calm Indian-summer afternoon, and the river is so high over the meadows, the pads and other low weeds so deeply buried, and the water so smooth and glassy withal that I am reminded of a calm April day during the freshets. The coarse withered grass, and the willows and button-bushes with their myriad balls, and whatever else stands on the brink, is reflected with wonderful distinctness. This shore thus seen from the boat is like the ornamented frame of a mirror. The button-balls, etc., are more distinct in the reflection, if I remember, because they have there for back-

ground the reflected sky, but the actual ones
are seen against the russet meadow. I even see
houses a mile off reflected in the meadow flood.
The cocks crow in barnyards, as if with new
lustiness. They seem to appreciate the day.
The river is three feet and more above the summer level. I see many pickerel dart away as I
push my boat over the meadows. They lie up
there now. There are already myriads of snow-
fleas on the water next the shore, and on the
cranberries we pick in the wreck, as if they were
peppered. When we ripple the surface, the undulating light is reflected from the waves upon
the bank and bushes and withered grass. Is
not this already November, when the yellow and
scarlet tints are gone from the forest? It is very
pleasant to float along over the smooth meadow, where every weed and each stem of coarse
grass that rises above the surface has another
answering to it, and even more distinct in the
water beneath, making a rhyme to it, so that
the most irregular form appears regular. A few
scattered dry and clean very light straw - colored grasses are a cheap and simple beauty, thus
reflected.

I slowly discover that this is a gossamer day.
I first see the fine lines stretching from one
weed, or grass-stem or rush, to another, sometimes seven or eight feet distant horizontally,

and only four or five inches above the water. When I look further, I find that they are every-where and on everything, sometimes forming conspicuous fine white gossamer webs on the heads of grasses. They are so abundant that they seem to have been suddenly produced in the atmosphere by some chemistry, spun out of air, I know not for what purpose. I remember that in Kirby and Spence it is not allowed that the spider can walk on the water to carry his web across from rush to rush, but here I see myriads of spiders on the water making some kind of progress, and at least with a line attached to them. True, they do not appear to walk well, but they stand up high and dry on the tips of their toes, and are blown along quite fast. They are of various sizes and colors, though mostly a greenish brown or else black, some very small. These gossamer lines are not visible unless be-tween you and the sun. We pass some black willows now, of course, quite leafless, and when they are between us and the sun, they are so completely covered with these fine cobwebs or lines, mainly parallel to one another, that they make one solid roof, a misty roof, against the sun. They are not drawn taut, but curved downward in the middle, like the rigging of a vessel, the ropes which stretch from mast to mast, as if the fleets of a thousand Lilliputian

nations were collected one behind another under
bare poles ; but when we have floated a few feet
farther, and thrown the willow out of the sun's
range, not a thread can be seen on it.   I landed
and walked up and down the causeway, and
found it the same there, the gossamer reaching
across the causeway, though not necessarily supported on the other side.   They streamed southward with the slight zephyr, as if the year were
weaving her shroud out of light.   There were
spiders on the rail [of the causeway] that produced them, similar to those on the water.   The
air appeared crowded with them.   It was a wonder they did not get into the mouth and nostrils,
or that we did not feel them on our faces, or continually going and coming among them did not
whiten our clothes more.   And yet one, with his
back to the sun, walking the other way, would
observe nothing of all this.   Methinks it is only
on these very finest days, late in the autumn,
that the phenomenon is seen, as if that fine
vapor of the morning were spun into these webs.
According to Kirby and Spence, " In Germany
these flights of gossamer appear so constantly in
autumn that they are there metaphorically called
' Der Fliegende Sommer,' the flying or departing summer."   What can possess these spiders,
thus to run all at once to every the least elevation, and let off this wonderful stream ?   Harris

tells me he does not know what it means. Sophia thought that thus, at last, they emptied themselves and wound up, or, I suggested, unwound themselves, cast off their mortal coil. It looks like a mere frolic spending and wasting of themselves, of their vigor, now that there is no further use for it, their July, perchance, being killed or banished by the frost.

Oct. 31, 1857. In the Lee farm swamp, by the old Sam Barrett mill-site, I see two kinds of ferns still green and much in fruit, apparently the *Aspidium spinulosum* (?) and *cristatum* (?). They are also common in the swamps now. They are quite fresh in those cold and wet places, and almost flattened down now. The atmosphere of the house is less congenial to them. In the summer you might not have noticed them. Now they are conspicuous amid the withered leaves. You are inclined to approach and raise each frond in succession, moist, trembling, fragile greenness. They linger thus in all moist, clammy swamps under the bare maples and grapevines and witch hazels, and about each trickling spring that is half choked with fallen leaves. What means this persistent vitality? Why were these spared when the brakes and osmundas were stricken down? They stay as if to keep up the spirits of the cold-blooded frogs which have not yet gone into the mud, that the summer may die with decent and graceful moderation. Is not the water of the spring improved by their presence? They fall back and droop here and there like the plumes of departing summer, of the departing year. Even in them I feel an argument for immortality. Death is so far from being universal. The same destroyer does not destroy all. How valuable they are, with the lycopodiums for cheerfulness. Greenness at the end of the year, after the fall of the leaf, a hale old age. To my eyes they are tall and noble as palm groves, and always some forest nobleness seems to have its haunt under their umbrage. All that was immortal in the swamp herbage seems here crowded into smaller compass, the concentrated greenness of the swamp. How dear they must be to the chickadee and the rabbit! the cool, slowly-retreating rear-guard of the swamp army. What virtue is theirs that enables them to resist the frost? If you are afflicted with melancholy at this season, go to the swamp, and see the brave spears of skunk-cabbage buds already advanced toward a new year. Their gravestones are not bespoken yet. Who shall be sexton to them? Is it the winter of their discontent? Do they seem to have lain down to die, despairing of skunk-cabbagedom? Mortal, human creatures must take a little respite in this fall of the year. Their spirits do flag a little. There is a little questioning of destiny, and thinking to go like cowards to where the weary shall be at rest. But not so with the skunk cabbage. Its withered leaves fall and are transfixed by a rising bud. Winter and death are ignored. The circle of life is complete. Are these false prophets? Is it a lie or a vain boast underneath the skunk-cabbage bud pushing it upwards and lifting the dead leaves with it? They rest with spears advanced. It is good for me to be here slumping in the mud, a trap covered with withered leaves, to see these green cabbage buds lifting the dry leaves in this watery, muddy place. They see over the brow of winter's hill. They see another summer ahead.

Nov. 1, 1851. It is a rare qualification to be able to state a fact simply and adequately, to digest some experience clearly, to say " yes " and " no " with authority, to make a square edge. A man must see before he can say. Statements are made but partially. Things are said with reference to certain conventions or institutions, not absolutely. A fact, truly and absolutely stated, is taken out of the region of common sense, and acquires a mythologic or universal significance. Say it and have done with it. Express it without expressing yourself. See not with the eye of science, which is barren, nor of youthful poetry, which is impotent. But taste the world and digest it. It would seem as if things got said but rarely and by chance. As you see, so at length will you say. When facts are seen superficially, they are seen as they lie in relation to certain institutions, perchance. I would have them expressed as more deeply seen, with deeper references, so that the hearer or reader cannot recognize them or apprehend their significance from the platform of common life, but it will be necessary that he be in a sense translated in order to understand them. At first blush, a man is not capable of reporting truth. To do that, he must be drenched and saturated with it. Then the truth will exhale from him naturally, like the odor of the muskrat from the coat of the trapper. What was enthusiasm in the young man must become temperament in the mature man. Without excitement, heat, or passion he will survey the world which excited the youth and threw him off his balance.

This on my way to Conantum, 2.30 P. M. It is a bright, clear, warm November day. I feel blessed. I love my life. I warm toward all nature. The crickets now sound faintly and from very deep in the sod. Fall dandelions look bright still. The grass has got a new greenness in spots. At this season there are stranger sparrows or finches about. The skunk cabbage is already pushing up again. It is a remarkable day for fine gossamer cobwebs. Here in the causeway, as I walk toward the sun, I perceive that the air is full of them, streaming from off the willows and spanning the road, all stretching across the road, and yet I cannot see them in any other direction, and feel not one.

It looks as if the birds would be incommoded. This shimmer moving along the gossamer lines as they are moved by the wind, gives the effect of a drifting storm of light. It is more like a fine snowstorm which drifts athwart your path than anything else. If there were no sunshine, I should never find out that they existed, I should not know that I was bursting a myriad barriers. Why should this day be so distinguished? What is the peculiar condition of the atmosphere to call forth this activity?

The river is peculiarly sky-blue to-day, not dark as usual. It is all in the air.

Saw a canoe birch by road beyond the Abel Minot house; distinguished it thirty rods off by the chalky whiteness of its limbs. It is of a more unspotted, transparent, and perhaps pinkish white than the common. Its branches do not droop and curl down like those of the other. There will be some loose curls of bark about it. The common birch is finely branched, and has frequently a snarly head; the canoe birch is a more open and free-growing tree. If at a distance you see the birch near its top forking into two or more white limbs, you may know it for a canoe birch. I have heard of a man in Maine who copied the whole Bible on to birch bark. It was much easier than to write that sentence which the birch tree stands for.

Nov. 1, 1852. Day before yesterday to the Cliffs in the misty rain. As I approached their edge, I saw the woods beneath, Fair Haven Pond, and the hills across the river, which owing to the mist was as far as I could see, and seemed much farther in consequence. I saw these between the converging branches of two white pines a rod or two from me on the edge of the rocks, and I thought there was no frame to a landscape equal to this, to see between two near pine boughs whose lichens are distinct, a distant forest and lake, the one, frame, the other, picture.

In November a man will eat his heart, if in any month.

It is remarkable how native man proves himself to the earth, after all, and the completeness of his life in all its appurtenances. His alliances how wide! He has domesticated not only beasts, but fowl, not only hens and geese and ducks and turkeys, but his doves winging their way to their dove-cotes over street and vil-

lage enhance the picturesqueness of his sky, to
say nothing of his trained falcons, his beautiful
scouts in the upper air.

He is lord of the fowl and the brute. The
dove, the martin, the bluebird, the swallow, and
in some countries, the hawk, have attached
themselves to his fortunes.

Nov. 1, 1853. Few come to the woods to see
how the pine lives and grows and spires, lifting
its evergreen arms to the light, to see its perfect
success. Most are content to behold it in the
shape of many broad boards brought to market,
and deem that its true success. The pine is no
more lumber than man is, and to be made into
boards and houses is no more its true and highest use than the truest use of a man is to be cut
down and made into manure. A pine cut down,
a dead pine, is no more a pine than a dead human carcass is a man. Is it the lumberman who
is the friend and lover of the pine, stands nearest to it, and understands its nature best? Is it
the tanner or turpentine distiller who posterity
will fable was changed into a pine at last? No,
no, it is the poet who makes the truest use of
the pine, who does not fondle it with an axe, or
tickle it with a saw, or stroke it with a plane.
It is the poet who loves it as his own shadow in
the air, and lets it stand. It is as immortal as
I am, and will go to as high a heaven, there to

tower above me still. Can he who has only discovered the value of whale-bone and whale-oil be said to have discovered the true uses of the whale ? Can he who slays the elephant for his ivory be said to have seen the elephant? No, these are petty and accidental uses. Just as if a stronger race were to kill us in order to make buttons and flageolets of our bones, and then prate of the usefulness of man. Every creature is better alive than dead, both men and moose and pine-trees, as life is more beautiful than death.

Nov. 1, 1855. P. M. Up Assabet, a-wooding. As I pushed up the river past Hildreth's, I saw a blue heron arise from the shore, and disappear round a bend in front ; the greatest of the bitterns (*Ardeæ*), with heavy undulating wings low over the water, seen against the woods, just disappearing round a bend in front ; with a great slate-colored expanse of wing, suited to the shadows of the stream, a tempered blue as of the sky and dark water commingled. This is the aspect under which the Musketaquid might be represented at this season : a long, smooth lake, reflecting the bare willows and button beeches, the stubble, and the wool grass on its tussock, a muskrat cabin or two conspicuous on its margin amid the unsightly tops of pontederia, and a bittern disappearing on undulating wing around a bend.

Nov. 1, 1857. I see much witch hazel, some of it quite fresh and bright. Its bark is alternate white and smooth reddish-brown, the small twigs looking as if gossamer had lodged on and draped them. What a lively spray it has, both in form and color! Truly it looks as if it would make divining rods, as if its twigs knew where the true gold was and could point to it. The gold is in the late blossoms. Let them alone, and they never point down to earth. They impart to the whole hillside a speckled, parti-colored look.

Nov. 1, 1858. As the afternoons grow shorter, and the early evening drives us home to complete our chores, we are reminded of the shortness of life, and become more pensive at least in this twilight of the year. We are prompted to make haste and finish our work before the twilight comes. I leaned over a rail on the Walden road, waiting for the evening mail to be distributed, when such thoughts visited me. I seemed to remember the November evening as a familiar thing come round again, and yet I could hardly tell whether I had ever known it, or only divined it. It appeared like a part of a panorama at which I sat spectator, a part with which I was perfectly familiar, just coming into view. I foresaw how it would look and roll along and was prepared to be pleased. Just such a piece of art merely, infinitely sweet and good, did it appear to me, and just as little were any active duties required of me. We are independent of all that we see. The hangman whom I have *seen* cannot hang me. The earth which I have *seen* cannot bury me. Such doubleness and distance does *sight* prove. Only the rich and such as are troubled with ennui are implicated in the maze of phenomena. You cannot see anything until you are clear of it. The long railroad causeway through the meadows west of me, the still twi-light, the dark bank of clouds in the horizon, the villagers crowding to the post-office, and then hastening home to supper by candle-light, had I not seen all this before? What new sweet was I to extract from it? Truly they mean that we should learn our lesson well. Nature gets thumbed like an old spelling book. Yet I sat the bench with perfect contentment, unwilling to exchange the familiar vision that was to be un-rolled for any treasure or heaven that could be imagined. I was no nearer to or farther off from my friends. We were sure to keep just so far apart in our orbits still, in obedience to the laws of attraction and repulsion, affording each other only steady, but indispensable starlight. It was as if I was promised the greatest novelty the world has ever seen or shall see, though the utmost possible novelty would be the difference between me and myself a year ago. This alone encouraged me, and was my fuel for the approaching winter. That we may behold the panorama with this slight improvement or change, this is what we sustain life for from year to year. And yet there is no more tempting novelty than this new November. No going to Europe or to another world is to be named with it. Give me the old familiar walk, post-office and all, with this ever new self, with this infinite expectation and faith which does not know when it is beaten. We 'll go nutting once more. We 'll pluck the nut of the world and crack it in the winter evenings. Theatres and all other sight-seeing are puppet shows in comparison. I will take another walk to the cliff, another row on the river, another skate on the meadow, be out in the first snow, and associate with the winter birds. Here I am at home. In the bare and bleached crust of the earth, I recognize my friend. One actual Frederick that you know is worth a million only read of. Pray, am I altogether a bachelor, or am I a widower, that I should go away and " leave my bride " ? This morrow that is ever knocking with irresistible force at our door, there is no such guest as that. I will stay at home and receive company. I want nothing new. If I can have but a tithe of the old secured to me, I will spurn all wealth

besides. Think of the consummate folly of attempting to go away from *here.* Here are all
the friends I ever had or shall have, and as
friendly as ever. Why, I never had a quarrel
with a friend, but it was just as sweet as unan-
imity could be. I do not think we budge an
inch forward or backward in relation to our
friends. How many things can you go away
from ? They see the comet from the northwest
coast just as plainly as we do, and the same
stars through its tail. Take the shortest way
round and stay at home. A man dwells in his
native valley like a corolla in its calyx, like an
acorn in its cup. Here, of course, is all that
you love, all that you expect, all that you are.
Here is your bride-elect, as close to you as she
can be got. Here is all the best and the worst
you can imagine. What more do you want ?
Foolish people think that what they imagine is
somewhere else. That stuff is not made in any
factory but their own.

Nov. 1, 1860. A perfect Indian summer
day, wonderfully warm, 72° + at 1 P. M., probably warmer at 2. The butterflies are out
again. I see the common yellow one, and the
Vanessa Antiopa, also yellow-winged grasshoppers with blackish eyes.

Nov. 2, 1840. It is well said that the " attitude of inspection is prone." The soul does

not inspect, but behold. Like the lily, or the crystal, or the rock, it looks in the face of the sky. Francis Howell says that in garrulous persons "the supply of thought seems never to rise much above the level of its exit." Consequently their thoughts issue in no jets, but incessantly dribble. In those who speak rarely, but to the purpose, the reservoir of thought is many feet higher than its issue. It takes the pressure of one hundred atmospheres to make one jet of eloquence.

Nov. 2, 1851. Saw a canoe birch beyond Nawshawtuck, growing out of the middle of a white-pine stump which still showed the marks of the axe; sixteen inches in diameter at its bottom, or at two feet from the ground where it had first taken root in the stump.

Nov. 2, 1852. Tall buttercups, red clover, houstonias, *Polygonum aviculare*, still. The month of chickadees and new swollen buds. At long intervals I see or hear a robin still.

Nov. 2, 1853. The beech leaves have all fallen except some about the lower part of the trees, and they make a fine thick bed on the ground. They are very beautiful, fine and perfect leaves, unspotted, not eaten by insects, of a handsome, clear leather color, like a book bound in calf, crisp and elastic. They cover the ground so perfectly and cleanly as to tempt you to recline on it, and admire the beauty of the smooth boles from that position, covered with lichens of various colors, green, etc. They impress you as full of health and vigor, so that their bark can hardly contain their spirits, but lies in folds or wrinkles about their ankles like a sack, with the *embonpoint*, wrinkles of fat, of infancy.

Nov. 2, 1854. P. M. By boat to Clamshell. I see larks hovering over the meadow, and hear a faint note or two, and a pleasant note from tree sparrows (?). Sailing past the bank above the railroad, close to the shore on the east side, just before a clear sunset, I see a fainter shadow of the boat, sail, myself, paddle, etc., directly above and upon the first, on the bank. What makes the second ? I at length discovered that it was the reflected sun which cast a higher shadow like the true one. As I moved to the west side, the upper shadow grew larger and less perceptible, and at last when I was so near the west shore that I could not see the reflected sun, it disappeared, but then there appeared one upside down in its place !

Nov. 2, 1857. P. M. To Bateman's Pond. It is very pleasant and cheerful nowadays, when the brown and withered leaves strew the ground and almost every plant is fallen or withered, to come upon a patch of polypody (as in abundance on hillside between Calla swamp and Bateman's Pond) on some rocky hillside in the woods, where in the midst of dry and rustling leaves, defying frost, it stands so freshly green and full of life. The mere greenness, which was not remarkable in the summer, is positively interesting now. My thoughts are with the polypody a long time after my body has passed. The brakes, the sarsaparilla, the osmundas, the Solomon's-seals, the lady's-slippers, etc., have long since withered and fallen. The huckleberries and blueberries, too, have lost their leaves. The forest floor is covered with a thick coat of moist brown leaves, but what is that perennial and spring-like verdure that clothes the rocks, of small green plumes pointing various ways? It is the cheerful community of the polypody. It survives at least as the type of vegetation, to remind us of the spring which shall not fail. These are the green pastures where I browse now. Why is not this form copied by our sculptors instead of the foreign acanthus leaves and bays? How fit for a tuft about the base of a column! The sight of this unwithering green leaf excites me like red at some seasons. Are not wood-frogs the philosophers who frequent these groves? Methinks I imbibe a cool, composed, frog-like philosophy when I behold them. The form of the

polypody is strangely interesting, it is even out-
landish. Some forms, though common in our
midst, are thus perennially foreign as the growth
of other latitudes. We all feel the ferns to be
further from us essentially and sympathetically
than the phænogamous plants, the roses and
weeds, for instance. It needs no geology nor
botany to assure us of that. The bare outline
of the polypody thrills me strangely. It only
perplexes me. Simple as it is, it is as strange
as an oriental character. It is quite independent of my race and of the Indian, and of all
mankind. It is a fabulous, mythological form,
such as prevailed when the earth and air and
water were inhabited by those extinct fossil
creatures that we find. It is contemporary
with them, and affects us somewhat as the
sight of them might do. Crossed over that high,
flat-backed, rocky hill, where the rocks, as usual
thereabouts, stand on their edges, and the grain,
running by compass east-northeast and west-
southwest, is frequently kinked up in a curious manner, reminding me of a curly head.
Call the hill Curly-pate.

Returning I see the red oak on R. W. E.'s
shore reflected in the bright sky crater. In the
reflection, the tree is black against the clear
whitish sky, though as I see it against the opposite woods, it is a warm greenish yellow. But

the river sees it against the bright sky and hence the reflection is like ink. The water tells me how it looks to it, seen from below.

I think that most men, as farmers, hunters, fishers, etc., walk along a river bank, or paddle along its stream without seeing the reflections. Their minds are not enough abstracted from the surface, from surfaces generally. It is only a reflecting mind that sees reflections. I am aware often that I have been occupied with shallow and commonplace thoughts, looking for something superficial, when I did not see the most glorious reflections, though exactly in the line of my vision. If the fisherman were looking at the reflection, he would not know when he had a nibble. I know from my own experience that he may cast his line right over the most elysian landscape and sky, and not catch the slightest notion of them. You must be in an abstract mood to see reflections, however distinct. I was even startled by the sight of that reflected red oak, as if it were a black water-spirit. When we are enough abstracted, the opaque earth itself reflects images to us, that is, we are imaginative, see visions.

Nov. 3, 1839. If one would reflect, let him embark on some placid stream, and float with the current. He cannot resist the muse. As we ascend the stream, plying the paddle with might and main, snatched and impetuous thoughts course through the brain. We dream of conflict, power and grandeur; but turn the prow down stream, and rock, tree, kine, knoll, assuming new and varying positions, as wind and water shift the scene, favor the liquid lapse of thought, far-reaching and sublime, but ever calm and gently undulating.

Nov. 3, 1840. The truth is only contained, never withheld, as a feudal castle may be the headquarters of hospitality, though the portal is but a span in the circuit of the wall. So of the three envelopes of the cocoanut, one is always so soft that it may be pierced with a thorn, and the traveler is grateful for the thick shell which held the liquor so faithfully.

Nov. 3, 1853. I make it my business to extract from Nature whatever nutriment she can furnish me, though at the risk of endless iteration. I milk the sky and the earth.

A man of many ideas and associations must pine in the woods. At the extreme north, the voyagers have to dance and act plays for employment. There is not enough of the garden in the wilderness, though I love to see a man sometimes from whom the usnea will hang as naturally as from a spruce. Our woods and fields are the perfection of parks and groves, and gardens and grottoes and arbors, and paths and parterres, and vistas and landscapes. They are the natural consequence of what art and refinement we as a people have. They are the common which each village possesses, the true paradise, in comparison with which all elaborately and willfully wealth-constructed parks and gardens are paltry imitations. No other creature effects such changes in nature as man. He changes by his presence the nature of the very trees. The poet's is not a logger's path, but a woodman's. The pioneer and logger have preceded him, and banished decaying wood and the spongy mosses which feed on it, and built hearths, and humanized nature for him.

Nov. 3, 1857. As I return from the Boulder Field, I see, between two of the boulders which are a dozen rods from me, a dozen feet high and nearly as much apart, the now winter-colored — that is, reddish (of oak leaves) — horizon of hills with its few white houses, four or five miles distant southward, as a landscape within the frame of a picture. But what a picture-frame ! These two great slumbering masses of rock, reposing like a pair of mastodons on the surface of the pasture, completely shutting out a mile of the horizon on each side, while between their adjacent sides, which are nearly perpendicular, I look to the now purified, dry, reddish, leafy horizon, with a faint tinge of blue from the distance.

To see a remote landscape between two near rocks !. I want no other gilding to my picture frame. There they lie as perchance they tumbled and split from off an iceberg. What better frame would you have? The globe itself, here named pasture, for ground and foreground, two great boulders for the sides of the frame, and the sky itself for the top. And for artist and subject, God and Nature! Such pictures cost nothing but eyes, and it will not bankrupt me to own them. They were not stolen by any conqueror as spoils of war, and none can doubt but they are really the works of an old master. What more, pray, will you see between any two slips of gilded wood in that pasture you call Europe and browse in sometimes? It is singular that several of these rocks should be thus split into twins. Even very low ones, just appearing above the surface, are divided and parallel, having a path between them.

Nov. 3, 1858. The jay is the bird of October. I have seen it repeatedly flitting amid the bright leaves, of a different color from them all, and equally bright, taking its flight from grove to grove. It, too, with its bright color, stands for some ripeness in the bird harvest; and its scream! it is as if it blew on the edge of an October leaf. It is never more in its element and at home than when flitting amid these brilliant colors. No doubt it delights in bright color, and so has begged for itself a brilliant coat. It is not gathering seeds from the sod, too busy to look around, while fleeing the country. It is wide awake to what is going on, on the qui vive. It flies to some bright tree and bruits its splendors abroad.

At base of Anursnack I find one or two fringed gentians yet open, but even the stems are generally killed.

How long we follow an illusion ! On meeting that one whom I call my friend, I find that I had imagined something that was not there. I am sure to depart sadder than I came. Nothing makes me so dejected as to have met my friends, for they make me doubt if it is possible to have any friends. I feel what a fool I am. I cannot conceive of persons more strange to me than they *actually* are ; not thinking, not believing, not doing as I do ; interrupted by me. My only distinction must be that I am the greatest bore they ever had. Not in a single thought agreed, regularly balking one another. But when I get far away, my thoughts return to them. That is the way I can visit them. Perhaps it is unaccountable to me why I care for them. Thus I am taught that my friend is not an actual person. When I have withdrawn and am alone, I forget the actual person, and remember only my ideal. Then I have a friend again. I am not so ready to perceive the illusion that is in Nature. I certainly come nearer, to say the least, to an actual and joyful intercourse with her. Every day I have more or less communion with her, *as I think.* At least, I do not feel as if I must withdraw out of nature. I feel like a welcome guest. Yet, strictly speaking, the same must be true of nature and of man ; our ideal is the only real. It is not the finite and temporal that satisfies or concerns us in either case.

I associate the idea of friendship, methinks, with the person the most foreign to me. This illusion is perpetuated like superstition in a country long after civilization has been reached. We are attracted toward a particular person, but no one has discovered the laws of this attraction. When I come nearest to that one *actually*, I am wont to be surprised at my selection. It may be enough that we have met *some time*, and now can never forget it. Some time or other we paid each other this wonderful compliment, looked largely, humanely, divinely on one another, and now are fated to be acquaintances forever. In the case of nature, I am not so conscious of this unsatisfied yearning.

Nov. 3, 1861. After a violent easterly storm in the night, which clears at noon, I notice that the surface of the railroad causeway composed of gravel is singularly marked, as if stratified, like some slate rocks on their edges, so that I can tell within a small fraction of a degree from what quarter the rain came. These lines, as it were of stratification, are perfectly parallel and straight as a ruler diagonally across the flat surface of the causeway for its whole length. Behind each little pebble, as a protecting boulder one eighth or one tenth of an inch in diameter, extends northwest a ridge of sand, an inch or more, which it has protected from being washed away, while the heavy drops driven almost horizontally have washed out a furrow on each side, and on all sides are these ridges, half an inch apart and perfectly parallel. All this is perfectly distinct to an observant eye, and yet could easily pass unnoticed by most. Thus each wind is self-registering.

Nov. 4, 1840. By your few words, show how insufficient would be many words. If, after conversation, I would reinstate my thought in its primary dignity and authority, I have recourse again to my first simple and concise statement. In breadth we may be patterns of conciseness, but in depth we may well be prolix.

Dr. Ware, Jr., said to-day in his speech at the meeting-house, " There are these three, sympathy, faith, patience ; " then proceeding in true ministerial style, "and the greatest of these is," but for a moment he was at a loss, and became a listener along with his audience, and concluded with, "Which is it? I don't know, pray take them all, brethren, and God help you."

Nov. 4, 1851. To Saw Mill Brook by turnpike, returning by Walden. It was quite a discovery when I first came upon this brawling mountain stream in Concord woods, for some fifty or sixty rods of its course as much obstructed by rocks, rocks out of all proportion to its tiny stream, as a brook can well be ; and the rocks are bared throughout the wood on either side, as if a torrent had anciently swept through here, so unlike the after character of the stream. Who would have thought that in tracing it up from where it empties into the larger Mill Brook in the open peat meadows, it would conduct him to such a headlong and impetuous youth. Perchance it should be called a " force." It suggests what various moods may attach to the same character. Ah, if I but knew that some minds, which flow so muddily in the lowland portion of their course, where they cross the highways, tumbled thus impetuously and musically, mixing themselves with the air in foam, but a little way back in the woods! that these dark and muddy pools where only the pout and the leech are to be found, issued from pure trout streams higher up! that the man's thoughts ever flowed as sparkling mountain water, that trout there loved to glance through his dimples, where the witch-hazel hangs over his stream! This stream is here sometimes quite lost amid the rocks, which appear as if they had been arched over it, but which it in fact has undermined and found its way beneath, and they have merely fallen arch-wise, as they were undermined. It is truly a raw and gusty day, and I hear a tree creak sharply like a bird, a phœbe. The hypericums stand red or lake over the brook. The jays with their scream are at home in the scenery. I see where trees have spread themselves over the rocks in a scanty covering of soil, been under-mined by the brook, then blown over, and, as they fell, lifted and carried with them all the soil, together with considerable rocks. So from time to time by these natural levers rocks are re-moved from the middle of the stream to the shore. The slender chestnuts, maples, elms, and white ash trees, which last are uncommonly numerous here, are now all bare of leaves, and a few small hemlocks, with their now thin but unmixed and fresh green foliage, stand over and cheer the stream, and remind me of winter, the snows which are to come and drape them and contrast with their green, and the chickadees that are to flit and lisp amid them. Ah, the beautiful tree, the hemlock, with its green canopy, under which little grows, not exciting the cupidity of the carpenter, whose use most men have not discovered. I know of some memorable ones worth walking many miles to see. These little cheerful hemlocks, the lisp of chickadees seems to come from them now, each standing with its foot on the very edge of the stream, reaching sometimes part way over its channel, and here and there one has lightly stepped across. These evergreens are plainly as much for shelter for the birds as for anything else. The fallen leaves are so thick they almost fill the bed of the stream and choke it. I hear the runnel gurgling under ground. As if the busy rill had ever tossed these rocks about! these storied rocks with their fine lichens and sometimes red stains as of Indian blood on them. There are a few bright ferns lying flat by the sides of the brook, but it is cold, cold, withering to all else. A whitish lichen on the witch-hazel rings it here. I glimpse the frizzled tail of a red squirrel with a chestnut in its mouth, on a white pine.

The ants appear to be gone into winter quarters. Here are two bushels of fine gravel, piled up in a cone, overpowering the grass, which tells of a corresponding cavity.

Nov. 4, 1852. Autumnal dandelion and yarrow. Must be out of doors enough to get experience of wholesome reality, as a ballast to thought and sentiment. Health requires this relaxation, this aimless life, this life in the present. Let a man have thought what he will of Nature in the house, she will still be novel out-doors. I keep out of doors for the sake of the mineral, vegetable, and animal in me.

How precious a fine day early in the spring; less so in the fall, less still in the summer and winter.

My thought is a part of the meaning of the world, and hence I use a part of the world as a symbol to express my thought.

Nov. 4, 1855. It takes a savage or wild taste to appreciate a wild apple. I remember two old maids to whose house I enjoyed carrying a purchaser to talk about buying their farm in the winter, because they offered us wild apples, though with an unnecessary apology for their wildness.

Nov. 4, 1857. To Pine Hill via Spanish Brook. I leave the railroad at Walden Crossing, and follow the path to Spanish Brook. How swift Nature is to repair the damage that man does! When he has cut down a tree, and left only a white-topped and bleeding stump, she comes at once to the rescue with her chemistry, and covers it decently with a first coat of gray, and in course of time she adds a thick coat of green-cup and bright coxcomb lichens, and it becomes an object of new interest to the lover of nature! Suppose it were always to remain a raw stump instead! It becomes a shelf on which this humble vegetation spreads and displays itself, and we forget the death of the larger in the life of the less.

I see in the path some rank thimble-berry shoots covered very thickly with their peculiar hoary bloom. It is only rubbed off in a few places down to the purple skin, by some passing hunter perchance. It is a very singular and delicate outer coat surely for a plant to wear. I find that I can write my name on it with a pointed stick very distinctly, each stroke, however fine, going down to the purple. It is a new kind of enameled card. What is this bloom and what purpose does it serve? Is there anything analogous in animated nature? It is the *coup de grace*, the last touch and perfection of any work, a thin elysian veil cast over it, through which it may be viewed. It is breathed on it by the artist, and thereafter his work is not to be touched without injury. It is the evidence of a ripe and completed work on which the unexhausted artist has breathed out of his superfluous genius. If it is a poem, it must be invested with a similar bloom by the imagination of the reader. It is the subsidence of superfluous ripeness, like a fruit preserved in its own sugar. It is the handle by which the imagination grasps it.

I climb Pine Hill just as the sun is setting this cool evening. As I sit with my back to a thick oak sprout whose leaves still glow with life, Walden lies, an oblong figure, below, endwise toward me. Its surface is slightly rippled, and dusky prolonged reflections extend wholly across its length, or half a mile. (I sit high.) The sun is once or twice its diameter above the horizon, and the mountains north of it stand out grand and distinct, a decided purple. But when I look critically, I distinguish a whitish mist (such is the color of the denser air) about their lower parts, while their tops are dark blue. (So the mountains have their bloom, and is not the bloom on fruits equivalent to that blue veil of air which distance gives to many objects?) I see one glistening reflection on the dusky and leafy northwestern earth, seven or eight miles off, betraying a window there, though no house can be seen. It twinkles incessantly as from a waving surface, owing probably to the undulation of the air. Now that the sun is actually setting, the mountains are dark blue from top to bottom. As usual, a small cloud attends the sun to the portals of the day, and reflects his brightness to us now that he is gone. But those grand and glorious mountains, how impossible to remember daily that they are there, and to live accordingly. They are meant to be a perpetual reminder to us, pointing out the way.

Nov. 4, 1858. On the 1st, when I stood on Poplar Hill, I saw a man far off by the edge of the river, splitting billets off a stump. Suspecting who it was, I took out my glass, and beheld Goodwin, the one-eyed Ajax, in his short blue frock, short and square-bodied, as broad as for his height he can afford to be, getting his winter's wood, for this is one of the phenomena of the season. As surely as the ants which he disturbs go into winter quarters in the stump when the weather becomes cool, so does Goodwin revisit the stumpy shores with his axe. As usual, his powder flask peeped out from a pocket on his breast, and his gun was slanted over a stump near by, and his boat lay a little farther along. He had been at work laying wall still farther off, and now, near the end of the day, he took himself to those pursuits which he loved better still. It would be no amusement to me to see a gentleman buy his winter wood. It is, to see Goodwin get his. I helped him tip over a stump or two. He said the owner of the land had given him leave to get them out, but it seemed to me a condescension for him to ask any man's leave to grub up these stumps. The stumps to those who can use them, I say, to those who will split them. He might as well ask leave of the farmer to shoot the musquash and the meadow hen. I might as well ask leave to look at the landscape. Near by were large hollows in the ground, now grassed over, where he had got out white-oak stumps in previous years. But strange to say, the town does not like to have him get his fuel in this way. They would rather the stumps should rot in the ground, or be floated down stream to the sea. They have, almost without dissent, agreed on a different mode of living, with their division of labor. They would have him stick to laying wall, and buy corded wood for fuel as they do. He has drawn up an old bridge sleeper, and cut his name on it for security, and now he gets into his boat and pushes off, saying he will go and see what Mr. Musquash is about.

Nov. 5, 1839. Æschylus. There was one man who lived his own healthy Attic life in those days. His words that have come down to us give evidence that their speaker was a seer in his day and generation. At this day they owe nothing to their dramatic form, nothing to stage machinery and the fact that they were spoken under these or those circumstances. All display of art for the gratification of a factitious taste, is silently passed by to come at the least particle of absolute and genuine thought they contain. The reader will be disappointed, however, who looks for traits of a rare wisdom or eloquence, and will have to solace himself, for the most part, with the poet's humanity, and what it was in him to say. He will discover that, like every genius, he was a solitary liver and worker in his day.

We are accustomed to say that the common-sense of this age belonged to the seer of the last, as if time gave us any vantage ground. But not so ; I see not but genius must ever take an equal start. . . . Common-sense is not so familiar with any truth, but genius will represent that truth in a strange light to it. Let the seer bring his broad eye down to the most stale and trivial fact, and he will make you believe it a new planet in the sky.

We are not apt to remember that we grow. It is curious to reflect how the maiden waits patiently and confidingly as the tender houstonia of the meadow for the slowly revolving years to work their will with her, to perfect and ripen her, like it to be fanned by the wind, watered by the rain, shined on by the sun, as if she, too, were a plant drawing in sustenance by a thousand roots and fibres. These young buds of mankind in the street are like buttercups in the meadows, surrendered to nature as they.

Nov. 5, 1840.　Truth is as vivacious, and will spread itself as fast, as the fungi, which you can by no means annihilate with your heel, for their sporules are so infinitely numerous and subtle as to resemble " thin smoke, so light that they may be raised into an atmosphere, and dispersed in so many ways by the attraction of the sun, by insects, wind, elasticity, adhesion, etc. ; that it is difficult to conceive a place from which they may be excluded."

Nov. 5, 1853.　Most of the muskrat cabins were lately covered by the flood, but now that it is gone down in a great measure, I notice that they have not been washed away or much injured, as a heap of manure would have been, they are so artificially constructed ; moreover, for the most part, they are protected as well as concealed by the button-bushes, willows, or weeds about them.　What exactly are they for ?　This is not the breeding season of the muskrat.　I think they are merely an artificial bank or air chamber near the water, houses of refuge.　But why do they need them more at this season than in summer ? it might be asked.　Perhaps they are constructed just before the rise of the water in the fall and winter, that they may not have to swim so far as the flood would require in order to eat their clams.

Nov. 5, 1855.　I hate the present modes of

living and getting a living. Farming and shop-
keeping and working at a trade or profession,
are all odious to me. I should relish getting
my living in a simple, primitive fashion. The
life which society proposes to me to live is so
artificial and complex, bolstered up on many
weak supports, and sure to topple down at last,
that no man surely can ever be inspired to live
it, and only "old fogies" ever praise it. At
best some think it their duty to live it. I believe
in the infinite joy and satisfaction of helping
myself and others to the extent of my ability.
But what is the use in trying to live simply,
raising what you eat, making what you wear,
building what you inhabit, burning what you
cut and dig, when those to whom you are allied
outwardly, want and will have a thousand other
things which neither you nor they can raise, and
nobody else, perchance, will pay for. The fel-
low-man to whom you are yoked is a steer that
is ever bolting right the other way. I was suggesting once to a man who was wincing under
some of the consequences of our loose and ex-
pensive way of living, " But you might raise
your own potatoes," etc. We had often done it
at our house and had some to sell. At which he
demurring, I said, setting it high, " You could
raise twenty bushels even." But said he, " I
use thirty-five." " How large is your family ? "

" A wife and three infant children." This was the real family. I need not enumerate those who were hired to help eat the potatoes and waste them. So he had to hire a man to raise his potatoes. Thus men invite the devil in, at every angle, and then prate about the Garden of Eden and the fall of man. I know many children to whom I would fain make a present on some one of their birthdays, but they are so far gone in the luxury of presents, have such perfect museums of costly ones, that it would absorb my entire earnings for a year to buy them something which would not be beneath their notice.

That white birch fungus always presents its face to the ground, parallel with it, for here are some on an upright dead birch whose faces or planes are at right angles with the axis of the tree, as usual, looking down, but others, attached to the top of the tree which lies prostrate on the ground, have their planes parallel with the axis of the tree, as if looking round the birch.

Nov. 5, 1857. Sometimes I would rather get a transient glimpse or side view of a thing than stand fronting it, as with these polypodies. The object I caught a glimpse of as I went by, haunts my thought a long time, is infinitely suggestive, and I do not care to front it and scrutinize it, for I know that the thing that really concerns me is not there, but in my relation to that.

That is a mere reflecting surface. It is not the polypody in my pitcher or herbarium, or which I may possibly persuade to grow on a bank in my yard, or which is described in the botanies, that interests me, but the one I pass by in my walks a little distance off, when in the right mood. Its influence is sporadic, wafted through the air to me. Do you imagine its fruit to stick to the back of the leaf all winter? At this season polypody is in the air. It is worth the while to walk in swamps now, to bathe your eyes in greenness. The terminal-shield fern is the handsomest and glossiest green.

I think the man of science makes the mistake, and the mass of mankind along with him, to suppose that you should give your chief attention to the phenomenon which excites you, as something independent of you, and not as it is related to you. The important fact is its effect on me. The man of science thinks I have no business to see anything else but just what he defines the rainbow to be, but I care not whether my vision is a waking thought or a dream remembered, whether it is seen in the light or in the dark. It is the subject of the vision, the truth alone that concerns me. The philosopher for whom rainbows, etc., can be explained away never saw them.

Nov. 5, 1858. The *Cornus florida* on the

Island is still full-leafed, and is now completely scarlet, though it was partly green on the twenty-eighth [of October]. It is apparently in the height of its color there now, or if more exposed perhaps it would have been on the first of November. This makes it the latest tree to change.

Nov. 5, 1860. I am struck by the fact that the more slowly trees grow at first, the sounder they are at the core, and I think the same is true of human beings. We do not wish to see children precocious, making great strides in their early years, like sprouts producing a soft and perishable timber, but better if they expand slowly at first, as if contending with difficulties, and so are solidified and perfected. Such trees continue and expand with nearly equal rapidity to an extreme old age.

Nov. 6, 1853. Climbed the wooded hill by Holden's spruce swamp, and got a novel view of the river and Fair Haven Bay through the almost leafless woods. How much handsomer a river or lake such as ours seen thus through a foreground of scattered or else partially leafless trees, though at a considerable distance this side of it, especially if the water is open, without a wooded shore or isles. It is the most perfect and beautiful of all frames, which yet the sketcher is commonly careful to brush aside. I mean a pretty thick foreground, a view of the distant water through the near forest, through a thousand little vistas, as we are rushing towards the former, that intimate mingling of wood and water which excites an expectation that the near and open view rarely realizes. We prefer that some part be concealed which our imagination may navigate.

Nov. 6, 1857. Minott is a very pleasing figure in nature. He improves any scenery, he and his comrades, Harry Hooper, John Wyman, Oliver Williams, etc. If he gets into a pond hole, he disturbs it no more than a water spirit for me.

Nov. 7, 1839. We are not commonly aware that there is a rising as well as a risen generation. It is a fact, the growing men or women which we do not commonly allow for or remember, who would disturb many a fair theory. Speak for yourself, old man. By what degrees of consanguinity is this succulent and rank-growing slip of manhood related to me? What is it but another herb, ranging all the kingdoms of Nature, drawing its sustenance by a thousand roots and fibres from all soils!

Nov. 7, 1840.

> I 'm guided in the darkest night
> By flashes of auroral light,
> Which overdart thy eastern home,
> And teach me not in vain to roam.

Thy steady light on t' other side
Pales the sunset, makes day abide,
And after sunrise, stays the dawn,
Forerunner of a brighter morn.

.   .   .   .

When others laugh, I am not glad,
When others cry, I am not sad.

.   .   .   .

I am a miser without blame,
Am conscience-stricken without shame,
An idler am I without leisure,
A busybody without pleasure.
I did not think so bright a day
Would issue in so dark a night,
I did not think such sober play
Would leave me in so sad a plight,
And I should be most sorely spent,
When first I was most innocent.

I thought by loving all beside,
To prove to you my love was wide,
And by the rites I soared above,
To show you my peculiar love.

Nov. 7, 1853. Three bluebirds still braving the cold winds, Acton Blues. Their blue uniform makes me think of soldiers who have received orders to keep the field and not go into winter quarters.

A muskrat's house on the top of a rock; [the soil?] too thin round the sides for a passage beneath, yet a small cavity at top, which makes me think they use them merely as a sheltered perch above water. They seize thus many cones to build on, as a hummock left by the ice. The wads of which this muskrat's house was composed were about six inches by four, rounded and massed at one end and flaking off at the other, and were composed chiefly of a little green moss-like weed, for the most part withered dark-brown, and having the strong odor of the fresh water sponge and conferva.

Nov. 7, 1855. I find it good to be out in this still, dark, mizzling afternoon. My walk or voyage is more suggestive and profitable than in bright weather. The view is contracted by the misty rain. The water is perfectly smooth, and the stillness is favorable to reflection. I am more open to impressions, more sensitive, not calloused or indurated by sun and wind, as if in a chamber still. My thoughts are concentrated. I am all compact. The solitude is real, too, for the weather keeps other men at home. This mist is like a roof and walls, over and around, and I walk with a domestic feeling. The sound of a wagon going over an unseen bridge is louder than ever, and so of other sounds. I am compelled to look at near objects. All things have a soothing effect. The very clouds and mists brood over me. My power of observation and contemplation is much increased. My attention does not wander. The world and my life are simplified. What now are Europe and Asia?

Nov. 7, 1857.　Minott adorns whatever part
of nature he touches.　Whichever way he walks
he transfigures the earth for me.　If a common
man speaks of Walden Pond to me, I see only a
shallow, dull-colored body of water, without reflections, or peculiar color, but if Minott speaks
of it, I see the green water and reflected hills at
once, for he *has been* there.　I hear the rustle
of leaves from woods which he goes through.

This has been another Indian-summer day.
Thermometer 58° at noon.

Nov. 7, 1858.　p. m.　To Bateman's Pond.
I leave my boat opposite the hemlocks, and as I
glance upwards between them, seeing the bare
but bright hillside beyond, I think, Now we are
left to the hemlocks and pines with their silvery
light, to the bare trees and withered grass.　The
very rocks and stones in the rocky road (that
beyond Farmer's) look white in the clear November light, especially after the rain.　We are
left to the chickadee's familiar notes, and the
jay for trumpeter.　What struck me was a certain emptiness beyond, between the hemlocks
and the hill, in the cool washed air, as if I
appreciated the absence of insects from it.　It
suggested, agreeably to me, a mere space in
which to walk briskly.　The fields are, as it
were, vacated.　The very earth is like a house
shut up for the winter, and I go knocking about

it in vain. But just then I heard a chickadee in a hemlock, and was inexpressibly cheered to find that an old acquaintance was yet stirring about the premises, and was, I was assured, to be there all winter. All that is evergreen in me revived at once.

The very moss (the little pine moss) in Hosmer's meadow is revealed by its greenness amid the withered grass and stubble.

Going up the lane beyond Farmer's, I was surprised to see fly up from the white stony ground two snow buntings, which alighted again close by. They had pale brown or tawny touches on the white breast, on each side of the head and on top of the head, in the last place with some darker color. Had light yellowish bills. They sat quite motionless within two rods, and allowed me to approach within a rod, as if conscious that the white rocks, etc., concealed them. It seemed as if they were attracted to our faces of the same color with themselves. One squatted flat, if not both. Their soft rippling notes, as they went off, reminded me of the northeast snowstorms to which erelong they are to be an accompaniment.

Looking southwest toward the pond just before sunset, I saw against the light what I took to be a shad-bush in full bloom, but without a leaflet. I was prepared for this sight after the very warm autumn, because this tree frequently puts forth leaves in October. Or it might be a young wild apple. Hastening to it, I found it was only the feathery seeds of the Virgin's Bower [*Clematis virginiana*], whose vine, so close to the branches, was not noticeable. They looked just like dense umbels of white flowers, and in this light, three or four rods off, were fully as light as white apple-blossoms. It is singular how one thing thus puts on the semblance of another. I thought at first I had made a discovery more interesting than the blossoming of apple trees in the fall. It carried me round to spring again, when the shad-bush, almost leafless, is seen waving its white blossoms amid the yet bare trees, the feathery masses, at intervals along the twigs, just like umbels of apple bloom, so caught and reflected the western light.

I pass a musquash house, apparently begun last night. The first mouthfuls of weeds were placed between some small button-bush stems which stood amid the pads and pontederia for a support, and to prevent their being washed away. Opposite I see some half concealed amid the bleached phalaris grass (a tall coarse grass), or, in some places, the blue joint.

Nov. 8, 1850. The stillness of the woods and fields is remarkable at this season of the

year. There is not even the creak of a cricket
to be heard. Of myriads of dry shrub-oak
leaves, not one rustles. Your own breath can
stir them, yet the breath of heaven does not suf-
fice to. The trees have the aspect of waiting
for winter. The sprouts which had shot up so
vigorously to repair the damage which the chop-
pers had done, have stopped short for the winter.
Everything stands silent and expectant. If I
listen, I hear only the note of a chickadee, our
most common bird at present, most identified
with our forests, or perchance the scream of a
jay, or from the solemn depths of the woods I
hear tolling far away the knell of one departed.
Thought rushes in to fill the vacuum. As you
walk, however, the partridge bursts away from
the foot of a shrub oak, like its own dry fruit ;
immortal bird! This sound still startles us.
The silent, dry, almost leafless, certainly fruitless woods, you wonder what cheer that bird can
find in them.

Nov. 8, 1851. Ah, those sun-sparkles on
Dudley Pond in this November air, what a
heaven to live in! Intensely brilliant as no
artificial light I have seen, like a dance of dia-
monds, coarse mazes of the diamond dance seen
through the trees. All objects shine to-day,
even the sportsmen seen at a distance, as if a
cavern were unroofed, and its crystals gave

entertainment to the sun.   This great see-saw of
brilliants, the ἀνήριθμον γέλασμα.   The squirrels
that run across the road sport their tails like
banners. · When I saw the bare sand at Cochituate, I felt my relation to the soil.   These are
my sands not yet run out.   Not yet will the
fates turn the glass.   In this sand my bones
will gladly lie.   Like the *Viola pedata*, I shall
be ready to bloom again here in my Indian-summer days.   Here, ever springing, never dying,
with perennial root I stand, for the winter of the
land is warm to me.   When I see the earth's
sands thrown up from beneath its surface, it
touches me inwardly, it reminds me of my origin,
for I am such a plant, so native to New England, methinks, as springs from the sand cast
up from below.

   Nov. 8, 1853.   10 A. M.   Our first snow.   The
children greet it with a shout, when they come
out at recess.   P. M.   It begins to whiten the
plowed ground now, but has not overcome the
russet of the grass ground.   Birds generally
wear the russet dress of nature at this season.
They have their fall, no less than the plants.
The bright tints depart from their foliage or
feathers, and they flit past like withered leaves
in rustling flocks.   The sparrow is a withered
leaf.   Perchance I heard the last cricket of the
season yesterday, — they chirp here and there at

longer and longer intervals till the snow quenches
their song, — and the last striped squirrel, too,
perchance, yesterday. They then do not go
into winter quarters till the ground is covered
with snow.

The partridges go off with a whirr, and then
sail a long way, level and low, through the woods
with that impetus they have got, displaying their
neat forms perfectly.

Nov. 8, 1857. A warm, cloudy, rain-threatening morning. About 10 A. M., a long flock
of geese are going over from northeast to southwest, or parallel with the general direction of the
coast, and great mountain ranges. The sonorous,
quavering sounds of the geese are the voice of
the cloudy air, a sound that comes from directly
between us and the sky, an aerial sound, and yet
so distinct, heavy and sonorous ; a clanking chain
drawn through the heavy air. I saw through
my window some children looking up, and
pointing their tiny bows into the heavens, and I
knew at once that the geese were in the air. It
is always an exciting event. The children, in-
stinctively aware of its importance, rushed into
the house to tell their parents. These travelers are revealed to you by the upward-turned
gaze of men. And though these undulating
lines are melting into the southwestern sky, the
sound comes clear and distinct to you as the

clank of a chain in a neighboring stithy. So they migrate, not flying from hedge to hedge, but from latitude to latitude, from state to state, steering boldly out into the ocean of the air. It is remarkable how these large objects, so plain when your vision is rightly directed, may be lost in the sky, if you look away for a moment, as hard to hit as a star with a telescope.

It is a sort of encouraging or soothing sound, to assuage their painful fears when they go over a town, as a man moans to deaden a physical pain. The direction of their flight each spring and autumn reminds us inlanders how the coast trends. In the afternoon I met Flood, who endeavored to draw my attention to a flock of geese in the mizzling air, but encountering me he lost sight of them, while I at length, looking that way, discovered them, though he could not. This was the third flock to-day. Now, if ever, then, we may expect some change in the weather.

P. M. To the swamp in front of the C. Miles house. I have no doubt that a good farmer, who of course loves his work, takes exactly the same kind of pleasure in draining a swamp, seeing the water flow out in his newly-cut ditch, that a child does in his mud dykes and water wheels. Both alike love to play with the natural forces.

There is quite a ravine by which the water of this swamp flows out eastward, and at the bottom of it many prinos berries are conspicuous, now apparently in their prime. These are appointed to be an ornament of this bare season between leaves and snow. The swamp pink's large, yellowish buds, too, are conspicuous now. I see also the swamp pyrus buds, expanded sometimes into small leaves. This then is a regular phenomenon. It is the only shrub, or tree that I know which so decidedly springs again in the fall, in the Indian summer. It might be called the Indian-summer shrub. The clethra buds, too, have decidedly expanded there, showing leaflets, but very small. Some of the new pyrus leaves are nearly full-grown. Would not this be a pretty device on some hale and cheery old man's shield, the swamp pyrus unfolding its leaves again in the fall? Every plant enjoys some preëminence, and this is its : the most forward to respond to the warmer season. How much spring there is in it! Its sap is most easily liquefied. It takes the least sun to thaw and develop it. It makes this annual sacrifice of its very first leaves to its love for the sun. While all other plants are reserved, this is open and confiding. I see it not without emotion. I, too, have my spring thoughts even in November. This I see in pleasant November days, when rills and birds begin to tinkle in winter fashion through the more open aisles of the swamps.

I do not know exactly what that sweet word is which the chickadee says when it hops near to me now in those ravines.

When the air is thick and the sky overcast, we need not walk so far. We give our attention to nearer objects, being less distracted from them. I take occasion to explore some near wood which my walks commonly overshoot.

Ah, my friends, I know you better than you think, and love you better, too. The day after never, we will have an explanation.

Nov. 8, 1858. P. M. To Boulder Field. . . . Nature has many scenes to exhibit, and constantly draws a curtain over this part or that. She is constantly repainting the landscape and all surfaces, dressing up some scene for our entertainment. Lately we had a leafy wilderness ; now bare twigs begin to prevail, and soon she will surprise us with a mantle of snow. Some green she thinks so good for our eyes that, like blue, she never banishes it entirely from our eyes, but has created evergreens.

It is remarkable how little any but a lichenist will observe on the bark of trees. The mass of men have but the vaguest and most indefinite notion of mosses, as a sort of shreds and fringes, and the world in which the lichenist dwells is much further from theirs than one side of this earth from the other. They see bark as if they saw it not. . . . Each phase of nature, while not invisible, is yet not too distinct and obstrusive. It is there, to be found when we look for it, but not demanding our attention. It is like a silent but sympathizing companion, in whose company we retain most of the advantages of solitude, with whom we can walk and talk, or be silent, naturally, without the necessity of talking in a strain foreign to the place. I know of but one or two persons with whom I can afford to walk. With most, the walk degenerates into a more vigorous use of your legs (ludicrously purposeless), while you are discussing some weighty argument, each one having his say, spoiling each other's day, worrying one another with conversation. I know of no use in the walking part in this case, except that we may *seem* to be getting on together toward some goal. But of course we keep our distance all the way ; jumping every wall and ditch with vigor in the vain hope of shaking our companion off, trying to kill two birds with one stone, though they sit at opposite points of the compass, to see nature and do the honors to one who does not.

I wandered over bare fields where the cattle, lately turned out, roamed restless and unsatisfied with the feed. I dived into a rust-

ling young oak wood where not a green leaf
was to be seen, and again I thought, They are
all gone surely, and have left me alone. Not
even a man Friday remains. What nutriment
can I extract from these bare twigs? Starva-
tion stares me in the face. "*Nay, nay,*" said a
nuthatch, making its way, head downward,
about a bare hickory close by, "The nearer the
bone, the sweeter the meat. Only the superfluous has been swept away. Now we behold the
naked truth. If at any time the weather is
too bleak and cold for you, keep the sunny side
of the trunk, for a wholesome and inspiring
warmth is there, such as the summer never
afforded. There are the winter mornings with
the sun on the oak wood-tops. While buds sleep
thoughts wake." "Hear! hear!" screamed the
jay from a neighboring tree, where I had heard
a tittering for some time, "winter has a concentrated and nutty kernel, if you know where to
look for it," and then the speaker shifted to another tree farther off and reiterated his asser-
tions, and his mate at a distance confirmed
them; and now I heard a suppressed chuckle
from a red squirrel that heard the last remark,
but had kept silent and invisible all the while.
The birds being gone, the squirrel came running
down a slanting bough, and as he stopped twirl-
ing a nut, called out rather impudently, "Look

here ! just get a snug-fitting fur coat and a pair
of fur gloves like mine, and you may laugh at
a northeast storm." Then he wound up with
a stray phrase in his own lingo, accompanied
by a flourish of his tail.

Nov. 9, 1850. I found many fresh violets
(*Viola pedata*) to-day in the woods.

Nov. 9, 1851. I would fain set down something beside facts. Facts should only be the
frame to my picture. They should be material
to the mythology which I am writing, not facts
to assist men to make money, farmers to farm
profitably in any common sense, facts to tell
who I am, and where I have been, or what I
have thought ; as now the bell rings for evening
meeting, and its volumes of sound, like smoke
which rises from where a cannon is fired, make
the tent in which I dwell. My facts shall all
be falsehoods to the common sense. I would so
state facts that they shall be significant, shall
be myths or mythologic, facts which the mind
perceived, thoughts which the body thought,
with these I deal. I cherish vague and misty
forms, vaguest when the cloud at which I gaze
is dissipated quite, and naught but the skyey
depths are seen.

James P. Brown's retired pond, now shallow
and more than half dried up, seems far away
and rarely visited, known to few, though not

far off. It is encircled by an amphitheatre of low hills, on two opposite sides covered with high pine woods, the two other sides with young white oaks and white pines respectively. I am affected by seeing there reflected this gray day, the gray stems of the pine wood on the hillside, and the sky; that mirror, as it were a permanent picture to be seen there, a permanent piece of idealism. I am a little surprised on beholding this reflection which I did not perceive for some minutes after looking into the pond, as if I had not regarded this as a constant phenomenon. What has become of Nature's common-sense and love of facts when in the very mud-puddles she reflects the skies and the trees? Does that procedure recommend itself entirely to the common-sense of men? Is that the way the New England farmer would have arranged it?

Now the leaves are gone, the birds' nests are revealed, the brood being fledged and flown. There is a perfect adaptation in the material used in constructing a nest. Here is one which I took from a maple on the causeway at Hubbard's bridge. It is fastened to the twigs by white woolen strings (out of a shawl?) which were picked up in the road, though it is more than half a mile from a house; and the sharp eyes of the bird have discovered plenty of horse-hairs out of the tail or mane with which to give it form by their spring, with meadow hay for body, and the reddish woolly material which invests the ferns in the spring, apparently, for lining.

Nov. 9, 1852. *Ranunculus repens, Bidens connata,* flat in a brook, yarrow, dandelion, autumnal dandelion, tansy, *Aster undulatus,* etc. A late three-ribbed golden-rod, with large serratures in the middle of the narrow leaves, ten or twelve rays, *Potentilla argentea.* Early part of November, time for walnutting.

Nov. 9, 1853. P. M. To Fair Haven Hill by boat with W. E. C. The muskrats have added a new story to their houses since the last flood which covered them, I mean that of October 31st, or thereabouts. They are uncommonly high, I think full four feet by five or more in diameter, a heaping cart - load. There are at least eight such within half a mile. It is remarkable how little effect the waves have on them, while a heap of manure or a haycock would be washed away or undermined at once. I opened one. It was composed of coarse grass, pontederia stems, etc., not altogether in mouthfuls. This was three and a half feet above water, others quite four. After taking off a foot, I came to the chamber. It was a regularly formed oval or elliptical chamber, about eighteen inches the longest way, and seven or

eight inches deep, shaped like a pebble, with
smooth walls of the weeds, and bottomed or
bedded with a very little drier grass, a mere
coating of it. It would hold four or five, closely
packed. The entrance, eight or nine inches
wide, led directly from the water at an angle of
45°, and in the water there were some green
and white stub ends of pontederia (?) stems, I
think, looking like flagroot. That thick wall, a
foot quite or more above, and eighteen inches
or two feet [below?], being of these damp
materials soon freezes, and makes a tight and
warm house. The walls are of such breadth
at the bottom that the water in the gallery
probably never freezes. If the height of these
houses is any sign of high or low water, this
winter it will be uncommonly high.

Nov. 9, 1855. 9 A. M. With Blake up Assabet. Saw in the pool at the Hemlocks what I
at first thought was a brighter leaf moved by
the zephyr on the surface of the smooth, dark
water, but it was a splendid male summer duck,
which allowed us to approach within seven or
eight rods. It was sailing up close to the
shore, and then rose and flew up the curving
stream. It was a perfect floating gem, and
Blake, who had never seen the like, was greatly
surprised, not knowing that so splendid a bird
was found in this part of the world. There it

was, constantly moving back and forth by invisible means, and wheeling on the smooth surface, showing now its breast, now its side, now its rear. It had a large, rich, flowing, green, burnished crest, a most ample head-dress, two crescents of dazzling white on the side of the head and the black neck, a pinkish red bill (with black tip) and similar irides, and a long white mark under and at wing - point on sides, the side, as if the form of wing at this distance, light bronze or greenish brown ; but, above all, its breast, when it turns into the right light, all aglow with splendid purple (?) or ruby (?) reflections like the throat of the humming-bird. It might not appear so, close at hand. This was the most surprising to me. What an ornament to a river, that glowing gem floating in contact with its waters ; as if the humming-bird should recline its ruby throat and its breast there ; like dipping a glowing coal in water. It so affected me. Unless you are thus near, and have a glass, the splendor and beauty of its colors will not be discovered.

I deal so much with my fuel, what with finding it, loading it, conveying it home, sawing and splitting it, get so many values out of it, that the heat it will yield when in the stove is of a lower temperature and less value in my eyes, though when I feel it I am reminded of all my adventures. I just turned to put in a stick. I had my choice in the box of gray chestnut rail, black and brown snag of an oak stump, dead white pine top, or else old bridge plank, and chose the last. Yes, I lose sight of the ultimate uses of the wood and work, the immediate ones are so great, and yet most of mankind, those called most successful in obtaining the necessaries of life, getting a living, obtain none of this except a mere vulgar and perhaps stupefying warmth. I feel disposed, to this extent, to do the getting a living and the living for any three or four of my neighbors who really want the fuel and will appreciate the act, now that I have supplied myself. I affect what would commonly be called a mean and miserable way of living. I thoroughly sympathize with all savages and gypsies in as far as they assert the original right of man to the productions of Nature and a place in her.

Nov. 9, 1857. Mr. [Jacob] Farmer tells me that one Sunday he went to his barn, having nothing to do, and thought he would watch the swallows, republican swallows. The old bird was feeding her young, and he sat within fifteen feet, overlooking them. There were five young, and as often as the bird came with a fly, the one at the door or opening took it, and then they all hitched round one notch, so that a new one was presented at the door, who received the next fly, and this was the invariable order, the same one never receiving two flies in succession. At last the old bird brought a very small fly, and the young one that swallowed it did not desert his ground, but waited to receive the next, but when the bird came with another of the usual size, she commenced a loud and long scolding at the little one, till it resigned its place, and the next in succession received the fly.

Nov. 9, 1858. The newspaper tells me that Uncannoonuc was white with snow for a short time on the morning of the 7th. Thus steadily but unobserved the winter steals down from the north till from our highest hills we can discern its vanguard. Next week perchance our own hills will be white. Little did we think how near the winter was. It is as if a scout had brought us word that an enemy was approaching in force, only a day's march distant. Manchester was the spy this time, who has a camp at the base of that hill. We had not thought seriously of winter, we dwelt in fancied security yet.

It is of no use to plow deeper than the soil is, unless you mean to follow up that mode of cultivation persistently, manuring highly and carting in muck, at each plowing making a soil, in short. Yet many a man likes to tackle weighty themes like immortality, but in his discourse he turns up nothing but yellow sand, under which what little fertile and available surface soil he may have is quite buried and lost. He should teach frugality rather, how to postpone the fatal hour; should plant a crop of beans. He might have raised enough of them to make a deacon of him, though never a preacher. Many a man runs his plow so deep in heavy or strong soil that it sticks fast in the furrow. It is a great art in the writer to improve from day to day just that soil and fertility which he has, to harvest that crop which his life yields, whatever it may be, not be straining as if to reach apples and oranges when he yields only ground-nuts. He should be digging, not soaring. Just as earnest as your life is, so deep is your soil. If strong and deep, you will sow wheat and raise bread of life in it.

Nov. 10, 1851. It appears to me that those things which most engage the daily attention of men, as politics, for instance, are, it is true, vital functions of human society, but should be unconsciously performed like the vital functions of the natural body. It is as if a thinker submitted himself to be rasped by the great gizzard of creation. Politics is, as it were, the gizzard of society, full of grit and gravel, and the two political parties are its two opposite halves which grind on each other. Not only individuals, but states, have thus a confirmed dyspepsia, which expresses itself, you can imagine by what sort of eloquence. Our life is not altogether a forgetting, but also, to a great extent, a remembering of that which, perchance, we should never have been conscious of, which should not be permitted to distract a man's waking hours. Why should we not meet, not always as dyspeptics, but sometimes as eupeptics? In our intercourse we refer to no true and absolute account of things, but there is ever a petty reference to man, to society, aye, often to Christianity. I come from the funeral of mankind to attend to a natural phenomenon. The significance of any fact in nature, of sun and moon and stars, is so much grander when not referred to man and his needs, but viewed absolutely. Then we catch sounds which are wafted from over the confines of time.

Nov. 10, 1858. Hearing in an oak wood near by a sound as if some one had broken a twig, I looked up and saw a jay, pecking at an acorn. There were several of them gathering acorns on a scarlet oak. I could hear them breaking them off. They then flew to a suitable limb, and placing the acorn under one foot, hammered away at it busily, looking round from time to time to see if any foe was approaching, and soon reached the meat, and nibbled at it, holding up their heads to swallow, while they held it very firmly with their claws. (Their hammering made a sound like the woodpecker's.) Nevertheless, it sometimes dropped to the ground before they had done with it.

Nov. 11, 1850. This afternoon I heard a single cricket singing, chirruping on a bank, the only one I have heard for a long time, like a squirrel, or a little bird, clear and shrill, — as I fancied, like an evening robin, singing in this evening of the year. A very fine and poetical strain for such a little singer. I had never before heard the cricket so like a bird. It is a remarkable note, the earth-song.

That delicate, waving, feathery dry grass which I saw yesterday is to be remembered with the autumn. The dry grasses are not dead for me. A beautiful form has as much life at one season as at another.

I notice that everywhere in the pastures minute young fragrant life-everlasting with only four or five flat-lying leaves and thread-like roots, all together as big as a fourpence, spots the ground, like winter rye and grass which roots itself in the fall against another year. These little things have bespoken their places for the next season. They have a little pallet of cotton or down in their centres, ready for an early start in the spring.

I saw an old bone in the woods covered with lichens, which looked like the bone of an old settler, which yet some little animal had recently gnawed. I saw plainly the marks of its teeth, so indefatigable is nature to strip the flesh from bones, and return them to dust again. No little rambling beast can go by some dry and ancient bone, but he must turn aside and try his teeth upon it. An old bone is knocked about till it becomes dust ; nature has no mercy on it. It was quite too ancient to suggest disagreeable associations. It survives like the memory of a man. With time all that was personal and offensive wears off. The tooth of envy may sometimes gnaw it and reduce it more rapidly, but it is much more a prey to forgetfulness.

Nov. 11, 1851. 2 P. M. A bright, but cold day, finger-cold. One must next wear gloves, put his hands in winter quarters. There is a cold, silvery light on the white pines as I go through J. P. Brown's field near Jenny Dugan's. I am glad of the shelter of the thick pine wood on the Marlboro' road, on the plain. The roar of the wind over the pines sounds like the surf on countless beaches, an endless shore, and at intervals it sounds like a gong resounding through halls and entries, that is, there is a certain resounding woodiness in the tone. The sky looks mild and fair enough from this shelter.

Every withered blade of grass and every dry weed as well as pine needle, reflects the light. The lately dark woods are open and light, the sun shines in upon the stems of trees which it has not shone on since spring. Around the edges of ponds the weeds are dead, and there, too, the light penetrates. The atmosphere is less moist and gross, and light is universally dispersed. We are greatly indebted to these transition seasons or states of the atmosphere, which show us thus phenomena that belong not to the summer or the winter of any climate. The brilliancy of the autumn is wonderful, this flashing brilliancy, as if the atmosphere were phosphoric.

When I have been confined to my chamber for the greater part of several days by some employment or perchance by the ague, till I felt weary and house-worn, I have been conscious of a certain softness to which I am otherwise commonly a stranger, in which the gates were loosened to some emotions; and if I were to become a confirmed invalid, I see how some sympathy with mankind and society might spring up. Yet what is my softness good for, even to tears? It is not I, but nature in me. I laughed at myself the other day to think that I cried while reading a pathetic story. I was no more affected in spirit than I frequently am, methinks. The tears were merely a phenomenon of the bowels, and I felt that that expression of my sympathy, so unusual with me, was something mean, and such as I should be ashamed to have the subject of it understand.

To-day you may write a chapter on the advantages of traveling, and to-morrow you may write another on the advantages of not traveling. The horizon has one kind of beauty and attraction to him who has never explored the hills and mountains in it, and another, I fear a less ethereal and glorious one, to him who has. That blue mountain in the horizon is certainly the most heavenly, the most elysian, which we have not climbed, on which we have not camped for a night. But our horizon, by such exploration, is only moved farther off, and if our whole life should prove thus a failure, the future which is to atone for all, where still there must be some success, will be more glorious still.

It is fatal to the writer to be too much possessed by his thought ; things must be a little remote to be described.

Nov. 11, 1853. 9 A. M. To Fair Haven by boat. The morning is so calm and pleasant, that I must spend the forenoon abroad. The river is smooth as polished silver. Some muskrat houses have received a slight addition in the night. The one I opened day before yesterday has been covered again, though not yet raised so high as before. I counted nineteen between Hubbard bathing place and Hubbard's further wood, this side the Hallowell place, from two to four feet high. I opened one. The floor of the chamber was two feet or more beneath the top, and one foot above the water. It was quite warm from the recent presence of the inhabitants.

Nov. 11, 1854. Minott heard geese go over night before last about 8 P. M. Therien, too, heard them "yelling like anything" over Walden, where he is cutting, the same evening.

Nov. 11, 1855. P. M. Up Assabet. The bricks of which the muskrat builds his house are little masses or wads of the dead weedy rubbish on the muddy bottom which it probably takes up with its mouth. It consists of various kinds of weeds, now confervæ by the slime, agglutinated and dried converbal threads, utricularia, hornwort, etc., — a streaming, tuft-like wad. The building of these cabins appears to be coincident with the commencement of their clam diet, for now their vegetable food, excepting roots, is cut off. I see many small collections of shells already left along the river's brink. Thither they resort with their clam, to open and eat it. But if it is the edge of a meadow which is being overflowed, they must raise it, and make a permanent dry stool there, for they cannot

afford to swim far with each clam. I see where
one has left half a peck of shells on perhaps
the foundation of an old stool or a harder clod
which the water is just about to cover. He has
begun his stool by laying two or three fresh wads
upon the shells, the foundation of his house.
Thus their cabin is apparently first intended
merely for a stool, and afterward, when it is
large, perforated as if it were the bank! There
is no cabin for a long way above the hemlocks,
where there is no low meadow bordering the
stream.

Nov. 11, 1858. Goodwin brings me this
morning a this year's loon which he has just
killed in the river, the Great Northern Diver,
but a smaller specimen than Wilson describes,
and somewhat differently marked. It is twenty-
seven inches long to end of feet, by forty-four,
bill three and three fourths to angle of mouth.
Above, bluish gray, with small white spots (two
at end of each feather). Beneath, pure white,
throat and all, except a dusky bar across the
vent. Bill, chiefly pale bluish and dusky. You
are struck by its broad, flat, sharp-edged legs,
made to cut through the water rather than to
walk with, set far back and naturally stretched
out backward, its long and powerful bill, conspicuous white throat and breast. Dislodged by
winter in the north, it is slowly traveling toward

a warmer climate, diving this morning in the cool river, which is now full of light, the trees and shrubs on its bank having long since lost their leaves. The neighboring fields are white with frost. Yet this hardy bird is comfortable and contented there, if the sportsmen will let it alone.

Nov. 11, 1859. October 24, riding home from Acton, I saw the withered leaves blown from an oak by the roadside, dashing off, gyrating, and surging upward into the air, so exactly like a flock of birds sporting with one another, that for a moment, at least, I could not be sure they were not birds, and it suggested how far the motions of birds, like those of these leaves, might be determined by currents of air, that is, how far the bird learns to conform to such currents.

Nov. 12, 1837. I yet lack discernment to distinguish the whole lesson of to-day, but it is not lost, it will come to me at last. My desire is to know *what* I have lived, that I may know *how* to live henceforth.

Nov. 12 [?], 1841. Music is only a sweet striving to express character. Now that lately I have heard of some traits in the character of a fair and earnest maiden whom I had known only superficially, but who has gone hence to make herself more known by distance, these strains sound like a wild harp music. There is apology enough for all the deficiency and short-coming in the world in the patient waiting of any bud of character to unfold itself.

Only character can command our reverent love. It is all mysteries in itself.

> What is it gilds the trees and clouds,
> And paints the heavens so gay,
> But yonder fast-abiding light
> With its unchanging ray.
>
> I 've felt within my inmost soul
> Such cheerful morning news,
> In the horizon of my mind
> I 've seen such morning hues,
>
> As in the twilight of the dawn
> When the first birds awake,
> Is heard within some silent wood
> When they the small twigs break;
>
> Or in the eastern skies is seen
> Before the sun appears,
> Foretelling of the summer heats
> Which far away he bears.

Walden. P. M. I seem to discern the very form of the wind when, blowing over the hills, it falls in broad flakes upon the surface of the pond, this subtle element obeying the law of the least subtle. I cannot but be encouraged by the blithe activity of the elements. Who hears the rippling of the rivers will not utterly despair of anything. The wind in the wood yonder sounds like an incessant waterfall, the water dashing and roaring among the rocks.

Nov. 12, 1851. Write often, write upon a thousand themes, rather than long at a time, not trying to turn too many feeble summersets in the air, and so come down upon your head at last. Antæus-like, be not long absent from the ground. Those sentences are good and well-discharged which are like so many little resiliences from the spring-floor of our life, each a distinct fruit and kernel springing from terra firma. Let there be as many distinct plants as the soil and the light can maintain. Take as many bounds in a day as possible, sentences uttered with your back to the wall. Those are the admirable bounds when the performer has lately touched the spring-board. A good bound into the air from the air is a good and wholesome experience, but what shall we say to a man's leaping off precipices in the attempt to fly. He comes down like lead. But let your feet be planted upon the rock, with the rock also at your back, and as in the case of King James and Roderick Dhu, you can say, —

> " Come one, come all, this rock shall fly
> From its firm base, as soon as I."

Such, uttered or not, is the strength of your sentences, sentences in which there is no strain, no fluttering inconstant and quasi aspiration, and ever memorable Icarian fall wherein your helpless wings are expanded merely by your swift descent into the pelagos beneath.

———— is one who will not stoop to rise. He wants something for which he will not pay the going price. He will only learn slowly by failure, not a noble, but disgraceful failure. This is not a worthy method of learning, to be educated by evitable suffering, like De Quincey, for instance. Better dive like a muskrat into the mud, and pull up a few weeds to sit on during the floods, a foundation of your own laying, a house of your own building, however cold and cheerless. Methinks the hawk that soars so loftily, and circles so steadily and apparently without effort, has earned this power by faithfully creeping on the ground as a reptile in a former state of existence. You must creep before you can run, you must run before you can fly. Better one effective bound upward with elastic limbs from the valley, than a jumping from the mountain-tops with attempt to fly. The observatories are not built high, but deep. The foundation is equal to the superstructure. It is more important to a distinct vision that it be steady, than that it be from an elevated point of view.

Walking through Ebby Hubbard's wood this afternoon with Minott, who was actually taking a walk for amusement and exercise, he said, on seeing some white pines blown down, that you might know that ground had been cultivated, for otherwise they would have rooted themselves more strongly. . . . He has a story for every woodland path. He has hunted in them all. Where we walked last, he had once caught a partridge by the wing.

7 P. M. To Conantum. A still cold night. The light of the rising moon in the east. The ground is frozen and echoes to my tread. There are absolutely no crickets to be heard now. They are heard, then, till the ground freezes. I hear no sound of any kind now at night, but sometimes some creature stirring, a rabbit, or skunk, or fox, betrayed by the dry leaves which lie so thick and light. The openness of the leafless woods is particularly apparent now by moonlight; they are nearly as light as the open field. It is worth the while always to go to the water, when there is but little light in the heavens, and see the heavens and the stars reflected. There is double the light that there is elsewhere, and the reflection has the force of a great silent companion. I thought to-night that I saw glow-worms in the grass on the side of the hill, was almost certain of it, and tried to lay my hands on them, but found it was the moonlight reflected from (apparently) the fine

frost crystals on the withered grass. They
were so fine that the reflections went and came
like glow-worms. The gleams were just long
enough for glow-worms, and the effect was precisely the same.

Nov. 12, 1852. 4 P. M. To Cliffs. It clears
up. A very bright rainbow, three reds, two
greens. I see its foot within half a mile in the
southeast, heightening the green of the pines.
From Fair Haven Hill, I see a very distant, long,
low, dark-blue cloud still left in the northwest
horizon, beyond the mountains, and against this
I see, apparently, a narrow white cloud resting
on every mountain, and conforming exactly to its
outline, as if the white, frilled edge of the main
cloud were turned up over them. In fact, the
massive dark-blue cloud beyond revealed these
distinct white caps resting on the mountains this
side, for twenty miles along the horizon.

The sun having set, my long, dark-blue cloud
has assumed the form of an alligator, and where
the sun has just disappeared it is split into two
tremendous jaws, between which glows the eternal city, its crenate lips all coppery-golden, its
serrate fiery teeth. Its body lies a slumbering
mass along the horizon.

Nov. 12, 1853. I cannot but regard it as a
kindness in those who have the steering of me,
that by the want of pecuniary wealth, I have

been nailed down to this my native region so long and steadily, and made to study and love this spot of earth more and more.   What would signify in comparison a thin and diffused love and knowledge of the whole earth instead, got by wandering?   Wealth will not buy a man a home in nature.   The man of business does not by his business earn a residence in nature.   It is an insignificant, a merely negative good to be provided with thick garments against cold and wet, an unprofitable and weak condition compared with being able to extract some exhilaration, some warmth even, out of cold and wet themselves, and to clothe them with our sympathy.   The rich man buys woolens and furs, and sits naked and shivering still, in spirit, but the poor lord of creation makes cold and wet to warm him, and be his garments.

The hylodes, as it is the first frog heard in the spring, so it is the last in the autumn.   I heard it last, I think, about a month ago.   I do not remember any hum of insects for a long time, though I heard a cricket to-day.

Nov. 12, 1858.   It is much the coldest day yet, and the ground is a little frozen and resounds under my tread.   All people move the brisker for the cold, are braced and a little elated by it.   They love to say, " Cold day, sir.'' Though the days are shorter, you get more work out of a hired man than before, for he must work to keep warm. . . . We are now reduced to browsing on buds and twigs, and methinks with this diet and this cold, we shall appear to the stall-fed thinkers like those unkempt cattle in meadows now, grazing the withered grass.   -

I think the change to some higher color in a leaf is an evidence that it has arrived at a late, more perfect, and final maturity, answering to the maturity of fruits, and not to that of green leaves, etc., which merely serve a purpose. The word ripe is thought by some to be derived from the verb to reap, so that what is ripe is ready to be reaped. The fall of the leaf is preceded by a ripe old age.

Nov. 12, 1859. The first sprinkling of snow, which for a short time whitens the ground in spots.

I do not know how to distinguish between our waking life and a dream. Are we not always living the life that we imagine we are? Fear creates danger, and courage dispels it.

There was a remarkable sunset, I think the twenty - fifth of October. The sunset sky reached quite from west to east, and it was the most varied in its forms and colors that I remember to have seen. At one time the clouds were softly and delicately rippled like the ripple marks on sand. But it was hard for me to see its beauty then, when my mind was filled with Captain Brown. So great a wrong as his fate implied overshadowed all beauty in the world.

Nov. 13, 1837. Sin destroys the perception of the beautiful. It is a sure evidence of the health and innocence of the beholder, if the senses are alive to the beauty of nature. This shall be the test of innocence, if I can hear a taunt, and look out on this friendly moon pacing the heavens in queen-like majesty, with the accustomed yearning.

Truth is ever returning into herself. I glimpse one feature to-day, another to-morrow, and the next day they are blended.

Nov. 13, 1839. Make the most of your regrets. Never smother your sorrow, but tend and cherish it, till it come to have a separate and integral interest. To regret deeply is to live afresh. By so doing you will find yourself restored to all your emoluments.

Nov. 13 [?], 1841. We constantly anticipate repose. Yet it surely can only be the repose that is in entire and healthy activity. It must be a repose without rust. What is leisure but opportunity for more complete and entire action? Our energies pine for exercise. The time we spend in the discharge of our duties is so much leisure, so that there is no man but has sufficient of it.

This ancient Scotch poetry at which its contemporaries so marveled, sounds like the uncertain lisping of a child. When man's speech
flows freest, it but stammers. There is never a
free and clear deliverance ; but read now when
the illusion of smooth verse is destroyed by the
antique spelling, and the sense is seen to stam-
mer and stumble all the plainer. To how few
thoughts do all these 'sincere efforts give utterance ? An hour's conversation with these men
would have done more. I am astonished to see
how meagre that diet is which has fed so many
men. The music of sound, which is all-sufficient
at first, is speedily lost, and then the fame of the
poet must rest on the music of the sense. A
great philosophical and moral poet would give
permanence to the language by making the best
sound convey the best sense.

Nov. 13, 1851. To Fair Haven Hill. A cold
and dark afternoon, the sun being behind clouds
in the west. The landscape is barren of objects,
the trees being leafless, and so little light in the
sky for variety ; such a day as will almost oblige
a man to eat his own heart, a day in which you
must hold on to life by your teeth. Now is the
time to cut timber for yokes and ox-bows, leaving the tough bark on, yokes for your own neck,
finding yourself yoked to matter and to time.
Truly hard times, these ! Not a mosquito left,

not an insect to hum. Crickets gone into winter quarters. Friends long since gone there, and you left to walk on frozen ground with your hands in your pockets. Ah, but is not this a glorious time for your deep inward fires? Will not your green hickory and white oak burn clear in this frosty air? Now is not your manhood taxed by the great Assessor? taxed for having a soul, a rateable soul? A day when you cannot pluck a flower, cannot dig a parsnip, nor pull a turnip, for the frozen ground. What do the thoughts find to live on? What avails you now the fire you stole from heaven? Does not each thought become a vulture to gnaw your vitals? No Indian summer have we had this November. I see but few traces of the perennial spring. We have not even the cold beauty of ice crystals and snowy architecture. Nothing but the echo of your steps on the frozen ground, which, it is true, is being prepared for immeasurable snows. Still there are brave thoughts within you that shall remain to rustle the winter through, like white-oak leaves upon your boughs, or like shrub oaks that remind the traveler of a fire upon the hillsides, or evergreen thoughts, cold even in midsummer, by their nature. These shall contrast the more fairly with the snow. Some warm springs shall still tinkle and fume, and send their column of vapor to the skies.

The mountains are of an uncommonly dark blue to-day. Perhaps this is owing not only to the great clearness of the atmosphere, which makes them seem nearer, but to the absence of the leaves. A little mistiness occasioned by warmth would set them further off. I see snow on the Peterboro' Hills reflecting the sun. It is pleasant thus to look from afar into winter. We look at a condition which we have not reached. Notwithstanding the poverty of the immediate landscape, in the horizon it is simplicity and grandeur. I look into valleys white with snow and now lit up by the sun, while all this country is in shade. There is a great gap in the mountain range just south of the two Peterboro' Hills. Methinks I have been through it, and that a road runs there. Humble as these mountains are compared with some, at this distance I am convinced they answer the purpose of Andes. Seen at this distance, I know of nothing more grand and stupendous than that great mountain gate or pass, a great cleft or sinus in the blue banks, as in a dark evening cloud, fit portal to lead from one country, from one quarter of the world to another, where the children of Israel might file through. Little does the New Hampshire farmer who drives over that road realize through what a sublime gap he is passing. You would almost as soon think of a road as winding through and over a dark evening cloud. This prospect of the mountains from our low hills is what I would rather have than pastures on the mountain-side such as my neighbors have, aye, than townships at their base. Instead of driving my cattle up there in May, I simply turn my eyes thither. They pasture there, and the grass they feed on never withers.

Just spent a couple of hours (8 to 10) with Miss Mary Emerson at Holbrook's; the wittiest and most vivacious woman I know, certainly that woman among my acquaintance whom it is most profitable to meet, the least frivolous, who will most surely provoke to good conversation. She is singular among women, at least, in being really and perseveringly interested to know what thoughtful people think. She relates herself surely to the intellectual wherever she goes. It is perhaps her greatest praise and peculiarity that she more surely than any other woman gives her companion occasion to utter his best thought. In spite of her own biases, she can entertain a large thought with hospitality, and is not prevented by any intellectuality in it, as women commonly are. In short, she is a genius, as woman seldom is, reminding you less often of her sex than any woman whom I know. Thus she is capable of a masculine appreciation of poetry and philosophy. I never talked with any other woman who I thought accompanied me so far in describing a poetic experience. Miss Fuller is the only other I think of in this connection, and of her rather from her fame than from my knowledge of her. Miss Emerson expressed to-night a singular want of respect for her own sex, saying that they were frivolous, almost without exception, that woman was the weaker vessel, etc. ; and that into whatever family she might go, she depended more upon the clown for society than upon the lady of the house. Men are more likely to have opinions of their own.

Just in proportion to the outward poverty is the inward wealth. In cold weather fire burns with a clearer flame.

Nov. 13, 1855. In mid - forenoon, 10.45, seventy or eighty geese, in three harrows, successively smaller, flying southwest, pretty well west, over the house. A completely overcast, occasionally drizzling forenoon. I at once heard their clangor, and rushed to and opened the window. The three harrows were gradually formed into one great one, before they were out of sight, the geese shifting their places without slacking their progress.

P. M. To Cardinal Shore. I saw in the pond by the roadside, a few rods before me, the sun shining bright, a mink swimming, the whole length of his back out. It was a rich brown fur, glowing internally as the sun fell on it, like some ladies' boas ; not black, as it sometimes appears, especially on ice. It landed within three rods, showing its long, somewhat cat-like neck, and I observed, was carrying something by its mouth, dragging it overland. At first I thought it a fish, maybe an eel, and when it had got half a dozen feet, I ran forward, and it dropped its prey, and went into the wall. It was a muskrat, the head and part of the legs torn off and gone, but the rest still fresh and quite heavy, including hind legs and tail. It had probably killed the muskrat in the brook, eaten so much, and was dragging the remainder to its retreat in the wall.

Nov. 13, 1858. It is wonderful what gradation and harmony there is in nature. The light reflected from bare twigs at this season, that is, since they began to be bare, in the latter part of October, is not unlike that from gossamer, and like that which will erelong be reflected from the ice that will incrust them. So the bleached herbage of the fields is like frost, and frost like snow, and one prepares for the other.

Nov. 14 [?], 1841. To find the sunset described by the old Scotch poet, Douglas, as I have seen it, repays me for many weary pages of antiquated Scotch. Nothing so restores and harmonizes antiquity and makes it blithe, as the

discovery of some natural sympathy. Why is
it that there is something melancholy in antiquity? We forget that it had any other future
than our present, as if it were not as near to
the future as ourselves. No, these ranks of
men to right and left, posterity and ancestry, are
not to be thridded by any earnest mortal. The
heavens stood over the heads of our ancestors as
near as to us. Any living word in their books
abolishes the difference of time. It need only
be considered from the present standpoint.

Nov. 14, 1851. In the evening I went to a
party. It is a bad place to go to, thirty or forty
persons, mostly young women, in a small room,
warm and noisy. Was introduced to two young
women. The first was as lively and loquacious
as a chickadee, had been accustomed to the
society of watering places, and therefore could
get no refreshment out of such a dry fellow as I.
The other was said to be pretty looking, but I
rarely look people in their faces, and, moreover,
I could not hear what she said, there was such a
clacking ; could not see the motion of her lips
when I looked that way. I could imagine better places for conversation, where there should
be a certain degree of silence surrounding you,
and less than forty talking at once. Why, this
afternoon even I did better. Old Mr. Joseph
Hosmer and I ate luncheon of cracker and

cheese together in the woods. I heard all he said, though it was not much, to be sure, and he could hear me ; and then he talked out of such a glorious repose, taking a leisurely bite at the cracker and cheese between his words, and so some of him was communicated to me, and some of me to him, I trust.

These parties, I think, are a part of the machinery of modern society that young people may be brought together to form marriage connections.

What is the use in going to see people whom yet you never see, and who never see you ?

I met a man yesterday afternoon in the road who behaved as if he were deaf, and I talked with him in the cold in a loud tone for fifteen minutes, but that uncertainty about his ears, and the necessity I felt to talk loudly, took off the fine edge of what I had to say, and prevented my saying anything satisfactory. It is bad enough when your neighbor does not understand you, but if there is any uncertainty as to whether he hears you, so that you are obliged to become your own auditor, you are so much the poorer speaker, and so there is a double failure.

Nov. 14, 1852. Still, yarrow, tall buttercup and tansy.

Nov. 14, 1855. Heard to-day in my chamber about 11 A. M. a singular sharp, crackling

sound by the window, which made me think of
an insect's snapping with its wings or striking
something.   It was produced by one of three
small pitch - pine cones which I gathered November 7th, and which lay in the sun on the win-
dow-sill.   I noticed a slight motion in the scales
at the apex, when suddenly, with a louder crackling, it burst, or the scales separated with a
crackling sound on all sides of it.   It was a
sudden and general bursting or expanding of all
the scales with a sharp, crackling sound, and
motion of the whole cone as by a force pent up
within it.   I suppose the strain only needed to
be relieved at one point for the whole to go off.

Nov. 14, 1857.   The principal flight of geese
was November 8th, so that the bulk of them
preceded this cold turn five days.   I find my
hands stiffened and involuntarily finding their
way to my pockets.   No wonder that the weather
is a standing subject of conversation, since we
are so sensitive.   If we had not gone through
several winters, we might well be alarmed at the
approach of cold weather.   With this keener
blast my hands suddenly fail to fulfill their office,
as it were, begin to die.   We must put on armor
against the new foe.   I can hardly tie and untie
my shoestrings.   What a story to tell an inhabitant of the tropics, perchance, that you went
to walk after many months of warmth, when

suddenly the air became so cold and hostile to your nature that it benumbed you, so that you lost the use of some of your limbs, could not untie your shoestrings !

Nov. 14, 1858. Now while the frosty air begins to nip your fingers and your nose, the frozen ground rapidly wears away the soles of your shoes, as sandpaper might. . The old she-wolf is nibbling at your very extremities. The frozen ground eating away the soles of your shoes is only typical of the vulture that gnaws your heart this month. Now all that moves migrates or has migrated, ducks are gone by, the citizen has sought the town.

Probably the witch hazel and many other flowers lingered till the eleventh, when it was colder. The last leaves and flowers (?) may be said to fall about the middle of November.

Snow and cold drive the doves to your door, and so your thoughts make new alliances.

Nov. 14, 1860. Yellow butterflies still.

Nov. 15, 1840. Over and above a man's business there must be a level of undisturbed serenity, only the more serene, as he is the more industrious, as within the reef encircling a coral isle there is always an expanse of still water where the depositions are going on which will finally raise it above the surface. He must preside over all he does. If his employment rob him of a serene outlook over his life, it is but idle, though it be measuring the fixed stars. He must know no distracting cares.

The bad sense is the secondary one.

Nov. 15 [?], 1841. A mild summer sun shines over forest and lake. The earth looks as fair this morning as the Valhalla of the gods. Indeed our spirits never go beyond nature. In the woods there is an inexpressible happiness. Their mirth is but just repressed. In winter when there is but one green leaf for many rods, what warm content is in them. They are not rude, but tender, even in the severest cold. Their nakedness is their defense. All their sights and sounds are elixir to my spirit. They possess a choice health. God is not more well. Every sound is inspiriting, and fraught with the same mysterious assurance from the creaking of the boughs in January to the soft sigh of the wind in July.

How much of my well-being, think you, depends on the condition of my lungs and stomach, such cheap pieces of Nature as they, which indeed she is every day reproducing with prodigality? Is that arrow indeed fatal which rankles in the breast of the bird on the bough, in whose eye all this fair landscape is reflected, and whose voice still echoes through the wood?

This is my argument in reserve for all cases.

My love is invulnerable. Meet me on that ground, and you will find me strong. When I am condemned, and condemn myself, I think straightway, But I love some things. Therein I am whole and entire. Therein I am God-propped.

When I see the smoke curling up through the woods from some farmhouse invisible, it is more suggestive of the poetry of rural and domestic life than a nearer inspection can be. Up goes the smoke as quietly as the dew exhales in vapor, as busy as the housewife below, disposing itself in circles and wreaths. It is contemporary with a piece of human biography, and waves as a feather in some man's cap. Under that rod of sky there is some plot a-brewing, some ingenuity has planted itself, and we shall see what it will do. It tattles of more things than the boiling of a pot. It is but one of man's breaths. All that is interesting in history or fiction is transpiring beneath that cloud. The subject of all life and death, of happiness and grief, goes thereunder. When the traveler in the forest, attaining to some eminence, discovers a column of smoke in the distance, it is a very gentle hint to him of the presence of man. It seems as if it would establish friendly relations between them without more ado.

Nov. 15, 1851. Here is a rainy day which keeps me in the house. I am pleased to read in

Stoerer's [?] " Life of Linnæus " (Trapp's trans-
lation) that his father, being the first learned
man of his family, changed his family name, and
borrowed that of Linnæus (Linden-tree man)
from a lofty linden tree which stood near his native place ; " a custom," he says, " not unfrequent
in Sweden, to take fresh appellations from natural
objects." What more fit than that the advent of
a new man into a family should acquire for it
and transmit to posterity a new patronymic !
Such a custom suggests, if it does not argue, an
unabated vigor in the race, relating it to those
primitive times when men did indeed acquire a
name as memorable and distinct as their characters. It is refreshing to find a man whom you
cannot feel satisfied to call John's son or John-
son's son, but by a new name applicable to himself alone, he being the first of his kind. We
may say there have been but so many men as
there are surnames, and of all the John Smiths
there has been but one true John Smith, and he
of course is dead. Get yourself, therefore, a
name, and better a nickname than none at all.
There was one enterprising boy came to school
to me whose name was " Buster," and an honor-
able name it was. He was the only boy in the
school, to my knowledge, who was named.

What shall we say of the comparative intellectual vigor of ancients and moderns, when we

read of Theophrastus, the father of botany, that he composed more than two hundred treatises in the third century before Christ and the seventeenth before printing, about twenty of which remain, and that these fill six volumes in folio printed at Venice ; among the last are two works on natural history, and one on the generation of plants.

" By his own avowal " [Pliny the elder's] " Natural History is a compilation from about twenty-five hundred different authors."

Nov. 15, 1853. After having some business dealings with men, I am occasionally chagrined, and feel as if I had done some wrong, and it is hard to forget the ugly circumstance. I see that such intercourse long continued would make one thoroughly prosaic, hard, and coarse. But the longest intercourse with Nature, though in her rudest moods, does not thus harden and make coarse. A hard, insensible man whom we liken to a rock, is indeed much harder than a rock. From hard, coarse, insensible men with whom I have no sympathy, I go to commune with the rocks, whose hearts are comparatively soft.

I was the other night elected a curator of our Lyceum, but was obliged to decline, because I did not know where to find good lecturers enough to make a course for the winter. We commonly think we cannot have a good journal in New

England, because we have not enough writers of ability. But we do not suspect likewise that we have not good lecturers enough to make a Lyceum.

This afternoon has wanted no condition to make it a gossamer day, it seems to me, but a calm atmosphere. Plainly the spiders cannot be abroad on the water, unless it is smooth. The one I witnessed this fall was at time of flood. May it be that they are driven out of their retreats like muskrats and snowfleas, and spin these lines for their support? Yet they work on the causeway, too.

Nov. 15, 1857. P. M. To Holden swamp and C. Miles swamp. My walk is the more lonely when I perceive that there are no ants upon the hillocks in field or wood. These are deserted mounds. They have commenced their winter sleep. The water is frozen solid in the leaves of the pitcher plant. This is the thickest ice I have seen. This water was most exposed in the cool swamp.

Going by my owl-nest oak, I saw that it had broken off at the hole, and the top fallen, but seeing in the cavity some leaves, I climbed up to see what kind of nest it was. I took out the leaves slowly, watching to see what spoils had been left with them. Some were pretty green, and all had evidently been placed there this fall.

When I had taken all out with my left hand, holding on to the top of the stump with my right, I looked round into the cleft, and there I saw sitting nearly erect at the bottom in one corner, a little *mus leucopus*, panting with fear, and with its large black eyes upon me. I held my face thus within seven or eight inches of it as long as I cared to hold on there, and it showed no sign of retreating. When I put in my hand, it merely withdrew downward into a snug little nest of hypnum and apparently the dirty-white, wool-like pappus of some plant, as big as a batting ball. Wishing to see its tail, I stirred it up again, when it suddenly rushed up the side of the cleft out over my shoulder and right arm, and leaped off, falling down through a thin hemlock spray some sixteen or eighteen feet to the ground on the hillside, where I lost sight of it. These nests, I suppose, are made when the trees are losing their leaves, as those of the squirrels are.

Nov. 15, 1859. A very pleasant Indian summer day. P. M. To Ledum swamp. I look up the river from the railroad bridge. It is perfectly smooth between the uniformly tawny meadows, and I see several muskrat cabins off Hubbard shore, distinctly outlined, as usual, in the November light. I hear in several places a faint cricket note, either a fine z-ing, or a distincter creak; also see and hear a grasshopper's crackling flight. The clouds were never more fairly reflected in the water than now, as I look up the cyanean reach from Clamshell. A fine gossamer is streaming from every fence, tree, and stubble, though a careless observer would not notice it. As I look along over the grass toward the sun at Hosmer's field beyond Lupine Hill, I notice the shimmering effect of the gossamer, which seems to cover it almost like a web, occasioned by its motion, though the air is so still. This is noticed at least forty rods off. I turn down Witherel Glade, only that I may bring its tufts of andropogon between me and the sun.

It is a fact proving how universal and widely related any transcendent greatness is, like the apex of a pyramid to all beneath it, that when I now look over my extracts of the noblest poetry, the best is oftenest applicable in part or wholly to this man's [Captain John Brown's] position. Almost any noble verse may be read either as his elegy or eulogy, or be made the text of an oration about him ; indeed such are now first discovered to be parts of a divinely established liturgy applicable to these rare cases for which the ritual of no church has provided, — the case of heroes, martyrs, and saints. This is the formula established on high, their burial service, to which every great genius has contributed its line or syllable. Of course the ritual of no church which is wedded to the state can contain a service applicable to the case of a state criminal unjustly condemned, a martyr. The sense of grand poetry read by the light of this event is brought out distinctly, like an invisible writing held to the fire.

Nov. 16, 1850. I am accustomed to regard the smallest brook with as much interest, for the time being, as if it were the Orinoco or Mississippi, and when a tributary rill empties into it, it is like the confluence of famous rivers I have read of. When I cross one on a fence, I love to pause in mid-passage and look down into the water, and study its bottom, its little mystery. There is none so small but you may see a pickerel regarding you with a wary eye, or a pigmy trout dart from under the bank, or in spring perchance a sucker will have found its way far up the stream. You are sometimes astonished to see a pickerel far up some now shrunken rill where it is a mere puddle by the roadside. I have stooped to drink at a clear spring no bigger than a bushel basket, in a meadow, from which a rill was scarcely seen to dribble away, and seen lurking at its bottom two little pickerel not so big as my finger, sole monarchs of this their ocean, and who probably would never visit a larger water.

I hear deep amid the birches some row among

the birds or the squirrels, where evidently some mystery is being developed to them. The jay is on the alert, mimicking every woodland note. "What *has* happened? who's dead?" The twitter retreats before you, and you are never let into the secret. Some tragedy surely is being enacted, but murder will out. How many little dramas are enacted in the depths of the woods at which man is not present!

There seems to be in the fall a sort of attempt at spring, a rejuvenescence, as if the winter were not expected by a part of nature. Violets, dandelions, and some other flowers blossom again, and mulleins and innumerable other plants begin again to spring, and are only checked by the increasing cold. There is a slight uncertainty whether there will be any winter this year.

Some of our richest days are those in which no sun shines outwardly, but so much the more a sun shines inwardly. I love nature, I love the landscape, because it is so sincere. It never cheats me, it never jests, it is cheerfully, musically earnest. I lie and rely on the earth.

The sweet-scented life-everlasting has not lost its scent yet, but smells like the balm of the fields.

The partridge-berry leaves checker the ground on moist hillsides in the woods. Are not *they* properly called checker-berries?

My journal should be the record of my love. I would write in it only of the things I love, my affection for an aspect of the world, what I love to think of. I have no more distinctness or pointedness in my yearnings than an expanding bud which does indeed point to flower and fruit, to summer and autumn, but is aware of the warm sun and spring influence only. I feel ripe for something, yet do nothing, can't discover what that thing is. I feel fertile merely. It is seedtime with me. I have lain fallow long enough.

Notwithstanding a sense of unworthiness which possesses me not without reason, notwithstanding that I regard myself as a good deal of a scamp, yet for the most part the spirit of the universe is unaccountably kind to me, and I enjoy perhaps an unusual share of happiness. But I question sometimes if there is not some settlement to come.

Nov. 16, 1851. It is remarkable that the highest intellectual mood which the world tolerates is the perception of the truth of the most ancient revelations, now in some respects out of date, but any direct revelation, any original thought, it hates like virtue. So far as thinking is concerned, surely original thinking is the divinest thing. We should reverently watch for the least motions, the least scintillations of thought in this sluggish world, and men should run to and fro on the occasion more than at an earthquake. We check and repress the divinity that stirs within us to fall down and worship the divinity that is dead without us. I go to see many a good man or good woman, so called, and utter freely that thought which alone it was given me to utter, but there was a man who lived a long, long time ago and his name was Moses, and another whose name was Christ, and if your thought does not, or does not appear to, coincide with what they said, the good man or good woman has no ears to hear you. They think they love God! It is only his old clothes, which they make scarecrows for the children. When will they come nearer to God than in these very children? A man lately preached here against the abuse of the sabbath, and recommended to walk in the fields and dance on that day. Good advice enough, which may take effect after a while. But with the mass of men, the reason is convinced long before the life is. They may see the church and the sabbath to be false, but nothing else to be true. One woman in the neighborhood says, " Nobody can hear Mr. ——— preach, hear him through, without seeing that he is a good man." " Well, is there any truth in what he says?" asks another. "Oh yes, it's true enough, but then it won't do, you know, it won't do. Now, there's our George, he's got the whole of it; and when I say, 'Come, George, put on your things, and go along to meeting,' he says, 'No, mother, I'm going out into the fields.' It won't do." The fact is, this woman has not character and religion enough to exert a controlling influence over her children by her example, and knows of no such police as the church and the minister.

If it were not for death and funerals, I think the institution of the church would not stand longer. The necessity that men be decently buried, our fathers and mothers, brothers and sisters and children (notwithstanding the danger that they be buried alive), will long, if not forever, prevent our laying violent hands on it. If salaries were stopped off, and men walked out of this world bodily at last, the minister and his vocation would be gone.

That sounds like a fine mode of expressing gratitude referred to by Linnæus. Hermann was a botanist who gave up his place to Tournefort, who was unprovided for. " Hermann," says Linnæus, " came afterwards to Paris, and Tournefort in honor of him ordered the fountains to play in the royal garden."

Nov. 16, 1852. 9 A. M. Sail up river to Lee's bridge. Colder weather and very windy, but still no snow. Very little ice along the edge of the river which does not melt before night. Muskrat houses completed; interesting objects, looking down a river-reach at this season, and our river should not be represented without one or two of these cones. They are quite conspicuous half a mile distant, and are of too much importance to be omitted in the river landscape. I see one duck. The pines on shore look very cold, reflecting a silvery light. The waves run high with white caps, and communicate a pleasant motion to the boat. At Lee's Cliff the *cerastium viscosum.* We sailed up Well-meadow brook. The water is singularly grayish, clear and cold, the bottom of the brook showing great nuphar roots, like its ribs, with some budding leaves.

The water is frozen in the pitcher-plant leaf. The swamp pink and blueberry buds attract.

Nov. 16, 1854. P. M. Sailed to Hubbard's bridge. Almost every muskrat's house is covered by the flood, though they were unusually high as well as numerous, and the river is not nearly so high as last year. I see where they have begun to raise them another story. A few cranberries begin to wash up, and rails, boards, etc., may now ·be collected by wreckers.

Nov. 16, 1858. Preaching? lecturing? Who are ye that ask for these things? What do you want to hear, ye puling infants? A trumpet

sound that would train you up to manhood? or
a nurse's lullaby? The preachers and lecturers
deal with men of straw, as they are men of straw
themselves. Why, a free-spoken man, of sound
lungs, cannot draw a long breath, without caus-
ing your rotten institutions to come toppling
down, by the vacuum he makes. Your church
is a baby-house made of blocks, and so of the
state. It would be a relief to breathe one's self
occasionally, among men. Freedom of speech!
It hath not entered into your hearts to conceive
what those words mean. The church, the state,
the school, the magazine, think they are liberal
and free! It is the freedom of a prison yard.
What is it you tolerate, you church to-day?
Not truth, but a life-long hypocrisy. The voice
that goes up from the monthly concerts is not so
brave and cheery as that which rises from the
frog-ponds of the land. Look at your editors of
popular magazines. I have dealt with two or
three of the most liberal of them. They are
afraid to print a *whole* sentence, a *sound* sentence, a free-spoken sentence. We want to get
30,000 subscribers, and will do anything to get
them. They consult the D. D.'s and all the
letters of the alphabet, before printing a sentence.

Nov. 17, 1837. If there is nothing new on
earth, still there is something new in the heav-

ens. We have always a resource in the skies. They are constantly turning a new page to view. The wind sets the types in their blue ground, and the inquiring may always read a new truth there.

Nov. 17, 1850. I found this afternoon in a field of winter rye, a snapping-turtle's egg, white and elliptical like a pebble, mistaking it for which I broke it. The little turtle was perfectly formed, even to the dorsal ridge, which was distinctly visible.

Nov. 17, 1851. All things tend to flow to him who can make the best use of them, even away from their legal owner. A thief, finding with the property of the Italian naturalist, Donati, whom he had robbed abroad, a collection of rare African seeds, forwarded them to Linnæus from Marseilles. Donati suffered shipwreck, and never returned.

Nov. 17, 1853. I notice that many plants about this season of the year or earlier, after they have died down at top, put forth fresh and conspicuous radical leaves against another spring ; so some human beings in the November of their days, exhibit some fresh radical greenness, which, though the frosts may soon nip it, indicates and confirms their essential greenness. When their summer leaves have faded and fallen, they put forth fresh radical leaves which sustain the life in their root still, against a new spring. The dry fields have, for a long time, been spotted with the small radical leaves of the fragrant life-everlasting, not to mention the large primrose, John's-wort, etc. Almost every plant, although it may show no greenness above ground, if you dig about it, will be found to have fresh shoots already pointing upward, and ready to burst forth in the spring.

Nov. 17, 1854. Paddled up river to Clamshell, and sailed back. I think it must have been a fishhawk which I saw hovering over the meadow and my boat (a raw, cloudy afternoon), now and then sustaining itself in one place, a hundred feet or more above the water, intent on a fish, with a hovering or fluttering motion of the wings, somewhat like a kingfisher. Its wings were very long, slender, and curved in outline of front edge, ⌒⌒ thus, perhaps. I think there was some white on rump. It alighted near the top of an oak within rifle-shot of me, afterward on the tip top of a maple by waterside, looking very large.

Nov. 17, 1855. It is interesting to me to talk with Rice, he lives so thoroughly and satisfactorily to himself. He has learned that rare art of living, the very elements of which most persons do not know. His life has been not a failure, but a success. Seeing me going to sharpen some plane irons, and hearing me complain of the want of tools, he said I ought to have a chest of tools. But I said it was not worth the while. I should not use them enough to pay for them. " You would use them more, if you had them," said he. " When I came to do a piece of work, I used to find commonly that I wanted a certain tool, and I made it a rule first always to make that tool. I have spent as much as $3,000 thus in my tools." Comparatively speaking, his life is a success ; not such a failure as most men's. He gets more out of any enterprise than his neighbors, for he helps himself more, and hires less. Whatever pleasure there is in it he enjoys. By good sense and calculation he has become rich, and has invested his property well, yet practices a fair and neat economy, dwells not in untidy luxury. It costs him less to live, and he gets more out of life than others. To get his living or keep it is not a hasty or disagreeable toil. He works slowly, but surely, enjoying the sweet of it. He buys a piece of meadow at a profitable rate, works it in pleasant weather, he and his son, when they are inclined, goes a-fishing or bee-hunting, or rifle-shooting quite as often, and thus the meadow gets redeemed, and potatoes get planted perchance, and he is very sure to have a good crop stored in his cellar in the fall, and some to sell. He always has the best of potatoes there. In the same spirit in which he and his son tackle up their Dobbin (he never keeps a fast horse) and go a-spearing or fishing through the *ice, they also tackle up and go to their Sudbury farm to hoe or harvest a little, and when they return they bring home in their hay-rigging a load of stumps which had impeded their labors, but may supply them with their winter wood. All the woodchucks they shoot or trap in the bean-field are brought home also. Thus their life is a long sport, and they know not what hard times are.

Labaume says that he wrote his journal of the campaign in Russia each night in the midst of incredible danger and suffering, with " a raven's quill and a little gunpowder mixed with some melted snow, in the hollow of my hand," the quill cut and mended with " the knife with which I had carved my scanty morsel of horse flesh." Such a statement promises well for the writer's qualifications to treat such a theme.

Nov. 17, 1858. P. M. Up Assabet. The muskrats are more active since the cold weather. I see more of them about the river now, swimming across back and forth, and diving in the middle where I lose them. They dive off the round-backed black mossy stones, which when small and slightly exposed look much like

themselves. In swimming, show commonly
three parts, with water between. One, sitting
in the sun, as if for warmth, on the opposite
shore to me, looks quite reddish-brown. They
avail themselves of the edge of the ice now
found along the sides of the river, to feed on.

The very sunlight on the pale-brown bleached
fields is an interesting object these cold days.
I naturally look toward it as to a wood fire.
Not only different objects are presented to our
attention at different seasons of the year, but
we are in a frame of body and of mind to appreciate different objects at different seasons. I see
one thing when it is cold and another when it
is warm.

We are interested at this season by the mani-
fold ways in which the light is reflected to us.
Ascending a little knoll covered with sweet fern,
the sun appearing but little above the sweet
fern, its light was reflected from a dense mass
of the bare, downy twigs of this plant in a surprising manner which would not be believed, if
described. It was quite like the sunlight reflected from grass and weeds covered with hoar
frost. Yet in an ordinary light, these are but
dark or dusky-looking with scarcely a noticeable
downiness. But as I saw them, there was a perfect halo of light resting on the knoll. I moved
to right or left. A myriad of surfaces are now

prepared to reflect the light. This is one of the hundred silvery lights of November. The setting sun, too, is reflected from windows more brightly than at any other season. " November lights " would be a theme for me.

Nature is moderate, and loves degrees. Winter is not all white and sere. Some trees are evergreen to cheer us, and on the forest floor our eyes do not fall on sere brown leaves alone, but some evergreen shrubs are placed there to relieve the eye. Mountain laurel, lambkill, checkerberry, wintergreen, etc., keep up the semblance of summer still.

Nov. 17, 1859. Another Indian-summer day, as fair as any we have had. I go down the railroad to Andromeda Ponds this afternoon.

I have been so absorbed of late in Captain Brown's fate as to be surprised wherever I detected the old routine surviving still, met persons going about their affairs indifferent. It appeared strange to me that the little dipper should be still diving in the river as of yore, and it suggested to me that this grebe might be diving here when Concord shall be no more. Any affecting human event may blind our eyes to natural objects.

How fair and memorable this prospect, when you stand opposite the sun, these ˙November afternoons, and look over the red andromeda swamp, a glowing, warm brown-red in the Indian summer sun, like a bed of moss in a hollow in the woods, with gray high-blueberry, and straw-colored grasses interspersed ; and when, going round it, you look over it in the opposite direction, it presents a gray aspect.

Nov. 18, 1837. Nature makes no noise. The howling storm, the rustling leaf, the pattering rain, are no disturbance. There is an essential and unexplored harmony in them. Why is it that thought flows with so deep and sparkling a current when the sound of distant music strikes the ear ? When I would muse I complain not of a rattling tune on the piano, a Battle of Prague even, if it be harmony, but an irregular, discordant drumming is intolerable.

When a shadow flits across the landscape of the soul, where is the substance ? Has it always its origin in sin ? and is that sin in me ?

Nov. 18, 1841. Some men make their due impression upon their generation because a petty occasion is enough to call forth all their energies; but are there not others who would rise to much higher levels, whom the world has never provoked to make the effort ? I believe there are men now living who have never opened their mouths in a public assembly, in whom nevertheless there is such a well of eloquence that the appetite of any age could never exhaust it, who pine for an occasion worthy of them, and will pine till they are dead, who can admire as well as the rest the flowing speech of the orator, but do yet miss the thunder and lightning, and visible sympathy of the elements which would garnish their own utterance. The age may well pine that it cannot put to use the gift of the gods. He lives on still unconcerned, not needing to be used. The greatest occasion will be the slowest to come.

If, in any strait, I see a man fluttered and his ballast gone, then I lose all hope of him, he is undone; but if he reposes still, though he do nothing else worthy of him, if he is still a man in reserve, there is then everything to hope of him.

Sometimes a body of men do unconsciously assert that their will is fate, that the right is decided by their fiat, without appeal, and when this is the case, they can never be mistaken; as when one man is quite silenced by the thrilling eloquence of another, and submits to be neg-. lected, as to his fate, because such is not the willful vote of the assembly, but their instinctive decision.

Nov. 18, 1851. Surveying these days the Ministerial lot. Now at sundown I hear the hooting of an owl, hōo hóo hóo-hōorer-hóo. It sounds like the hooting of an idiot or a maniac broke loose.. This is faintly answered in a different strain, apparently from a greater distance, almost as if it were the echo, that is, so far as the *succession* is concerned. I heard it last evening. The men who help me, call it the hooting owl, and think it is the cat-owl. It is a sound admirably suited to the swamp and to the twilight woods, suggesting a vast undeveloped nature which men have not recognized.

The chopper who works in the woods all day for many weeks or months at a time, becomes intimately acquainted with them in his way. He is more open, in many respects, to the impressions they are fitted to make than the naturalist who goes to see them. He is not liable to exaggerate insignificant features. He really forgets himself, forgets to observe, and at night he *dreams* of the swamp, its phenomena and events. Not so the naturalist; enough of his unconscious life does not pass there. A man can hardly be said to be *there*, if he *knows* that he is there, or to go there if he knows where he is going. The man who is bent upon his work is frequently in the best attitude to observe what is irrelevant to his work. (*Mem.* Wordsworth's observations on relaxed attention.) You must be conversant with things for a long time to know much about them, like the moss which has hung from the spruce, and as the partridge and the rabbit are acquainted with the thickets, and at length have acquired the color of the places they frequent. If the man of science can put all his knowledge into propositions, the woodman has a great deal of incommunicable knowledge.

Nov. 18, 1852.   Yarrow and tansy still.

Nov. 18, 1853.   Conchologists call those shells "which are fished up from the depths of the ocean" and are never seen on the shore, *pelagii*, but those which are cast on shore and are never so delicate and beautiful as the former, on account of exposure and abrasion, *littorales.* So is it with the thoughts of poets.   Some are fresh from the deep sea, radiant with unimagined beauty, — *pelagii ;* but others are comparatively worn, having been tossed by many a tide, scaled off, abraded, and eaten by worms, — *littorales.*

Nov. 18, 1854.   Saw sixty geese go over the Great Fields in one waving line broken from time to time. by their crowding on each other and vainly endeavoring to form into a harrow, honking all the while.

Nov. 18, 1855.   Men foolishly prefer gold to that of which it is the symbol, simple, honest, independent labor.   Can gold be said to buy food, if it does not buy an appetite for food? It is fouler and uglier to have too much than not to have enough.

Nov. 18 [?], 1857.   Much cold slate-colored cloud, bare twigs seen gleaming toward the light like gossamer, pure green of pines where old leaves have fallen, reddish or yellowish-brown oak leaves rustling on the hillsides, very pale brown, bleaching almost hoary fine grass or hay in the fields, akin to the frost which has killed it, and flakes of clear yellow sunlight falling on it here and there, — such is November. The fine grass killed by the frost, and bleached till it is almost silvery, has clothed the fields for a long time.

Now, as in the spring, we rejoice in sheltered and sunny places. Some corn is left out still.

Flannery is the hardest-working man I know. Before sunrise and long after sunset he is taxing his unweariable muscles. The result is a singular cheerfulness. He is always in good spirits. He often overflows with his joy, when you perceive no occasion for it. If only the gate sticks, some of it bubbles up and overflows in his passing comment on that accident. How much mere industry proves! There is a sparkle often in his passing remark, and his voice is really like that of a bird.

In one light, these are old and worn-out fields that I ramble over, and men have gone to law about them long before I was born, but I trust that I ramble over them in a new fashion, and redeem them.

There are many ways of feeling one's pulse.

In a healthy state, the constant experience is a pleasurable sensation or sentiment. For instance, in such a state I find myself in perfect connection with nature, and the perception and remembrance even, of any natural phenomena is attended with a gentle, pleasurable excitement. Prevailing sights and sounds make the impression of beauty and music on me. But in sickness all is deranged. I had yesterday a kink in my back and a general cold, and as usual it amounted to a cessation of life. I lost for the time my support or relation to nature. Sympathy with nature is an evidence of perfect health. You cannot perceive beauty but with a serene mind. The cheaper your amusements, the safer and surer. They who think much of theatres, operas, and the like, are beside themselves. Each man's necessary path, though as obscure and apparently uneventful as that of a beetle in the grass, is the way to the deepest joys he is susceptible of. Though he converses only with moles and fungi, and disgraces his relatives, it is no matter, if he knows what is steel to his flint. Many a man who should rather describe his dinner imposes on us with a history of the Grand Khan.

Nov. 18, 1858. P. M. To Conantum. I look south from the Cliff, the westering sun just out of sight behind the hill. Its rays from those bare twigs across the pond are bread and cheese to me. So many oak leaves have fallen that the white birch stems are more distinct amid the young oaks. I see to the bone, see those bare birches prepared to stand the winter through on the hillsides. They never sing, What's this dull town to me? The maples skirting the meadows in dense phalanxes, look like light infantry advanced for a swamp fight. Ah, dear *November*, you must be sacred to the *nine*, surely. The willow catkins already peep out one fourth of an inch. Early crowfoot is reddened at Lee's.

Nov. 19, 1839.

> Light-hearted, thoughtless, shall I take my way,
> When I to thee this being have resigned,
> Well knowing, on some future day,
> With usurer's craft, more than myself to find.

Nov. 19 [?], 1857. I see where a mouse, which had a hole under a stump, has eaten out clean the inside of the little seeds of the *Prinos verticillata* berries. What pretty fruit for them, these bright berries! They run up the twigs in the night, and gather this shining fruit, take out the small seeds, and eat these kernels at the entrance to their burrows. The ground is strewn with them there.

Nov. 20, 1850. Desor, who has been among the Indians at Lake Superior this summer, told me the other day that they had a particular name for each species of tree, as of the maple, but they had but one word for flowers. They did not distinguish the species of the last.

It is often the unscientific man who discovers the new species. It would be strange if it were not so. But we are accustomed properly to call that only a scientific discovery which knows the relative value of the thing discovered, and uncovers a fact to mankind.

Nov. 20, 1851. It is often said that melody can be heard farther than noise, and the finest melody farther than the coarsest. I think there is truth in this, and that accordingly those strains of the piano which reach me here in my attic stir me so much more than the sounds which I should hear if I were below in the parlor, because they are so much purer and diviner melody. They who sit farthest off from the noisy and bustling world are not at pains to distinguish what is sweet and musical, for that alone can reach them, that chiefly comes down to posterity.

Hard and steady and engrossing labor with the hands, especially out of doors, is invaluable to the literary man, and serves him directly. Here I have been for six days surveying in the woods, and yet when I get home at evening somewhat weary at last, and beginning to feel that I have nerves, I find myself more susceptible than usual to the finest influences, as music and poetry. The very air can intoxicate me, or the least sight or sound, as if my finer senses had acquired an appetite by their fast.

Mr. J. Hosmer tells me that one spring he saw a red squirrel gnaw the bark of a maple, and then suck the juice, and this he repeated many times.

Nov. 20, 1853. I once came near speculating in cranberries. Being put to it to raise the wind, and having occasion to go to New York, to peddle some pencils which I had made, as I passed through Boston I went to Quincy market and inquired the price of cranberries. The dealer took me down cellar, asked if I wanted wet or dry, and showed me them. I gave it to be understood that I might want an indefinite quantity. It made a slight sensation among the dealers, and for aught I know, raised the price of the berry for a time. I then visited various New York packets, and was told what would be the freight on deck and in the hold, and one skipper was very anxious for my freight. When I got to New York, I again visited the markets as a purchaser, and " the best of eastern cranberries " were offered me by the barrel at a cheaper rate than I could buy them in Boston. I was obliged to manufacture $1,000 worth of pencils, and slowly dispose of, and finally sacrifice them, in order to pay an assumed debt of $100.

What enhances my interest in dew (I am thinking of summer) is the fact that it is so distinct from rain, formed most abundantly after bright, starlight nights, a product especially of the clear, serene air, the manna of fair weather, the upper side of rain, as the country above the clouds. That nightly rain, called dew, gathers and falls in so low a stratum that our heads tower above it like mountains in an ordinary shower. It only consists with comparative fair weather above our heads. Those warm volumes of air forced high up the hillsides in summer nights are driven thither to drop their dew, like kine to their yards to be milked, that the moisture they hold may be condensed, and so dew formed before morning on the tops of the hills. A writer in " Harper's Magazine," vol. vii., p. 505, says that the mist at evening does not rise, " but gradually forms higher up in the air." He calls it, the moisture of the air become visible, says there is most dew in clear nights because clouds prevent the cooling down of the air, they radiate the heat of the earth back to it, and that a strong wind, by keeping the air in motion, prevents its heat from passing off. He says also that bad conductors of heat have always most dew on them, and that wool or swan's down are "good for experimenting on the quantity of dew falling," weighed before and after ; thinks it not safe to walk in clear nights, especially after midnight when the dew is most abundantly forming, better in cloudy nights, which are drier ; also thinks it not prudent to venture out until the sun begins to rise, and warms the air ; but I think this prudence begets a tenderness that will catch more cold at noonday than the opposite hardiness at midnight.

Nov. 21, 1853. Is not the dew but a humble, gentler rain, the nightly rain, above which we raise our heads, and unobstructedly behold the stars? The mountains are giants which tower above the rain, as we above the dew on the grass. It only wets their feet.

Nov. 20, 1854. 7 A. M. To Boston. 9 A. M. Boston to New York by express train. See the reddish soil (red sandstone?) all through Connecticut. Beyond Hartford a range of rocky hills crossing the State on each side the railroad. The second one very precipitous, and apparently terminating at East Rock, New Haven. Pleasantest part of the whole route between Springfield and Hartford along the river, perhaps including the hilly region this side of Springfield. Reached Canal Street at 5 P. M., or candle-light. Started for Philadelphia from foot of Liberty Street at 6 P. M., by Newark, Bordentown, and Camden Ferry, all in the dark ; saw only the glossy paneling of the cars reflected out into the dark like the magnificent lit façade of a row of edifices reaching all the way to Philadelphia, except when we stopped, and a lantern or two showed us a ragged boy and the dark buildings of some New Jersey town. Arrived at 10 P. M. Time, four hours from New York, thirteen from Boston, fifteen from Concord. Put up at Jones's Exchange Hotel, 77 Dock Street. Lodgings, thirty-seven cents and a half per night ; meals, separate. Not to be named with French's in New York.

Nov. 21, 1854. Was admitted into the building of the Academy of Natural Sciences. Its collection of birds said to be the largest in the world. They belonged to the son of Massena (Prince of Essling ?), and were sold at auction, bought by a Yankee for $22,000, over all the crowned heads of Europe, and presented to the Academy. Other collections also are added to this. The Academy has received great donations.

Furness described a lotus identical with an Egyptian one, as found somewhere down the river below Philadelphia.

Lodged at the United States Hotel, opposite the Girard (formerly United States) bank.

Nov. 22, 1854. Left at 7.30 A. M., for New

York. Saw Greeley. He took me to the New Opera House, where I heard Grisi and her troupe. He appeared to know and be known by everybody. Was admitted free to the opera, and we were led by a page to various parts of the house at different times.

Nov. 20, 1857. In books, that which is most generally interesting is what comes home to the most cherished private experience of the greatest number. It is not the book of him who has traveled farthest on the surface of the globe, but of him who has lived the deepest, and been the most at home. If an equal emotion is excited by a familiar homely phenomenon as by the pyramids, there is no advantage in seeing the pyramids. It is on the whole better, as it is simpler, to use the common language. We require that the reporter be very firmly planted before the facts which he observes, not a mere passer-by, hence the facts cannot be too homely. A man is worth most to himself and to others, whether as an observer, or poet, or neighbor, or friend, who is most contented and at home. There his life is the most intense, and he loses the fewest moments. Familiar and surrounding objects are the best symbols and illustrations of his life. If a man who has had deep experiences should endeavor to describe them in a book of travels, it would be to use the language of a wandering tribe instead of a universal language. The poet has made the best roots in his native soil, and is the hardest to transplant. The man who is often thinking that it would be better to be somewhere else than where he is, excommunicates himself. Here I have been these forty years learning the language of these fields that I may the better express myself. If I should travel to the prairies, I should much less understand them, and my past life would serve me but ill to describe them. Many a weed stands for more of life to me than the big trees of California would if I should go there. We need only travel enough to give our intellects an airing. In spite of Malthus and the rest, there will be plenty of room in this world, if every man will mind his own business. I have not heard of any planet running against another yet.

P. M. To Ministerial Swamp. Some bankswallows' nests are exposed by the caving of the bank at Clamshell. The very smallest hole is about two and a half inches wide horizontally, and barely one high. All are much wider than high. One nest, with an egg in it still, is completely exposed. The cavity at the end is shaped like a thick hoe-cake or lens, about six inches wide and somewhat more than two thick vertically. The nest is a regular but shallow one, made simply of stubble, about five inches in diameter and three quarters of an inch thick.

Returning, I see, methinks, two gentlemen plowing a field as if to try an agricultural experiment. As it is very cold and windy, both plowman and driver have their coats on. But when I get nearer, I hear the driver speak in a peculiarly sharp and petulant manner to the plowman, as they are turning the furrow, and I know at once that they belong to those two races which are so slow to amalgamate. Thus my little Idyl is disturbed.

In the large Wheeler field, *Ranunculus bulbosus* in full bloom.

The hardy tree sparrow has taken the place of the chipping and song sparrow, so much like the former that most do not know it is another. His faint lisping chip will keep up our spirits till another spring.

I observed this afternoon how some bullocks had a little sportiveness forced upon them. They were running down a steep declivity to water, when, feeling themselves unusually impelled by gravity downward, they took the hint even as boys do, flourished round gratuitously, tossing their hind-quarters into the air, and shaking their heads at each other ; but what increases the ludicrousness of it to me is the fact that such capers are never accompanied by a smile. Who does not believe that their step is less elastic, their movement more awkward, from their long domesticity ?

Nov. 20, 1855. Again I hear that sharp, crackling, snapping sound, and hastening to the window I find that another of the pitch-pine cones, gathered November 7th, lying in the sun, or which the sun has scorched, has separated its scales very slightly at the apex. It is only discoverable on a close inspection, but while I look the whole cone opens its scales with a smart crackling, and rocks, and seems to bristle up, scattering the dry pitch on the surface. They all thus fairly loosen and open, though they do not at once spread wide open. It is almost like the disintegration of glass. As soon as the tension is relaxed in one part, it is relaxed in every part.

Nov. 20, 1858. P. M. To Ministerial Swamp. [Martial Miles] says that a marsh hawk had a nest in his meadow several years, and though he shot the female three times, the male, with but little delay, returned with a new mate. He often watched these birds, and saw that the female could tell when the male was coming, a long way off. He thought the male fed her and the young all together. She would utter a scream when she perceived him, and rising into the air (before or after the scream ?), she turned

over with her talons uppermost, while he passed
some three rods above, and caught without fail
the prey which he let drop, and then carried it
to her young. He had seen her do this many
times, and always without failing.

I go across the great Wheeler pasture. It is
a cool but pleasant November afternoon. The
glory of November is in its silvery, sparkling
lights, the air is so clear, and there are so many
bare, polished, bleached or hoary surfaces to reflect the light. Few things are more exhilarating, if it is only moderately cold, than to walk
over bare pastures, and see the abundant sheeny
light, like a universal halo, reflected from the
russet and bleached earth. The earth shines
perhaps more than in spring, for the reflecting
surfaces are less dimmed now. It is not a red,
but a white light. There are several kinds of
twigs, this year's shoots of shrubs, which have a
slight down, or haziness, hardly perceptible in
ordinary lights, though held in the hand, but
which seen toward the sun reflect a sheeny, silvery light. Such are not only the sweet-fern,
but the hazel in a less degree, alder twigs, and
even the short huckleberry twigs, also lespedeza
stems. It is as if they were covered with a
myriad fine spiculæ, which reflect a dazzling
white light exceedingly warming to the spirits
and imagination. This gives a character of

snug warmth and cheerfulness to the swamp, as if it were a place where the sun consorted with rabbits and partridges. Each individual hair on every such shoot above the swamp is bathed in glowing sunlight, and is directly conversant with the day god.

As I returned over Conantum summit yesterday just before sunset, and was admiring the various rich browns of the shrub-oak plain across the river, which seemed to me more wholesome and remarkable, as more permanent than the late brilliant colors, I was surprised to see a broad halo traveling with me, and always opposite the sun to me, at least one fourth mile off, and some three rods wide on the shrub oaks.

The rare, wholesome and permanent beauty of withered oak leaves of various hues of brown, mottling a hillside, especially seen when the sun is low, Quaker colors, sober ornaments, beauty that quite satisfies the eye, — the richness and variety are the same as before, the colors different, more incorruptible and lasting.

Sprague of Cohasset states to the Natural History Society Sept. 1, 1858, that the light under the tail of the common glow-worm "remained for fifteen minutes after death."

Nov. 21, 1850. The witch hazel blossom on Conantum has, for the most part, lost its ribbons now.

I saw the sun falling on a distant white-pine wood whose gray and moss-covered stems were visible amid the green, in an angle where this forest abutted on a hill covered with shrub oaks. It was like looking into dreamland. It is one of the avenues to my future. Certain coincidences like this are accompanied by a certain flash as of hazy lightning flooding all the world suddenly with a tremulous, serene light which it is difficult to see long at a time.

I saw Fair Haven Pond with its island, and a strip of perfectly still and smooth water in the lee of the island, and two hawks, fish-hawks, perhaps, sailing over it. I did not see how it could be improved. Yet I do not see what these things can be. I begin to see such an object when I cease to understand it, and see that I did not realize or appreciate it before, but I get no further than this. How adapted these forms and colors to my eye! A meadow and an island! What are these things? Yet the hawks and the ducks keep so aloof! and nature is so reserved! I am made to love the pond and the meadow, as the wind is made to ripple the water.

Nov. 21, 1851. Better men than they hire to come here never lecture. Why don't they ask Edmund Hosmer or George Minott? I would rather hear them decline than most of these hirelings lecture.

Nov. 21 [?], 1857. P. M. Up Assabet. Just
above the grape-hung birches, my attention was
drawn to a singular looking dry leaf or parcel
of leaves on the shore about a rod off. Then I
thought it might be the dry and yellowed skeleton of a bird with all its ribs ; then, the shell of
a turtle, or possibly some large dry oak leaves
peculiarly curled and cut ; and then all at once
I saw that it was a woodcock, perfectly still,
with its head drawn in, standing on its great
pink feet. I had apparently noticed only the
yellowish-brown portions of the plumage, referring the dark-brown to the shore behind it. May
it not be that the yellowish-brown markings of
the bird correspond somewhat to its skeleton ?
At any rate, with my eye steadily on it from a
point within a rod, I did not for a considerable
time suspect it to be a living creature. Exam-
ining the shore after it had flown with a whis-
tling flight, I saw that there was a clear shore of
mud between the water and the edge of ice crystals about two inches wide, melted so far by the
lapse of the water, and all along the edge of the
ice, for a rod or two at least, there was a hole
where it had thrust its bill down, probing every
half inch, frequently closer. Some animal life
must be collected at that depth just in that narrow space, savory morsels for this bird. . . . The
chubby bird darted away zigzag, carrying its

long tongue-case carefully before it over the witch hazel bushes. This is its walk, the portion of the shore, the narrow strip still left open and unfrozen between the water's edge and the ice.

Nov. 21, 1860. Another finger-cold evening, which I improve in pulling my turnips, the usual amusement of such weather, before they shall be frozen in. It is worth while to see how green and lusty they are yet, still adding to their stock of nutriment for another year, and between the green and also withering leaves it does me good to see their great crimson round or scalloped tops sometimes quite above ground, they are so bold. They remind you of rosy cheeks in cold weather, and indeed there is a relationship. Even pulling turnips when the first cold weather numbs your fingers, like every other kind of harvestry, is interesting, if you have been the sower, and have not sown too many.

Nov. 22, 1851. At the brook [Saw Mill Brook] the partridge berries checker the ground with their leaves, now interspersed with red berries. The cress at the bottom of the brook is doubly beautiful now, because it is green while most other plants are sere. It rises and falls and waves with the current.

As I returned through Hosmer's field, the sun was just setting beneath a black cloud by which it had been obscured, and as it had been a cold and windy afternoon, its light, which fell suddenly on some white pines between me and it, lighting them up like a shimmering fire, and also on the oak leaves and chestnut stems, was quite a circumstance.   It was, from the contrast between the dark and comfortless afternoon, and this bright and cheerful light, almost fire.   The eastern hills and woods, too, were clothed in a still golden light.   It was a sort of Indian summer in the day, which thus far has been denied to the year.   After a cold, gray day, this cheering light almost warms us by its resemblance to fire.

Nov. 22, 1853.   Geese went over yesterday and to-day, also.

If there is any one with whom we have a quarrel, it is most likely such a person makes a demand on us which we disappoint.

I was just thinking it would be fine to get a specimen leaf from each changing tree and shrub and plant in autumn, in September and October, when it had got its brightest, characteristic color, intermediate in its transition from the green to the russet or brown state, the color of its ripeness, outline it, and copy its color exactly with paint in a book, a book which should be a memorial of October, be entitled October Hues, or Autumnal Tints.   I remember especially the beautiful yellow of the *Populus grandidentata* and the tints of the scarlet maple. What a memento such a book would be, beginning with the earliest reddening of the leaves, woodbine, ivy, etc., and the lake of radical leaves, down to the latest oaks. I might get the impression of their veins and outlines in summer, and after, color them.

Nov. 22, 1858. About the first of November, a wild pig from the West, said to weigh three hundred pounds, jumped out of a car at the depot, and made for the woods. The owner had to give up the chase at once not to lose his passage, while some railroad employees pursued the pig even to the woods one and a half miles off, but there the pig turned and pursued them so resolutely that they ran for their lives, and one climbed a tree. The next day being Sunday, they turned out in force with a gun and a large mastiff, but still the pig had the best of it, fairly frightened the men by his fierce charges, and the dog was so wearied and injured by the pig that the men were obliged to carry him in their arms. The pig stood it better than the dog, ran between the gun-man's legs, threw him over and hurt his shoulder, though pierced in many places by a pitchfork. At the last accounts, he had been driven or baited into a barn in Lincoln, but no one durst enter, and they were preparing to shoot him. Such pork might be called venison.

He was caught at last in a snare, and so conveyed to Brighton.

Nov. 22, 1860. P. M. To northwest part of Sudbury. The *Linaria Canadensis* [Wild Toad-flax] is still freshly blooming. It is the freshest flower I notice now. Considerable ice lasting all day on the meadows and cold pools.

This is a very beautiful November day, a cool but clear crystalline air, through which even the white pines, with their silvery sheen, are an affecting sight. It is a day to behold and to ramble over the stiffening and withered surface of the tawny earth. Every plant's down glistens with a silvery light along the Marlboro' road, the sweet fern, the lespedeza, and bare blueberry twigs, to say nothing of the weather-worn tufts of *Andropogon scoparius.* A thousand bare twigs gleam like cobwebs in the sun. I rejoice in the bare, bleak, hard, and barren-looking surface of the tawny pastures, the firm outline of the hills, so convenient to walk over, and the air so bracing and wholesome. Though you are finger-cold toward night, and you cast a stone on your first ice, and see the unmelted crystals under every bank, it is glorious November weather. You enjoy not only the bracing coolness, but all the heat and sunlight there is, reflected back to you from the earth. The sandy road itself lit by the November sun is beautiful. Shrub oaks

and young oaks generally, and hazel bushes, and
other hardy shrubs are your companions, as if it
were an iron age, yet in simplicity, innocence,
and strength, a golden one.

It is glorious to consider how independent man
is of all enervating luxuries, and the poorer he is
in respect to them, the richer he is. Summer is
gone with its infinite wealth, and still nature
is genial to man. Though he no longer bathes
in the stream, or reclines on the bank, or plucks
berries on the hills, still he beholds the same in-
accessible beauty around him. What though he
has no juice of the grape stored up for him in
cellars, the air itself is wine of an older vin-
tage, and far more sanely exhilarating than any
cellar affords. It is ever some gouty senior, and
not a blithe child that drinks or cares for that
so famous wine. Though so many phenomena
which we lately admired have now vanished,
others are more remarkable and interesting than
before. The smokes from distant chimneys, not
only greater because more fire is required, but
more distinct in the cooler atmosphere, are a
very pleasing sight, and conduct our thoughts
quickly to the roof and hearth and family beneath, revealing the homes of men.

Maynard's yard and frontage, and all his
barns and fences are singularly neat and substantial, and the high road is in effect converted

into a private way through his grounds. It suggests unspeakable peace and happiness. Yet, strange to tell, I noticed that he had a tiger instead of a cock for a vane on his barn, and he himself looked overworked. He had allured the surviving forest trees to grow into ancestral trees about his premises, and so attach themselves to him as if he had planted them. The dirty highway was so subdued that it seemed as if it were lost there. He had all but stretched a bar across it. Each traveler must have felt some misgivings, as if he were trespassing. However, the farmer's life expresses only such content as an ox in his yard, chewing the cud.

What though your hands are numb with cold, your sense of enjoyment is not benumbed. You cannot even find an apple but it is sweet to taste. Simply to see a distant horizon through a clear air, the firm outline of a distant hill, or a blue mountain-top through some new vista, this is wealth enough for one afternoon. We journeyed to the foreign land of Sudbury, to see how the Sudbury men, the Hayneses and the Puffers and the Brighams live; we traversed their pastures and their wood-lots, and were home again at night.

Nov. 23, 1850. To-day it has been finger-cold. Unexpectedly I found ice by the side of the brooks this afternoon nearly an inch thick. The difference in temperature of various localities is greater than is supposed. If I was surprised to find ice on the sides of the brooks, I was much more surprised to find a pond in the woods, containing an acre or more, quite frozen over, so that I walked across it. It was a cold corner where a pine wood excluded the sun. In the larger ponds and the river, of course there is no ice yet. This is a shallow, reedy pond. I lay down on the ice and looked through at the bottom. The plants appeared to grow more uprightly than on the dry land, being sustained and protected by the water. Caddis-worms were everywhere crawling about in their handsome quiver-like sheaths or cases.

I find it to be the height of wisdom not to endeavor to oversee myself, and live a life of prudence and common-sense, but to see over and above myself, entertain sublime conjectures, to make myself the thoroughfare of thrilling thoughts, live all that can be lived. The man who is dissatisfied with himself, what can he not do?

Nov. 23, 1852. This morning the ground is white with snow, and it still snows. This is the first time it has been fairly white this season, though once before, many weeks ago, it was slightly whitened for ten or fifteen minutes. Already the landscape impresses me with a greater sense of fertility. There is something genial even in the first snow, and Nature seems to relent a little of her November harshness. Men, too, are disposed to give thanks for the bounties of the year all over the land, and the sound of the mortar is heard in all houses, and the odor of summer savory reaches even to poets' garrets. This, then, may be considered the end of the flower season for this year, though this snow will probably soon melt again. Among the flowers which may be put down as lasting thus far, as I remember, in the order of their hardiness, are yarrow, tansy, these very fresh and common, cerastium [mouse-ear chickweed], autumnal dandelion, dandelion, and perhaps tall buttercup, the last four scarce. The following seen within a fortnight : a late three - ribbed golden-rod, blue-stemmed golden-rod (these two perhaps within a week), *Potentilla argentea, Aster undulatus, Ranunculus repens, Bidens connata*, and Shepherd's purse. I have not looked for witch hazel nor *Stellaria media* [common chickweed] lately.

I had a thought in a dream last night, which surprised me by its strangeness, as if it were based on an experience in a previous state of existence, and could not be entertained by my waking self. Both the thought and the language were equally novel to me, but I at once discovered it to be true, and to coincide with my experience in this state.

Nov. 23, 1853. 6 A. M. To Swamp Bridge Brook mouth. The cocks are the only birds I hear. But they are a host. They crow as freshly and bravely as ever, while poets go down stream, degenerate into science and prose.

By eight o'clock the misty clouds disperse, and it turns out a pleasant, calm, and spring-like morning. The water, going down, but still spread far over the meadows, is seen from the window perfectly smooth and full of reflections. What lifts and lightens and makes heaven of earth is the fact that you see the reflection of the humblest weed against the sky, but you cannot put your head low enough to see the substance so. The reflection enchants us, just as an echo does.

If I would preserve my relation to nature, I must make my life more moral, more pure and innocent. The problem is as precise and simple as a mathematical one. I must not live loosely, but more and more continently.

The Indian summer, said to be more remarkable in this country than elsewhere, no less than the reblossoming of certain flowers, the peep of the hylodes, and sometimes the faint warble of some birds, is the reminiscence or rather the return of spring, the year renewing its youth.

At 5 P. M. I saw flying southwest high overhead a flock of geese, and heard the faint honking of one or two. They are in the usual harrow
form, twelve in the shorter line, and twenty-four
in the longer, the latter abutting on the former
at the fourth bird from the front. This is the
sixth flock I have seen or heard of since the
morning of the 17th, that is, within a week.

Nov. 23, 1860. Most of us are still related to
our native fields as the navigator to undiscovered
islands in the sea. We can any autumn discover a new fruit there which will surprise us
by its beauty or sweetness. So long as I saw
one or two kinds of berries in my walks whose
names I did not know, the proportion of the
unknown seemed indefinitely, if not infinitely,
great. Famous fruits imported from the East
or South and sold in our markets, as oranges,
lemons, pineapples, and bananas, do not concern
me so much as many an unnoticed wild berry,
whose beauty annually lends a new charm to
some wild walk, or which I have found to be
palatable to an outdoor taste. The tropical
fruits are for those who dwell within the tropics.
Their fairest and sweetest parts cannot be ex-
ported nor imported. Brought here, they chiefly
concern those whose walks are through the market - place. It is not those far - fetched fruits
which the speculator imports, that concern us

chiefly, but rather those which you have fetched yourself from some far hill or swamp, journeying all the long afternoon, in the hold of a basket, consigned to your friends at home, the first of the season. As some beautiful or palatable fruit is perhaps the noblest gift of Nature to man, so is a fruit with which one has in some measure identified himself by cultivating or collecting it one of the most suitable presents to a friend. It was some compensation for Commodore Porter, who may have introduced some cannon-balls and bombshells into parts where they were not wanted, to have introduced the Valparaiso squash into the United States. I think that this eclipses his military glory.

Nov. 24, 1850. Plucked a buttercup to-day. I have certain friends whom I visit occasionally, but I commonly part from them early, with a certain bitter-sweet sentiment. That which we love is so mixed and entangled with that we hate in one another that we are more grieved and disappointed, aye, and estranged from one another, by meeting than by absence. Some men may be my acquaintances merely, but one whom I have been accustomed to idealize, to have dreams about as a friend, and mix up intimately with myself, can never degenerate into an acquaintance. I must know him on that higher ground, or not know him at all.

We do not confess and explain because we would fain be so intimately related as to understand each other without speech. Our friend must be broad. His must be an atmosphere coextensive with the universe, in which we can expand and breathe. For the most part, we are smothered and stifled by one another. I go to see my friend and try his atmosphere. If our atmospheres do not mingle, if we repel each other strongly, it is of no use to stay.

Nov. 24, 1851. Found on the south side of the [Ministerial] swamp the *Lygodium palmatum,* which Bigelow calls the only climbing fern in our latitude.

Nov. 24, 1857. Some poets have said that writing poetry was for youths only, but not so. In that fervid and excitable season we only get the impulse which is to carry us onward in our future career. Ideals are exhibited to us then distinctly which all our lives after we may aim at, but not attain. The mere vision is little compared with the steady, corresponding endeavor thitherward. It would be vain for us to be looking ever at promised lands toward which we were not meanwhile steadily and earnestly traveling, whether the way led over a mountain top or through a dusky valley. In youth, when we are most elastic, we merely receive an impulse in the proper direction. To suppose this is equivalent to having traveled the road, or obeyed the impulse faithfully throughout a lifetime, is absurd. We are shown fair scenes in order that we may be tempted to inhabit them, and not simply tell what we have seen.

Nov. 24, 1858. It is a lichen day, with a little moist snow falling. The great green lungwort lichen shows now on the oaks (strange that there should be none on the pines close by), and the fresh, bright chestnut fruit of other kinds, glistening with moisture, brings life and immortality to light.

When I looked out this morning, the landscape presented a very pretty wintry sight, little snow as there was. Being very moist, it had lodged on every twig, and every one had its counterpart in a light, downy white one, twice or thrice its own depth, resting on it.

Here is an author who contrasts love for " the beauties of the person " with that for " excellences of the mind," as if these were the alternatives. I must say that it is for neither of these that I should feel the strongest affection. I love that one with whom I sympathize, be she " beautiful " or otherwise, of excellent mind or not.

Nov. 24, 1859. How pretty amid the downy and cottony fruits of November the head of the white anemone, raised a couple of feet from the ground on slender stalks, two or three together,

— small heads of yellowish-white down compact and regular as a thimble beneath, but, at this time, diffusive and bursting forth above, somewhat like a little torch with its flame.

Nov. 24, 1860. The first spitting of snow, a flurry or squall, from out a gray or slate-colored cloud that came up from the west. This consisted almost entirely of pellets an eighth of an inch or less in diameter. They drove along almost horizontally, or curving upward like the outline of a breaker before the strong and chilling wind. The plowed fields were for a short time whitened with them. The green moss about the bases of trees was very prettily spotted white with them, and also the large beds of cladonia in the pastures. They come to contrast with the red cockspur lichens on the stumps which you had not noticed before. Striking against the trunks of the trees on the west side, they fell and accumulated in a white line at the base. Though a slight touch, this was the first wintry scene of the season. The air was so filled with these snow pellets that we could not see a hill half a mile off, for an hour. The hands seek the warmth of the pockets, and fingers are so benumbed that you cannot open your jackknife. The rabbits in the swamp enjoy it as well as you. Methinks the winter gives them more liberty, like a night. I see where a boy has set a box trap, and baited it with half an apple, and, a mile off, come across a snare set for a rabbit or partridge in a cowpath in a pitch-pine wood, near where the rabbits have nibbled the apples which strew the wet ground. How pitiable that the most many see of a rabbit should be the snare some boy has set for one!

The bitter-sweet of a white-oak acorn which you nibble in a bleak November walk over the tawny earth, is more to me than a slice of imported pineapple. We do not think much of table fruits. They are especially for aldermen and epicures. They do not feed the imagination. That would starve on them. These wild fruits, whether eaten or not, are a dessert for the imagination.

Nov. 25, 1850. This afternoon, late and cold as it is, has been a sort of Indian summer. Indeed, I think we have summer days from time to time the winter through, and that it is often the snow on the ground which makes the whole difference. This afternoon the air was indescribably clear and exhilarating, and though the thermometer would have shown it to be cold, I thought there was a finer and purer warmth than in summer, a wholesome, intellectual warmth in which the body was warmed by the mind's contentment, — the warmth hardly sensuous, but rather the satisfaction of existence.

The landscape looked singularly clean and pure and dry, the air like a pure glass being laid over the picture, the trees so tidy and stripped of their leaves ; the meadow and pastures clothed with clean, dry grass, looked as if they had been swept ; ice on the water and winter in the air; but yet not a particle of snow on the ground. The woods, divested in great part of their leaves, are being ventilated. It is the season of perfect works, of hard, tough, ripe twigs, not of tender buds and leaves. The leaves have made their wood, and a myriad new withes stand up all around, pointing to the sky, and able to survive the cold. It is only the perennial that you see, the iron age of the year.

I saw a muskrat come out of a hole in the ice. He is a man wilder than Ray or Melvin. While I am looking at him, I am thinking what he is thinking of me. He is a different sort of man, that is all. He would dive when I went nearer, then reappear again, and had kept open a place five or six feet square, so that it had not frozen, by swimming about in it. Then he would sit on the edge of the ice, and busy himself about something, I could not see whether it was a clam or not. What a cold-blooded fellow ! thoughts at a low temperature, sitting perfectly still so long on ice covered with water, mumbling a cold, wet clam in its shell. What safe, low, moderate thoughts he must have! He does not get upon stilts. The generation of muskrats do not fail. They are not preserved by the legislature of Massachusetts.

I experience such an interior comfort, far removed from the sense of cold, as if the thin atmosphere were rarefied by heat, were the medium of invisible flames, as if the whole landscape were one great hearthside, that where the shrub-oak leaves rustle on the hillside, I seem to hear a crackling fire and see the pure flames, and I wonder that the dry leaves do not blaze into yellow flames.

When I got up high on the side of the cliff, the sun was setting like an Indian summer sun. There was a purple tint in the horizon. It was warm on the face of the rocks, and I could have sat till the sun disappeared, to dream there. It was a mild sunset such as is to be attended to. Just as the sun shines on us warmly and serenely, our creator breathes on us and re-creates us.

Nov. 25, 1852. At Walden. I hear at sundown what I mistake for the squawking of a hen, for they are firing at chickens hereabouts, but it proved to be a flock of wild geese going south.

Nov. 25, 1853. Just after the sun set tonight, I observed the northern part of the heavens was covered with fleecy clouds which abruptly terminated in a straight line stretching east and west directly over my head, the western end being beautifully rose-tinted. Half an hour later, this cloud had advanced southward, showing clear sky behind it in the north, until its southern edge was seen at an angle of 45° by me, but though its line was straight as before, it now appeared regularly curved like a segment of a melon rind, as usual.

Nov. 25, 1857. p. m. To Hubbard's Close, and thence through woods to Goose Pond and Pine Hill. A clear, cold, windy afternoon. The cat crackles with electricity when you stroke her, and the fur rises up to your touch. This is November of the hardest kind, bare frozen ground covered with pale brown or straw-colored herbage, a strong, cold, cutting north wind which makes me seek to cover my ears, a perfectly clear and cloudless sky. The cattle in the fields have a cold, shrunken, shaggy look, their hair standing out every way, as if with electricity, like the cat's. Ditches and pools are fast skimming over, and a few slate-colored snowbirds with thick, shuffling twitter, and fine-chipping tree sparrows flit from bush to bush in the otherwise deserted pastures. This month taxes a walker's resources more than any other. For my part, I should sooner think of going into

quarters in November than in winter. If you do
feel any fire at this season out of doors, you may
depend upon it, it is your own. It is but a short
time these afternoons before the night cometh in
which no man can walk. If you delay to start
till three o'clock, there will be hardly time left
for a long and rich adventure, to get fairly out
of town. November Eat-heart, is that the name
of it? Not only the fingers cease to do their
office, but there is often a benumbing of the
faculties generally. You can hardly screw up
your courage to take a walk when all is thus
tightly locked or frozen up, and so little is to be
seen in field or wood. I am inclined to take to
the swamps or woods as the warmest place, and
the former are still the openest. Nature has
herself become, like the few fruits she still
affords, a very thick-shelled nut with a shrunken
meat within. If I find anything to excite a
warming thought abroad, it is an agreeable disappointment, for I am obliged to go willfully
and against my inclination at first, the prospect
looks so barren, so many springs are frozen up,
not a flower, perchance, and few birds left, not
a companion abroad in all these fields for me.
I seem to anticipate a fruitless walk. I think
to myself hesitatingly, shall I go there, or there,
or there? and cannot make up my mind to any
route, all seem so unpromising, mere surface-

walking and fronting the cold wind, so that I have to force myself to it often, and at random. But then I am often unexpectedly compensated, and the thinnest yellow light of November is more warming and exhilarating than any wine they tell of. The mite which November contributes becomes equal in value to the bounty of July. I may meet with something that interests me, and immediately it is as warm as in July, as if it were the south instead of the northwest wind that blew.

I do not know if I am singular when I say that I believe there is no man with whom I can associate, who will not, comparatively speaking, spoil my afternoon. That society or encounter may at last yield a fruit which I am not aware of, but I cannot help suspecting that I should have spent those hours more profitably alone.

I notice a thimble-berry vine forming an arch four feet high which has firmly rooted itself at the small end.

The roar of the wind in the trees over my head sounds as cold as the wind feels.

I shiver about awhile on Pine Hill, waiting for the sun to set. The air appears to me dusky now after four, these days. The landscape looks darker than at any other season, like arctic scenery. There is the sun a quarter of an hour high, shining on it through a per-

fectly clear sky, but to my eye it is singularly
dark or dusky. And now the sun has disappeared, there is hardly less light for half a minute. I should not know when it was down, but
by looking that way, as I stand at this height.

Returning I see a fox run across the road in
the twilight. He is on a canter, but I see the
whitish tip of his tail. I feel a certain respect
for him, because, though so large, he still main-
tains himself free and wild in our midst, and is
so original, so far as any resemblance to our
race is concerned. Perhaps I like him better
than his tame cousin, the dog, for it.

It is surprising how much, from the habit
of regarding writing as an accomplishment, is
wasted on form. A very little information or
wit is mixed up with a great deal of convention-
alism in the style of expressing it, as with a
sort of preponderating paste or vehicle. Some
life is not simply expressed, but a long-winded
speech is made, with an occasional attempt to
put a little life into it.

Nov. 25, 1858. While most keep close to
their parlor fires this cold and blustering
Thanksgiving afternoon, and think with compassion of those who are abroad, I find the
sunny south side of the swamp as warm as is
their parlor, and warmer to my spirit. Aye,
there is a serenity and warmth here, which the

parlor does not suggest, enhanced by the sound of the wind roaring on the northwest side of the swamp a dozen or so rods off. What a wholesome and inspiring warmth is this !

Pass Tarbell's. The farmer, now on the down-hill of life, at length gets his new barn and barn cellar built, far away in some unfrequented vale. This for twoscore years he has struggled for. This is his poem done at last, to get the means to dig that cavity and rear those timbers aloft. How many millions have done just like him, or failed to do it ! There is so little originality, and just as little, and just as much fate, so to call it, in literature. With steady struggle, with alternate failure and success, he at length gets a barn cellar completed, and then a tomb. You would think there was a tariff on thinking and originality.

Nov. 25, 1860. Last night and to-day, very cold and blustering. Winter weather has come suddenly this year. The house was shaken by wind last night, and there was a general deficiency of bed-clothes. This morning some windows were as handsomely decorated with frost as ever in winter. I wear mittens or gloves, and my greatcoat. There is much ice on the meadows now, the broken edges shining in the sun. Now for the phenomena of winter. As I go up the meadow-side toward Clamshell I

see a very great collection of crows far and wide
on the meadows, evidently gathered by this cold
and blustering weather. Probably the moist
meadows where they feed are frozen up against
them. They flit before me in countless numbers, flying very low on account of the strong
northwest wind that comes over the hill, and a
cold gleam is reflected from the back and wings
of each, as from a weather - stained shingle.
Some perch within three or four rods of me,
and seem weary. I see where they have been
pecking the apples of the meadow - side, — an
immense cohort of cawing crows which sudden
winter has driven near to the habitations of man.
When I return after sunset, I see them collecting, and hovering over and settling in the
dense pine woods, as if about to roost there. . . .

How is any scientific discovery made? Why,
the discoverer takes it into his head first. He
must all but see it. . . .

How often you make a man richer in spirit,
in proportion as you rob him of earthly luxuries
and comforts.

Nov. 26, 1837. I look around for thoughts,
when I am overflowing, myself. While I live
on, thought is still in embryo, it stirs not within
me. Anon it begins to assume shape and come-
liness, and I deliver it, and clothe it in its garment of language. But, alas! how often when

thoughts choke me, do I resort to a spat on the back, or swallow a crust, or do anything but expectorate them.

Nov. 26, 1857. Minott's is a small, square, one-storied, unpainted house, with a hipped roof, and at least one dormer window, a third of the way up the south side of a long hill, which is some fifty feet high, and extends east and west. A traveler of taste may go straight through the village, without being detained a moment by any dwelling, either the form or surroundings being objectionable ; but very few go by this house without being agreeably impressed, and therefore led to inquire who lives in it. Not that its form is so incomparable, nor even its weather-stained color, but chiefly, I think, because of its snug and picturesque position on the hillside, fairly lodged there where all children like to be, and its perfect harmony with its surroundings and position. For if, preserving this form and color, it should be transplanted to the meadow below, nobody would notice it, more than a schoolhouse which was lately of the same form. It is there because somebody was independent, bold enough to carry out the happy thought of placing it high on the hillside. It is the locality, not the architecture, that takes us captive. There is exactly such a site (only, of course, less open on either side) between this house and the next westward, but few, if any, even of the admiring travelers, have thought of this as a house-lot, or would be bold enough to place a cottage there. Without side fences, or graveled walk, or flower-plots, that simple sloping bank before it is pleasanter than any front yard, though many a visitor, and many times the master, has slipped and fallen on the steep path. From its position and exposure, it has shelter and warmth and dryness and prospect. He overlooks the road, the meadow and brook, and houses beyond, to the distant Fair Haven. The spring comes earlier to that door-yard than any other, and summer lingers longest there.

Nov. 26, 1859. To the Colburn farm woodlot. The chickadee is the bird of the wood, the most unfailing. When in a windy or in any day you have penetrated some thick wood like this, you are pretty sure to hear its cheery note. At this season, it is almost its sole inhabitant. I see to-day one brown creeper busily inspecting the pitch pines. It begins at the base, and creeps rapidly upward by starts, adhering close to the bark, and shifting a little from side to side often till near the top, then suddenly darts off downward to the base of another tree where it repeats the same course. This has no black cockade like the nuthatch.

Nov. 27, 1853. Now a man will eat his heart, if ever, now while the earth is bare, barren, and cheerless, and we have the coldness of winter without the variety of ice and snow. Methinks the variety and compensation are in the stars. How bright they are now in contrast with the dark earth!

Nov. 27, 1855. P. M. By river to J. Farmer's. He gave me the head of a gray rabbit which his boy had snared. This rabbit is white beneath the whole length, reddish brown on the sides, and the same spotted with black, above; the hairs coarse and homely, yet the fur beneath thick and slate-colored, as usual; well defended from the cold; sides, I might say, *pale*-brick color, the brown part. The fur under the feet dirty yellowish, as if stained by what it trod upon.

Farmer said that his grandfather, who could remember one hundred and twenty-five years before this, told him that they used to catch wolves in Carter's pasture by the North River, east of Dodge's Brook, in this manner: they piled up logs cob-house fashion, beginning with a large base, eight or ten feet square, and narrowing successively each tier, so as to make steps for the wolves to the top, say ten feet high. Then they put a dead sheep within. A wolf soon found it in the night, sat down outside, and howled till he called his comrades to him, and then they ascended step by step, and jumped down within; but when they had done eating, they could not get out again. They always found one of the wolves dead, and supposed he was punished for betraying the others into this trap. A man in Brighton, whom he fully believes, told him that he built a bower near a dead horse, and placed himself within, to shoot crows. One crow took his station as sentinel on the top of a tree, and thirty or forty alighted upon the horse. He fired and killed seven or eight. But the rest, instead of minding him, immediately flew to their sentinel, and pecked him to pieces before his eyes. Also Mr. Joseph Clark told him that as he was going along the road, he cast a stick over the wall and hit some crows in a field, whereupon they flew directly at their sentinel· on an apple-tree and beat and buffeted him away to the woods as far as he could see.

Nov. 27, 1857. Standing before Stacy's large glass windows, this morning, I saw that they were gloriously ground by the frost. I never saw such beautiful feather and fir like frosting. His windows are filled with fancy articles and toys for Christmas and New Year's presents, but this delicate and graceful outside frosting surpassed them all infinitely. I saw countless feathers with very distinct midribs and fine pinnæ. The half of a trunk seemed to rise in each case up along the sash, and these feathers branched off from it all the way, sometimes nearly horizontally. Other crystals looked like fine plumes, of the natural size. If glass could be ground to look like this, how glorious it would be. You can tell which shopman has the hottest fire within, by the frost being melted off. I was never so struck by the gracefulness of the curves in vegetation, and wonder that Ruskin does not refer to frost work.

Nov. 27, 1859. The Greeks and Romans made much of honey, because they had no sugar ; olive oil also was very important. Our poets. (?) still sing of honey (though we have sugar) and oil, though we do not produce and scarcely use it.

Nov. 28, 1837. Every tree, fence, and spire of grass that could raise its head above the snow was this morning covered with a dense hoar frost. The trees looked like airy creatures of darkness caught napping. On this side, they were huddled together, their gray hairs streaming, in a secluded valley, which the sun had not yet penetrated, and on that they went hurrying off in Indian file by hedgerows and watercourses, while the shrubs and grasses, like elves and fairies of the night, sought to hide their diminished heads in the snow. The branches and taller grasses were covered with a wonderful ice-foliage answering leaf for leaf to their summer dress. The centre, diverging, and even more minute fibres, were perfectly distinct, and the edges regularly · indented. These leaves were on the side of the twig or stubble opposite to the sun (when it was not bent toward the east), meeting it, for the most part, at right angles, and there were others standing out at all possible angles upon this, and upon one another.

It struck me that these ghost leaves, and the green ones whose form they assume, were creatures of the same law. It could not be in obedience to two several laws, that the vegetable juices swelled gradually into the perfect leaf on the one hand, and the crystalline particles trooped to their standard in the same admirable order on the other.

The river viewed from the bank above appeared of a yellowish green color, but on a nearer approach, this phenomenon vanished, and yet the landscape was covered with snow.

Nov. 28, 1853. Settled with J. Munroe & Co., and on a new account placed twelve of my books with him on sale. I have paid him directly out of pocket, since the book was published, two hundred and ninety dollars, and taken a receipt for it. This does not include postage, proof-sheets, etc. I have received from other quarters about fifteen dollars. This has been the pecuniary value of the book.

Dr. Harris described to me his finding a new species of cicindēla [glow-worm] at the White Mountains this fall, the same of which he had found a specimen there some time ago, supposed to be very rare, found at Peter's River and Lake Superior; but he proves it to be common near the White Mountains.

Nov. 28, 1857. Spoke to Skinner about that wild-cat which he says he heard a month ago in Ebby Hubbard's woods. He was going down to Walden in the evening (with a companion) to see if geese had not settled in it, when they heard this sound, which his companion, at first, thought made by a coon, but Skinner said it was a wild-cat. He says he has heard them often in the Adirondack region, where he has purchased furs. He told his companion he would hear it again soon, and he did, somewhat like the domestic cat, a low sort of growling, and then a sudden quick-repeated caterwaul, or *yow-yow-yow* or *yang-yang-yang*. He says they utter this from time to time when on the track of some prey.

Nov. 28, 1858. A gray, overcast, still day, and more small birds, tree sparrows and chickadees, than usual about the house. There have been a very few fine snowflakes falling for many hours, and now, by 2 P. M., a regular snowstorm has commenced, fine flakes falling steadily, and rapidly whitening all the landscape. In half an hour the russet landscape is painted white, even to the horizon. Do we know of any other so silent and sudden a change?

I cannot now walk without leaving a track behind me. That is one peculiarity of winter walking. Anybody may follow my trail. I have walked, perhaps, a particular wild path along some swamp side all summer, and thought to myself, I am the only villager that ever comes here. But I go out shortly after the first snow has fallen, and lo, here is the track of a sportsman and his dog in my secluded path, and probably he preceded me in the summer as well. But my hour is not his, and I may never meet him.

Nov. 28, 1859. Saw Abel Brooks with a half-bushel basket on his arm. He was picking up chips on his and neighboring lots, had got about two quarts of old and blackened pine chips, and with these was returning home at dusk more than a mile, — such a petty quantity as you would hardly have gone to the end of your yard for, and yet he said he had got more than two cords of them at home, which he had collected thus, and sometimes with a wheelbarrow. He had thus spent an hour or two, and walked two or three miles in a cool November evening, to pick up two quarts of pine chips scattered through the woods. He evidently takes real satisfaction in collecting his fuel, perhaps gets more heat of all kinds out of it than any man in town. He is not reduced to taking a walk for exercise, as some are. It is one thing to own a wood-lot as he does who perambulates its bounds almost daily, so as to have worn a path about it, and another to own one as many a person does, who hardly knows where it is. Evidently the quantity of chips in his basket is not essential. It is the chipping idea which he pursues. It is to him an unaccountably pleasing occupation, and no doubt he loves to see his pile grow at home. Think how variously men spend the same hour in the same village. The lawyer sits talking with his client after twilight, the trader is weighing sugar and salt, while Abel Brooks is hastening home from the woods with his basket half full of chips. I think I should prefer to be with Brooks. He was literally as smiling as a basket of chips.

Nov. 29, 1839. Many brave men have there been, thank fortune, but I shall never grow brave by comparison. When I remember myself, I shall forget them.

Cambridge, Nov. 29, 1841. One must fight his way after a fashion, even in the most civil and polite society. The most truly kind and generous have to be won by a sort of valor, for the seeds of suspicion as well as those of confidence lurk in every spadeful of earth. Officers of respectable institutions turn the cold shoulder to you, though they are known as genial and well-disposed persons. They cannot imagine you to be other than a rogue. It is that instinctive principle which makes the cat show her talons, when you take her by the paw. Certainly that valor which can open the hearts of men is superior to that which can only open the gates of cities. You must let people see that they serve themselves more than you.

Nov. 29, 1850. Still misty, drizzling weather without snow or ice. The pines standing in the ocean of mist seen from the Cliffs are trees in every stage of transition from the actual to the imaginary. The near are more distant, the distant more faint, till at last they are a mere shadowy cone in the distance. You can command only a circle of thirty or forty rods in diameter. As you advance, the trees gradually come out of the mist, and take form before your eyes. You are reminded of your dreams. Life looks like a dream. You are prepared to see visions.

Nov. 29, 1853. P. M. To J. P. Brown's Pond Hole. J. Hosmer showed me a pestle which his son had found this summer, while plowing on the plain between his house and the river. It has a rude bird's head, a hawk's or eagle's, the beak and eyes (the latter a mere prominence) serving for a knob or handle. It is affecting as a work of art by a people who have left so few traces of themselves, a step beyond the common arrow-head and pestle and axe, something more fanciful, a step beyond pure utility. As long as I find traces of works of convenience merely, however much skill they show, I am not so much affected as when I discover works which evince the exercise of fancy and taste, however rude. It is a great step to find a pestle whose handle is ornamented with a bird's-head knob. It brings the maker still nearer to the races which so ornament their umbrellas and cane handles. I have then evidence in stone that men lived here who had fancies to be pleased, and in whom the first steps toward a complete culture were taken. It implies so many more thoughts such as I have. The arrow-head, too, suggests a bird, but a relation to it not in the least godlike. But here an Indian has patiently sat, and fashioned a stone in a likeness of a bird, and added some pure beauty to that pure utility, and so far has begun to

leave behind him war and even hunting, — to
redeem himself from the savage state.   Enough
of this would have saved him from extermina-
tion.

It has been cloudy and milder this afternoon,
but now I begin to see in the western horizon a
clear crescent of yellowish sky, and suddenly a
glorious yellow sunlight falls on all the eastern
landscape, russet fields and hillsides, evergreens
and rustling oaks, and single leafless trees.   In
addition to the clearness of the air at this season, the light is all from one side, and none
being absorbed or dissipated in the heavens, but
it being reflected both from the russet earth and
the clouds, it is intensely bright.   All the limbs
of a maple seen far eastward rising over a hill are
wonderfully distinct and lit.   I think we have
some such sunsets as this, and peculiar to the
season, every year.   I should call it the russet
afterglow of the year.   It may not be warm,
but must be clear and comparatively calm.

Nov. 29, 1857.   P. M.   To Assabet Bath, and
down bank.   Again I am struck by the singularly wholesome colors of the withered oak
leaves, especially the shrub oak, so thick and firm
and unworn, without speck, clear reddish-brown,
sometimes paler or yellowish-brown, the whitish
under sides contrasting with the upper in a very
cheerful manner, as if the tree or shrub rejoiced

at the advent of winter. It exhibits the fashion-
able colors of the winter on the two sides of its
leaves. It sets the fashions; colors good for
bare ground or for snow, grateful to the eyes of
rabbits and partridges. This is the extent of its
gaudiness, red-brown and misty-white, and yet
it is gay. The colors of the brightest flowers
are not more agreeable to my eye. Then there
is the rich dark brown of the black oak, large
and somewhat curled leaf on sprouts, with its
light, almost yellowish-brown under side. Then
the salmonish hue of white-oak leaves, with the
under sides less distinctly lighter. Many, however, have faded already.

Nov. 29, 1858. P. M. To Hill. About three
inches of snow fell last night. How light and
bright the day now; methinks it is as good as a
half hour added to the day. White houses no
longer stand out and stare in the landscape.
The pine woods snowed up look more like the
bare oak woods with their gray boughs. The
river meadows show now far off a dull straw
color or pale brown amid the general white,
where the coarse sedge rises above the snow;
and distant oak woods are now indistinctly reddish. It is a clear and pleasant winter day.
The snow has taken all the November out of the
sky. Now, blue shadows and green rivers (both
which I see), and still winter life. I see par-

tridge and mice and fox tracks, and crows sit silent on a bare oak top.

Nov. 29, 1859. To Copan. Saw quite a flock of snow buntings, not yet very white. They rose from the midst of a stubble field unexpectedly. The moment they settled after wheeling around they were perfectly concealed, though quite near. I could only hear their rippling note from the earth from time to time.

Nov. 29, 1860. If a man has spent all his days about some business by which he has merely got to be rich, as it is called, has got much money, many houses and barns and wood-lots, then his life has been a failure, I think. But if he has been trying to better his condition in a higher sense than this, has been trying to be somebody, that is, to invest himself, and get a patent for it, so that all may see his originality, though he should never get above board (and great inventors, you know, commonly die poor), I shall think him comparatively successful.

You would think that some men had been tempted to live in this world at all, only by the offer of a bounty by the general government, a bounty on living. I told such a man the other day that I had got a Canada lynx here in Concord, and his instant question was, " Have you got the reward for him ? " " What reward ? " " Why, the ten dollars which the State offers."

As long as I saw him, he neither said nor thought anything about the lynx, but only about the reward. You might have inferred that ten dollars was something rarer in his neighborhood than a lynx even, and that he was anxious to see it on that account. I had thought that a lynx was a bright-eyed, four-legged, furry beast, of the cat kind, very current indeed, though its natural gait is by leaps. But he knew it to be a draft drawn by the cashier of the Wild Cat Bank on the State Treasury, payable at sight. Then I reflected that the first currency was of leather, or a whole creature (whence *pecunia*, from *pecus*, a herd), and since leather was at first furry, I easily understood the connection between a lynx and ten dollars, and found that all money was traceable right back to the Wild Cat Bank. But the fact was that instead of receiving ten dollars for the lynx, I had paid away some dollars in order to get him, so you see, I was away back in a gray antiquity, behind the institution of money, further than history goes. Yet though money can buy no fine fruit whatever, and we are never made truly rich by the possession of it, the value of things is commonly estimated by the amount of money they will fetch. A thing is not valuable, for example, a fine situation for a house, until it is convertible into so much money, that is, can cease to be what

it is and become something else which you prefer.
So you will see that all prosaic people who possess only the common sense, who believe chiefly
in this kind of wealth, are speculators in fancy
stocks, and continually cheat themselves; but
poets and all discerning people who have an object in life, and know what they want, speculate
in real values. The mean and low values of
anything depend on its convertibility into something else, that is, have nothing to do with its
intrinsic value. The world and our life have
practically a similar value only to most. A
man has his price at the South, is worth so many
dollars, and so he has at the North. Many a
man has set out by saying, I will make so many
dollars by such a time, or before I die, and that
is his price, as much as if he were knocked off
for it by a Southern auctioneer.

Tuesday, Nov. 30, 1841. Cambridge. When
looking over the dry and dusty volumes of the
English poets, I cannot believe that those fresh
and fair creations I had imagined are contained
in them. English poetry, from Gower down,
collected into an alcove, and so from the library
window compared with the commonest nature,
seems very mean. Poetry cannot breathe in
the scholar's atmosphere. The Aubreys and
Hickeses, with all their learning, profane it yet
indirectly by their zeal. You need not envy

his feelings who for the first time had cornered up poetry in an alcove. I can hardly be serious with myself when I remember that I have come to Cambridge after poetry. I think if it would not be a shorter way to a complete volume to step at once into the field or wood, with a very low reverence to students and librarians. On running over the titles of these books, looking from time to time at their first pages or farther, I am oppressed by an inevitable sadness. One must have come into a library by an oriel window as softly and undisturbed as the light which falls on the books through the stained glass, and not by the librarian's door, else all his dreams will vanish. Can the Valhalla be warmed by steam and go by clock and bell?

Good poetry seems so simple and natural a thing that when we meet it, we wonder that all men are not always poets. Poetry is nothing but healthy speech. Though more than any other, the poet stands in the midst of nature, yet more than any other can he stand aloof from her. The best lines, perhaps, only suggest that this man simply saw or heard or felt what seems the commonest fact in my experience.

Nothing is so attractive and unceasingly curious as character. There is no plant that needs such tender treatment, there is none that will endure so rough. It is the violet and the oak.

It is divine and related to the heavens, as the earth is by the aurora. It has no acquaintance and no companion. It goes silent and unobserved longer than any planet in space, but when at length it does show itself, it seems like the flowering of all the world, and its before unseen orbit is lit up like the track of a meteor. I hear no good news ever, but some trait of a noble character. It reproaches me plaintively. I am mean in contrast, but again am thrilled and elevated so that I can see my own meanness, and again still, that my own aspiration is realized in that other. You reach me, my friend, not by your kind or wise words uttered to me here or there ; but as you retreat, perhaps after .years of vain familiarity, some gesture or unconscious action in the distance speaks to me with more emphasis than all those years. I am not concerned to know what eighth planet is wandering in space up there, or when Venus or Orion rises, but if in any cot east or west, and set behind the woods, there is any planetary character illuminating the earth.

> Packed in my mind lie all the clothes
> Which outward nature wears,
> For, as its hourly fashions change,
> It all things else repairs.
>
> My eyes look inward, not without,
> And I but hear myself,

And that new wealth which I have got
Is part of my own pelf.

For while I look for change abroad,
I can no difference find,
Till some new ray of peace uncalled
Illumes my inmost mind.

As when the sun streams through the wood
Upon a winter's morn,
Where'er his silent beams may stray,
The murky night is gone.

How could the patient pine have known
The morning breeze would come,
Or simple flower anticipate
The insect's noonday hum,

Till that new light, with morning cheer,
From far streamed through the aisles,
And nimbly told the forest trees
For many stretching miles ?

Nov. 30, 1851.   Another cold and windy afternoon, with some snow, not yet melted, on the
ground.   Under the south side of a hill between
Brown's and Tarbell's, in a warm nook, disturbed three large gray squirrels and some partridges, which had all sought out this bare and
warm place.   While the squirrels hid themselves
in the treetops, I sat on an oak stump by an
old cellar hole, and mused.   This squirrel is
always an unexpectedly large animal to see
frisking about.   My eye wanders across the valley to the pine woods which fringe the opposite

side, and finds in their aspect something which
addresses itself to my nature. Methinks that in
my mood I was asking nature to give me a sign.
I do not know exactly what it was that attracted
my eye. I experienced a transient gladness, at
any rate, at something which I saw. I am sure
that my eye rested with pleasure on the white
pines now reflecting a silvery light, the infinite
stories of their boughs, tier above tier, a sort of
basaltic structure, a crumbling precipice of pine
horizontally stratified. Each pine is like a great
green feather stuck in the ground. A myriad
white-pine boughs extend themselves horizontally,
one above and behind another, each bearing its
burden of silvery sunlight, with darker seams
between them, as if it were a great crumbling
piny precipice thus stratified. On this my eyes
pastured while the squirrels were up the trees
behind me. That, at any rate, it was that I
got by my afternoon walk, a certain recognition
from the pine, some congratulation. Where is
my home? It is indistinct as an old cellar-hole
now, a faint indentation merely in a farmer's
field, which he has plowed into, rounding off its
edges, years ago, and I sit by the old site on
the stump of an oak which once grew there.
Such is nature where we have lived. Thick
birch groves stand here and there, dark brown
now, with white. lines here and there. The *Ly-*

godium palmatum [climbing fern] is quite abundant on that side of the swamp, twining round the golden-rods, etc.

Nov. 30, 1852. To Pine Hill. The buds of the *Populus tremuloides* show their down as in early spring, and the early willows. From Pine Hill, Wachusett is seen over Walden. The country seems to slope up from the west end of Walden to the mountain. Already a little after four o'clock, the sparkling windows and vanes of the village seen under and against the faintly purple-tinged, slate-colored mountains, remind me of a village in a mountainous country at twilight, where early lights appear. I think that this sparkle. without redness, a cold glitter, is peculiar to this season.

Nov. 30, 1853. 8 A. M. To river to examine roots. I ascertain this morning that the white root with eyes, and slaty-tinged fibres, and sharp leaves rolled up, found gnawed off and floating about muskrat houses is the root of the great yellow lily. The leaf-stalk is yellow, while that of the white lily is a downy or mildewy blue-black. The yellow-lily root is then, it would seem, a principal item in the vegetable diet of the muskrat. I find that those large triangular or rhomboidal or shell-shaped eyes or shoulders on this root are the bases of leaf-stalks which have rotted off, but toward the upper end of the root are still seen decaying. They are a sort of abutment on which the leaf-stalk rested. The fine black dots on them are the bases of the fine threads or fibres of the leaf-stalk, which in the still living leaf-stalk are distinguished by their purple color. These eyes, like the leaves, of course, are arranged spirally across the roots in parallel rows, in quincunx order, so that four make a diamond figure.

Nov. 30, 1855. This evening I received Cholmondeley's gift of Indian books, forty-four volumes in all, which came by the Canada.

On the twenty-seventh, when I made my last voyage for the season, I found a large round pine log about four feet long, floating, and brought it home. Off the larger end I sawed two wheels about a foot in diameter, and seven or eight inches thick, and I fitted to them an axletree made of a joist which I also found in the river. Thus I had a convenient pair of wheels on which to get my boat up and roll it about. I was pleased to get my boat in by this means rather than on a borrowed wheelbarrow. It was fit that the river should furnish the material, and that in my last voyage on it, when the ice reminded me that it was time to put it in winter quarters.

Nov. 30, 1856. Minott told me on Friday of an oldish man and woman who had brought to a muster here once a great leg of bacon boiled, to turn a penny with. The skin, as thick as sole leather, was flayed and turned back, displaying the tempting flesh. A tall, raw-boned, omnivorous heron of a Yankee came along and bargained with the woman, who was awaiting a customer, for as much of that as he could eat. He ate and ate and ate, making a surprising hole, greatly to the amusement of the lookers-on, till the woman in her despair, unfaithful to her engagement, appealed to the police to drive him off.

Minott Pratt tells me that he watched the fringed gentian this year, and it lasted till the first week in November.

Nov. 30, 1857. A still, warm, cloudy, rain-threatening day. Surveying the J. Richardson lot. The air is full of geese. I saw five flocks within an hour, about 10 A. M., containing from thirty to fifty each, afterward two more flocks, making in all from two hundred and fifty to three hundred, at least, all flying southwest over Goose and Walden Ponds. You first hear a faint honking from one or two in the northeast, and think there are but few wandering there, but look up and see forty or fifty coming on, in a more or less broken harrow, wedging their way southwest. I suspect they honk more, at any rate they are more broken and alarmed, when

passing over a village, and are seen falling into
their ranks again, assuming the perfect harrow
form. Hearing only one or two honking, even
for the seventh time, you think there are but
few till you see them. According to my calcu-
lation, ten or fifteen hundred may have gone
over Concord to-day. When they fly low and
near, they look very black against the sky.
Nov. 30, 1858. p. m. To Walden with C.,
and Fair Haven Hill. It is a pleasant day, and
the snow melting considerably. Though Walden is open, it is a perfect winter scene ; this
withdrawn, but ample recess in the woods, with
all that is necessary for a human residence, yet
never referred to by the London " Times " and
Galignani's " Messenger," as some of those arctic
bays are. Some are hastening to Europe, some
to the West Indies, but here is a bay never
steered for. These nameless bays, where the
" Times " and the " Tribune " have no correspondent, are the true bays of All Saints for me.
Green pines on this side, brown oaks on that,
the blue sky overhead, and the white counter-
pane all around. It is an insignificant fraction
of the globe which England and Russia and the
filibusters have overrun. The open pond close
by, though considerably rippled to-day, affects
me as a peculiarly mild and genial object by
contrast with this frozen pool, and I sit down on

the shore in the sun, on the bare rocks. There seems to be a milder air above it, as the water within it is milder. Going west through Wheeler's Owl wood toward Weird Dell, Well Meadow Field, I beheld a peculiar winter scene, seen many times before, but forgotten. The sun, rather low, is seen through the wood with a cold, dazzling, white lustre, like that of burnished tin, reflected from the silvery needles of the pine. No powerful light streams through, but you stand in the quiet and somewhat sombre aisles of a forest cathedral, where cold green masses alternate with pale-brown, but warm, leather-colored ones; you are inclined to call them red, reddish tawny, almost ruddy. These are the internal decorations, while dark trunks streaked with sunlight rise on all sides, and a pure white floor stretches around, and perhaps a single patch of yellow sunlight is seen on the white shaded floor.

Did ever clouds flit and change, form and dissolve so fast as in this clear cold air? for it is rapidly growing colder, and at such a time, with a clear air, wind, and shifting clouds, I never fail to see mother-o'-pearl tints abundant in the sky.

Coming over the side of Fair Haven Hill at sunset, we saw a long, large, dusky cloud in the northwest horizon, apparently just this side of

Wachusett, or at least twenty miles off, which was snowing, when all the rest was clear sky. It was a complete snow cloud. It looked like rain falling at an equal distance, except that the snow fell less directly, and the upper outline of a part of the cloud was more like that of a dusky mist. It was not much of a snowstorm, just enough to partially obscure the mountains about which it was falling, while the cloud was apparently high above them, or it may have been a little this side. The cloud was of a dun color, and at its south end, where the sun was just about to set, it was all aglow on its under side with a salmon fulgor, making it look warmer than a furnace, at the same time that it was snowing. It was a rare and strange sight, that of a snowstorm twenty miles off, on the verge of a perfectly clear sky. Thus local is all storm, surrounded by serenity and beauty. The terrestrial mountains were made ridiculous beneath that stupendous range. The sun seen setting through the snow-carpeted woods, with shimmering pine needles, or dark green spruces, and warm brown oak leaves for screens. With the advent of snow and ice, so much cold white, the browns are warmer to the eye. All the red that is in oak leaves and huckleberry twigs comes out.

I cannot but still see in my mind's eye those

little striped breams poised in Walden's glaucous water. They balance all the rest of the world in my estimation at present, for this is the bream I have just found, and, for the time being, I neglect all its brethren, and am ready to kill the fatted calf on its account. For more than two centuries have men fished here, and have not distinguished this permanent settler of the township. It is not like a new bird, a transient visitor that may not be seen again for years, but there it dwells and has dwelt permanently, who can tell how long? When my eyes first rested on Walden, the striped bream was poised in it, though I did not see it, and when Tahatawan paddled his canoe there. How wild it makes the pond and the township to find a new fish in it. America renews her youth here. But in my account of the bream, I cannot go a hair's breadth beyond the mere statement that it exists, the miracle of its existence. My contemporary and neighbor, yet so different from me! I can only poise my thought there by its side, and try to think *like* a bream for a moment. I can only think of precious jewels, of music, poetry, beauty, and the mystery of life. I only see the bream in its orbit, as I see a star, but I care not to measure its distance or weight. The bream appreciated floats in the pond, as the centre of the system, another image of God. Its life no

man can explain, more than he can his own. I
want you to perceive the mystery of the bream.
I have a contemporary in Walden. It has fins
where I have legs and arms. I have a friend
among the fishes, at least a new acquaintance.
Its character will interest me, I trust, and not its
clothes and anatomy. I do not want it to eat.
Acquaintance with it is to make my life more
rich and eventful. It is as if a poet or an an-
chorite had moved into the town, whom I can
see from time to time, and think of yet oftener.

Though science may sometimes compare herself to a child picking up pebbles on the sea-
shore, that is a rare mood with her. Ordinarily
her practical belief is that it is only a few pebbles which are not known, weighed and measured.
A new species of fish signifies hardly more than
a new name. See what is contributed in the
scientific reports. One counts the fin-rays, another measures the intestines, a third daguerreo-
types a scale, etc.; as if all but this were done,
and these were very rich and generous contribu-
tions to science. Her votaries may be seen wandering along the shore of the ocean of Truth,
with their backs toward it, ready to seize on the
shells which are cast up. You would say that
the scientific bodies were terribly put to it for
objects and subjects. A dead specimen of an
animal, if it is only well preserved in alcohol, is

just as good for science as a living one preserved
in its native element.   What is the amount of
my discovery to me?   It is not that I have got
one in a bottle, and that it has a name in a book,
but that I have a little fishy friend in the pond.
How was it when the youth first discovered
fishes?   Was it the number of their fin-rays or
other arrangement, or the place of the fish in
some system that made the boy dream of them?
Is it these things that interest mankind in the
fish, the inhabitant of the water?   No, but a
faint recognition of a living contemporary, a
provoking mystery.   One boy thinks of fishes,
and goes a-fishing from the same motive that his
brother searches the poets for rare lines.   It is
the poetry of fishes which is their chief use, their
flesh is their lowest use.   The beauty of the fish,
that is what it is best worth while to measure.
Its place in our systems is of comparatively little
importance.   Generally the boy loses some of
his perception and his interest in the fish, and
degenerates into a fisherman or an ichthyolo-
gist.

Nov. 30, 1859.   I am one of a committee of
four (Simon Brown, ex - Lieutenant - Governor,
R. W. Emerson, myself, and John Keyes, late
High Sheriff) instructed by a meeting of citi-
zens to ask liberty from the selectmen to have
the bell of the first parish tolled at the time

Captain Brown is being hanged, and while we shall be assembled in the Town House to express our sympathy with him. I applied to the selectmen yesterday. After various delays, they at length answer me to-night that they " are uncertain whether they have any control over the bell, but that, in any case, they will not give their consent to have the bell tolled." Beside their private objections, they are influenced by the remarks of a few individuals ; ———— said that he had heard " five hundred " damn me for it, and that he had no doubt, if it were done, some counter demonstration would be made, such as firing minute guns. A considerable part of Concord are in the condition of Virginia to-day, afraid of their own shadows.

It is quite warm to-day, and as I go home on the railroad causeway, I hear a hylodes peeping.

Dec. 1, 1850. I saw a little green hemisphere of moss which looked as if it covered a stone, but, thrusting my cane into it, I found it was nothing but moss about fifteen inches in diameter, and eight or nine inches high. When I broke it up, it appeared as if the annual growth was marked by successive layers half an inch deep, each. The lower ones were quite rotten, but the present year's quite green, the intermediate, white. I counted fifteen or eighteen. It was quite solid, and I saw that it continued solid as it grew by branching occasionally just enough to fill the newly gained space, and the tender extremities of each plant, crowded close together, made the firm and compact surface of the bed. There was a darker line separating the growths, where I thought the surface had been exposed to the winter. It was quite saturated with water, though firm and solid.

Dec. 1, 1852. To Cliffs. The snow keeps off unusually. The landscape is of the color of a russet apple, which has no golden cheek. The sunset sky supplies that. But, though it is crude to bite, it yields a pleasant acid flavor. The year looks back to summer, and a summer smile is reflected in her face. There is in these days a coolness in the air which makes me hesitate to call them Indian summer. At this season, I observe the form of the buds which are prepared for spring, the large bright yellow and reddish buds of the swamp pink, the already downy ones of the *Populus tremuloides* and the willows, the red ones of the blueberry, etc., also the catkins of the alders and birches.

Dec. 1, 1853. Those trees and shrubs which retain their withered leaves though the winter, shrub oaks, and young white, red, and black oaks, the lower branches of larger trees of the last mentioned species, hornbeams, young hickories, etc., seem to form an intermediate class between deciduous and evergreen trees. They may almost be called the ever-reds. Their leaves, which are falling all winter long, serve as a shelter to rabbits and partridges, and other winter birds and quadrupeds. Even the chickadees love to skulk amid them, and peep out from behind them. I hear their faint, silvery, lisping notes, like tinkling glass, and occasionally a sprightly *day-day-day*, as they inquisitively hop nearer and nearer to me. ˙They are a most honest and innocent little bird, drawing yet nearer to us as the winter advances, and deserve best of all of the walker.

Dec. 1, 1856. P. M. By path around Walden. With this little snow of the 29th ultimo there is yet pretty good sledding, for it lies solid. I see the pale-faced farmer out again on his sled for the five thousandth time. Cyrus Hubbard, a man of a certain New England probity and worth, immortal and natural, like a natural product, like the sweetness of a nut, like the toughness of hickory. He, too, is a redeemer for me. How superior actually to the faith be professes! He is not an office-seeker. What an institution, what a revelation is a man! We are wont foolishly to think that the creed a man professes is more significant than the fact he is. It matters not how hard the conditions seemed, how mean the world, for a man is a prevalent force, and a new law himself. He is system whose law is to be observed. The old farmer condescends to countenance still this nature and order of things. It is a great encouragement that an honest man makes this world his abode. He rides on the sled drawn by oxen world-wise, yet comparatively so young, as if they had seen scores of winters. The farmer spoke to me, I can swear, clean, cold, moderate, as the snow. He does not melt the snow where he stands. Yet what a faint impression that encounter may make on me after all! Moderate, natural, true, as if he were made of earth, stone, wood, snow. I thus meet in this universe kindred of mine, composed of these elements. I see men like frogs. Their peeping I partially understand.

I go by Haden's and take S. Wheeler's woodpath to railroad. Slate-colored snow-birds flit before me in the path, feeding on the seeds, the countless little brown seeds that begin to be scattered over the snow, so much the more obvious to bird and beast. A hundred kinds of indigenous grain are harvested now, broadcast upon the surface of the snow. Thus, at a critical season, these seeds are shaken down on to a clean, white napkin, unmixed with dirt and rubbish, and off this the little pensioners pick them. Their clean table is thus spread a few

inches or feet above the ground. . . . Will
wonder become extinct in me ? Shall I become
insensible as a fungus ?

A ridge of earth, with the red cock's - comb
lichen on it, peeps out still at the rut's edge.

The dear wholesome color of shrub-oak leaves,
so clean and firm, not decaying, but which have
put on a kind of immortality, not wrinkled and
thin like the white-oak leaves, but full-veined
and plump as nearer earth. Well-tanned leather
on the one side, sun - tanned, color of colors,
color of the cow and the deer, silver-downy beneath, turned toward the late bleached and russet fields. What are acanthus leaves, and the
rest, to this ? Emblem of my winter condition.
I love and could embrace the shrub oak, with
its scanty garment of leaves rising above the
snow, lowly whispering to me, akin to winter
thoughts, and sunsets, to all virtue; coverts
which the hare and the partridge seek, and I too
seek. What cousin of mine is the shrub oak ?
Rigid as iron, clean as the atmosphere, hardy as
virtue,- innocent and sweet as a maiden, is the
shrub oak. In proportion as I know and love
it, I am natural and sound as a partridge. I
felt a positive yearning toward one bush this
afternoon. There was a match found for me at
last. I fell in love with a shrub oak. Tenacious
of its leaves which shrivel not, but retain a cer-

tain wintry life in them, firm shields painted in
fast colors, a rich brown. The deer-mouse, too,
knows the shrub oak, and has its hole in the
snow by the shrub oak's stem. Now, too, I remark in many places ridges and fields of fine
russet or straw-colored grass rising above the
snow, and beds of empty, straw-colored heads of
everlasting, and ragged looking Roman wormwood. The blue curls' chalices stand empty,
and waiting evidently to be filled with ice. I
see great thimble-berry bushes rising above the
snow, with still a rich, rank bloom on them, as
in July, hypæthral mildew, elysian fungus! To
see the bloom on the thimble-berry stem lasting
into midwinter! What a salve that would
make, collected and boxed.

No, I am a stranger in your towns. I am not
at home at French's or Lovejoy's, or Savery's.
I can winter more to my mind amid the shrub
oaks. I have made arrangements to stay with
them. The shrub oak, lowly, loving the earth,
and spreading over it, tough, thick-leaved, leaves
firm and sound in winter, rustling like leather
shields, leaves fair and wholesome to the eye,
clean and smooth to the touch. Tough to support the snow, not broken down by it, well-nigh
useless to man, a sturdy phalanx, hard to break
down, product of New England soil, bearing
many striped acorns; well named *shrub oak,*

low, robust, hardy, indigenous, well-known to
the striped squirrel and the partridge and the
rabbit. The squirrels nibble its nuts, sitting
upon an old stump of its larger cousin. What
is Peruvian bark to your bark! How many
rents I owe to you, how many eyes put out!
How many bleeding fingers! How many shrub-
oak patches I have been through, stooping,
winding my way, bending the twigs aside, guid-
ing myself by the sun, over hills and valleys and
plains, resting in clear grassy spaces!

How can any man suffer long? for a sense of
want is a prayer, and all prayers are answered.

Dec. 1, 1857. p. m. Walking in Ebby Hubbard's woods, I hear a red squirrel barking at
me amid the pine and oak tops, and now I
see him coursing from tree to tree. How se-
curely he travels there fifty feet from the ground,
leaping from the slender, bending twig of one
tree across an interval of three or four feet, and
catching at the nearest twig of the next, which
so bends under him, that it is hard at first to
get up. His traveling is a succession of leaps
in the air at that height, without wings! And
yet he gets along about as rapidly as on the
ground.

I hear the fainted possible *quivet* from a nuthatch quite near me on a pine. I thus always
begin to hear the bird on the approach of winter,

as if it did not breed, but merely wintered, here.
[Added later.] · Hear it all the fall, and occasionally through the summer of '59.

Dec. 2, 1839. A rare landscape immediately suggests a suitable inhabitant, whose breath shall be its wind, whose moods its seasons, and to whom it will always be fair. To be chafed and worried, and not as serene as nature, does not become one whose nature is as steadfast as she. We do all stand in the front ranks of the battle every moment of our lives. Where there is a brave man, there is the thickest of the fight, there the post of honor. Not he who procures a substitute to go to Florida is exempt from service. He gathers his laurels in another field. Waterloo is not the only battle-ground. As many and fatal guns are pointed at my breast now, as are contained in the English arsenals.

Dec. 2, 1852. The pleasantest day of all. Started in boat before 9 ᴀ. ᴍ., down river to Billerica with W. E. C. Not wind enough for a sail. I do not remember when I have taken a sail or a row on the river in December before. We had to break the ice about the boathouse for some distance. Still no snow. The banks are white with frost. The air is calm and the water smooth. The distant sounds of cars, cocks, hounds, etc., as we glide past N. Barrett's farm remind me of spring. It is an anticipation,

a looking through winter to spring. There is a
certain resonance and elasticity in the air that
makes the least sound melodious as in spring.
The old unpainted houses under the trees look
as if winter had come and gone. A side of one
is painted as if with the pumpkin pies left over
after Thanksgiving, it is so singular a yellow.
The river has risen since the last rain a few
feet, and partially floods the meadow. See still
two ducks there. Hear the jay in distant copses,
and the *Fringilla linaria* flies and mews over.
Some parts of the meadow are covered with ice,
through which we row, which yet lasts all day.
The waves we make in the river nibble and
crumble its edge, and produce a rustling of the
grass and seeds, as if a muskrat were stirring.
We land behind Tarbell's, and walk inland.
How warm in the hollows! The outline of the
hills is very agreeable there, ridgy hills with
backs to them. A perfect cowpath winds along
the side of one. These creatures have such weight
to carry that they select the easiest course. Again
embark. It is remarkably calm and warm in
the sun, now that we have brought a hill between
us and the wind. There goes a muskrat. He
leaves so long a ripple behind that in this light
you cannot tell where his body ends, and think
him longer than he is. This is a glorious river-
reach. At length we pass the bridge. Every-

where the muskrat houses line the shores, or what was the shore, some three feet high, and regularly sharp, as the Peak of Teneriffe. C. says, " Let us land ; ' the angle of incidence should be equal to the angle of reflection.' " We did so. By the island where I formerly camped, half a mile or more above the bridge on the road from Chelmsford to Bedford, we saw a mink, slender, black at ten rods distance (Emmonds says they are a dark, glossy brown), very like a weasel in form. He alternately ran along the ice and swam in the water, now and then holding up his head and long neck, and looking at us, — not so shy as a muskrat ; I should say very black. The muskrats would curl up into a ball on the ice, decidedly reddish brown. The ice made no show, being thin and dark. The mink's head is larger in proportion to the body than the muskrat's, not so sharp and rat-like. Left our boat just above the last-named bridge on west side. A bright, dazzling sheen for miles on the river as you look up. it. Crossed the bridge, turned into a path on the left, and ascended a hill a mile and a half off, between us and Billerica, somewhat off from the river. The Concord affords the water prospects of a larger river, like the Connecticut even, hereabouts. I found a spear-head by a mysterious little building. On the west side of the river in Billerica here is a grand range of hills, somewhat cliffy, covered with young oaks, whose leaves now give it a red appearance even when seen from Ball's Hill. It is one of the most interesting and novel features in the river scenery.

Men commonly talk as if genius were something proper to an individual. I esteem it but a common privilege, and if one does not enjoy it now, he may congratulate his neighbor that *he* does. There is no place for man-worship. We understand very well a man's relation, not to *his* genius, but to *the* genius.

Returning, the water is smoother and more beautiful than before. The ripples we make produce ribbed reflections or shadows on the dense but leafless bushes on shore, thirty or forty rods distant, very regular, and so far they seem motionless and permanent. All the water behind us, as we row, and even on the right and left at a distance, is perfectly unruffled, we move so fast, but before us down stream it is all in commotion from shore to shore. There are some fine shadows on those grand red oaken hills in the north. When a muskrat comes to the surface too near you, how quickly and with what force he turns and plunges again, making a sound in the calm water as if you had thrown into it a large stone with violence. Long did it take to sink the Carlisle bridge. The reflections after sunset were distinct and glorious, the heaven into which we unceasingly rowed. I thought now that the angle of reflection was greater than the angle of incidence. It grew cooler ; the stars came out soon after we turned Ball's Hill, and it became difficult to distinguish our course. The boatman knows a river by reaches. Got home in the dark, our feet and legs numb and cold with sitting and inactivity, having been about eight miles by river, etc. It was some time before we recovered the full use of our cramped legs. I forgot to speak of the after-glows. The twilight in fact had several stages, and several times after it had grown dusky, acquired a new transparency, and the trees on the hillsides were lit up again.

Dec. 2, 1853. The skeleton, which at first sight produces only a shudder in all mortals, becomes at last, not only a pure, but a sugges-tive and pleasing object to science. The more we know of it, the less we associate it with any goblin of our imagination. The longer we keep it, the less likely it is that any such will come to claim it. We discover that the only spirit which haunts it is a universal Intelligence which has created it in harmony with all nature. Sci-ence never saw a ghost, nor does it look for any, but it sees everywhere the traces, and is itself the agent, of a Universal Intelligence.

Dec. 2, 1856. Saw Melvin's lank, bluish-white, black-spotted hound, and Melvin with his gun near by, going home at eve. He follows hunting, praise be to him, as regularly in our tame fields as the farmers follow farming ; persistent genius, how I respect and thank him for it. I trust the Lord will provide us with another Melvin when he is gone. How good in him to follow his own bent, and not continue at the sabbath-school all his days ! What a wealth he thus becomes to the neighborhood. Few know how to take the census. I thank my stars for Melvin, who is such a trial to his mother. He is agreeable to me as a tinge of russet on the hillside. I would fain give thanks morning and evening for my blessings. Awkward, gawky, loose-hung, dragging his legs after him, he is my contemporary and neighbor. He is of one tribe, I of another, and we are not at war.

How quickly men come on to the highways with their sleds, and improve the first snow. The farmer has begun to play with his sled as early as any of the boys. I see him already with mittens on and thick boots well-greased, and fur cap, and red comforter about his throat, though it is not yet cold, walking beside his team with contented thoughts. This drama every day in the streets ! This is the theatre I go to. There he goes with his venture behind him, and often he gets aboard for a change.

Dec. 2, 1857. I find that according to the deed of Duncan Ingraham to John Richardson in 1797, my old beanfield at Walden Pond then belonged to George Minott. (C. Minott thinks he bought it of an Allen.) This was Deacon George Minott, who lived in the house next below the East Quarter schoolhouse, and was a brother of my grandfather-in-law. He was directly descended from Thomas Minott, who, according to Shattuck, was secretary of the abbot of Walden (!) in Essex, and whose son George was born at Saffron Walden (!) and was afterwards one of the early settlers of Dorchester.

Dec. 3, 1853. P. M. Up river by boat to Clamshell Hill. I see that muskrats have not only erected cabins, but since the river rose have in some places dug galleries a rod into the bank, pushing the sand behind them into the water. So they dig these now as places of retreat merely, or for the same purpose as the cabins apparently. One I explored this afternoon was formed in a low shore at a spot where there were weeds to make a cabin of, and was apparently never completed, perhaps because the shore was too low. Some of the clamshells, probably opened by the muskrats, and left lying on their half-sunken cabins where they are kept wet by the waves, show very handsome rainbow tints. . . . It is a somewhat saddening reflection that the beautiful colors of this shell, for want of light, cannot be said to exist, until its inhabitant has fallen a prey to the spoiler, and it is thus left a wreck upon the strand. Its beauty then beams forth, and it remains a splendid cenotaph to its departed tenant, suggesting what glory he has gone to. Though fitted to be, it is not a gem " of purest ray serene," so long as it remains in " the dark, unfathomed caves of ocean," but only when it is tossed up to light. It is as if the occupant had not begun to live, until the light, with whatever violence, is let into its shell with these magical results. These shells beaming with the tints of the sky and the rainbow commingled, suggest what pure serenity has occupied them. There the clam dwells within a little pearly heaven of its own.

Look at the trees, bare or rustling with sere brown leaves, except the evergreens; the buds dormant at the foot of the leaf-stalks; look at the fields, russet and withered, and the various sedges and weeds with dry, bleached culms : such is our relation to nature at present, such plants are we. We have no more sap, nor verdure, nor color now. I remember how cheerful it has been formerly to sit round a fire outdoors amid the snow, and while I felt some cold, to feel some warmth also, and see the fire gradually increasing and prevailing over damp steaming and dripping logs, and making a warm hearth for me. Even in winter we maintain a temperate cheer, a serene inward life, not destitute of warmth and melody.

Dec. 3, 1840. Music, in proportion as it is pure, is distant. The strains I now hear seem at an inconceivable distance, yet remotely within me. Remoteness throws all sound into my inmost being, and it becomes music, as the slumbrous sounds of the village, or the tinkling of the forge from across the water or the fields. To the senses, that is farthest from me which addresses the greatest depth within me.

Dec. 3, 1856. Mizzles and rains all day, making sloshy walking, which sends us all to the shoemaker's. Bought me a pair of cowhide boots to be prepared for winter walks. The shoemaker praised them, because they were made a year ago. I feel like an armed man now. The man who has bought his boots feels like him who has got in his winter's wood. There they stand beside me in the chamber, expectant, dreaming of far woods and wood paths, of frost - bound or sloshy roads, or of being bound with skate-straps and clogged with ice-dust.

For years my appetite was so strong that I browsed on the pine forest's edge seen against the winter horizon. How cheap my diet still!

Dry sand that has fallen in the railroad cuts, and slid on the snow beneath, is a condiment to my walk. I ranged about like a gray moose looking at the spiring tops of the trees, and fed my imagination on them, — far away, ideal trees, not disturbed by the axe of the wood - cutter. Where was the sap, the fruit, the value of the forest for me but in that line where it was relieved against the sky! That was my wood-lot; the silvery needles of the pine straining the light.

A man killed at the fatal Lincoln Bridge died in the village the other night. The only words he uttered while he lingered in his delirium were " All right," probably the last he uttered when he was struck. Brave, prophetic words to go out of the world with! Good as " I still live."

How I love the simple, reserved countrymen, my neighbors, who mind their own business and let me alone, who never waylaid nor shot at me, to my knowledge, when I crossed their fields, though each one has a gun in his house. For nearly twoscore years, I have known at a distance these long-suffering men, whom I never spoke. to, who never spoke to me, and now I feel a certain tenderness for them, as if this long probation were but the prelude to an eternal friendship. What a long trial we have withstood, and how much more admirable we are to

each other, perchance, than if we had been bed-
fellows.   I am not only grateful because Homer,
and Christ, and Shakespeare have lived, but I
am grateful for Minott, and Rice, and Melvin,
and Goodwin, and Puffer even.   I see Melvin
all alone filling his sphere in russet suit, which
no other would fill or suggest.   He takes up as
much room in nature as the most famous.

Six weeks ago I noticed the advent of chickadees, and their winter habits.   As you walk
along a woodside, a restless little flock of them,
whose notes you hear at a distance, will seem to
say, "Oh, there he goes, let's pay our respects to
him!" and they will flit after and close to you,
and naïvely peck at the nearest twig to you, as
if they were minding their own business all the
while, without any reference to you.

Dec. 3, 1857.   Surveying the Richardson lot
which bounds on Walden Pond, I turned up a
rock near the pond to make a bound with, and
found under it and attached to it, a collection of
black ants (say one fourth of an inch long), and
an inch in diameter, collected around one monster black ant, as big as four or five at least,
and a small parcel of yellowish eggs (?).   The
large ant had no wings, and was probably the
queen.   The ants were quite lively, though but
little way under the rock.   The eggs (?) adhered to the rock, when turned up.

Dec. 3, 1858. I improve every opportunity to go into a grist-mill, any excuse to see its cobweb tapestry. I put questions to the miller, as an excuse for staying, while my eye rests delighted on the cobwebs above his head, and perchance on his hat.

Dec. 3, 1859. Suddenly quite cold, and freezes in the house. Rode with a man this morning, who said that if he did not clean his teeth when he got up, it made him sick all the rest of the day, but he had found, by late experience, that when he had not cleaned his teeth for several days, they cleaned themselves. I assured him that such was the general rule, that when, from any cause, we were prevented from doing what we had commonly thought indispensable for us to do, things cleaned or took care of themselves.

—— was betrayed by his eyes, which had a glaring film over them, and no serene depth into which you could look. Inquired particularly the way to Emerson's, and the distance, and when I told him, said he knew it as well as if he saw it. Wished to turn and proceed to his house. Said, " I know I am insane," and I knew it too. He also called it " nervous excitement." At length when I made a certain remark, he said, " I don't know but you are Emerson ; are you ? you look somewhat like him." He said as much, two or three times, and added once, " but then Emerson would not lie." Finally put his questions to me, of Fate, etc., as if I *were* Emerson. Getting to the woods, I remarked upon them, and he mentioned my name, but never to the end suspected who his companion was. Then proceeded to business, " since the time was short," and put to me the questions he was going to put to Emerson. His insanity exhibited itself chiefly by his incessant excited talk, scarcely allowing me to interrupt him, but once or twice apologizing for his behavior. What he said was for the most part connected and sensible enough.

When I hear of John Brown and his wife weeping at length, it is as if the rocks sweated.

Dec. 3, 1860. Talking with —— and —— to-day, they declared that John Brown did wrong. When I said that I thought he was right, they agreed in asserting that he did wrong because he threw his life away, and that no man had a right to undertake anything which he knew would cost him his life. I inquired if Christ did not foresee that he would be crucified, if he preached such doctrines as he did, but they both (though as if it were their only escape) asserted that they did not believe he did. Upon which a third party threw in, " You do not think he had as much foresight as Brown." Of course, they as good as said that if Christ had foreseen that he would be crucified, he would have "backed out." Such are the principles and the logic of the mass of men.

It is to be remembered that by good deeds or words you encourage yourself, who always have need to witness or hear them.

Dec. 4, 1840. I seem to have experienced a joy sometimes like that with which yonder tree for so long has budded and blossomed, and reflected the green rays. The opposite shore of the pond, seen through the haze of a September afternoon, as it lies stretched out in gray content, answers to some streak in me.

Dec. 4, 1856. I notice that the swallow-holes in the bank behind Dennis's, which is partly washed away, are flat - elliptical, three times or more as wide horizontally as they are deep vertically, or about three inches by one.

Saw and heard cheep faintly one little tree sparrow, the neat, chestnut-crowned and winged, and white - barred bird, so clean and tough, made to withstand the winter. This color reminds one of the upper side of the shrub-oak leaf. The *Fringilla hiemalis* also. I love the few homely colors of Nature at this season, her strong, wholesome browns, her sober and primeval grays, her celestial blue, her vivacious green, her pure cold snowy white. Thus Nature

feeds her children cheaply with color. I have
no doubt that it is an important relief to the
eyes which have long rested on snow, to rest on
brown oak leaves and the bark of trees. We
want the greatest variety within the smallest
compass, and yet without glaring diversity, and
we have it in the colors of the withered oak
leaves ; the white, so curled, shriveled, and pale ;
the black (?), more flat and glossy, and darker
brown ; the red, much like` the black, but, per-
haps, less dark and less deeply cut. The scarlet still occasionally retains some blood in its
veins.

Smooth white reaches of ice, as long as the
river on each side, are threatening to bridge
over its dark-blue artery, any night. They
remind me of a trap set for it, which the frost
will spring. Each day, at present, the wriggling river nibbles off the edges of the trap
which have advanced in the night. It is a
close contest between day and night.

Already you see the tracks of sleds leading
by unusual routes, where will be seen no trace
of them in summer, into far fields and woods,
crowding aside and pressing down the snow,
to where some heavy log or stone has thought
itself secure, and the spreading tracks, also, of
the heavy, slow-paced oxen, and the well-shod
farmer who turns out his feet. Erelong, when

the cold is stronger, these tracks will lead the walker deep into remote swamps impassable in summer. All the earth is a highway then.

Sophia says that just before I came home, Min caught a mouse, and was playing with it in the yard. It had got away from her once or twice and she had caught it again, and now it was stealing off again, as she was complacently watching it with her paws tucked under her, when her friend, Riorden's stout cock, stepped up inquisitively, looked down at it with one eye, turning its head, then picked it up by the tail, gave it two or three whacks on the ground, and giving it a dexterous toss in the air, caught it in its open mouth, and it went, head foremost and alive, down its capacious throat in the twinkling of an eye, never again to be seen in this world ; Min all the while, with paws comfortably tucked under her, looking on unconcerned. What matters it one mouse, more or less, to her ? The cock walked off amid the currant-bushes, stretched his neck up and gulped once or twice, and the deed was accomplished. Then he crowed lustily in celebration of the exploit. It might be set down among the *Gesta gallorum.* There were several human witnesses. It is a question whether Min ever understood where that mouse went to. She sits composedly sentinel, with paws tucked under her, a good part of her days at present, by some ridiculous little hole, the possible entry of a mouse.

He who abstains from visiting another for magnanimous reasons, enjoys better society alone.

My first botany, as I remember, was " Bigelow's Plants of Boston and Vicinity," which I began to use about twenty years ago, looking chiefly for the popular names, and the short references to the localities of plants, even without any regard to the plant. I also learned the names of many, but without using any system, and forgot them soon. I was not inclined to pluck flowers, but preferred to leave them where they were, and liked them best there. I was never in the least interested in plants in the house. But from time to time we look at nature with new eyes. About half a dozen years ago, I found myself again attending to plants with more method, looking out the name of each one, and remembering it. I began to bring them home in my hat, a straw one with a scaffold lining to it, which I called my botany box. I never used any other, and when some whom I visited were evidently surprised at its dilapidated look, as I deposited it on their front entry table, I assured them it was not so much my hat, as my botany box. I remember gazing with interest at the swamps about those days, and wondering if I could ever attain to such familiarity with plants that I should know the species of every twig and leaf in them, should be acquainted with every plant (except grasses and cryptogamous ones), summer and winter, that I saw. Though I knew most of the flowers, and there were not in any particular swamp more than half a dozen shrubs that I did not know, yet these made it seem like a maze of a thousand strange species, and I even thought of commencing at one end, and looking it faithfully and laboriously through, till I knew it all. I little thought that in a year or two I should have attained to that knowledge without all that labor. Still, I never studied botany, and do not to-day, systematically, the most natural system is still so artificial. I wanted to know my neighbors, if possible, to get a little nearer to them. I soon found myself observing when plants first blossomed and leaved, and I followed it up early and late, far and near, several years in succession, running to different sides of the town and into neighboring towns, often between twenty and thirty miles in a day. I often visited a particular plant four or five miles distant half a dozen times within a fortnight, that I might know exactly when it opened, besides attending at the same time to a great many others in different directions, and some of them equally distant. At the same time I had an eye for birds and whatever else might offer.

Dec. 4, 1859. Awake to winter, and snow two or three inches deep, the first of any consequence.

Dec. 5, 1853. P. M. Got my boat in. The river frozen over thinly in most places, and whitened with snow which was sprinkled on it this noon.

4 P. M. To Cliffs. Now for short days and early twilight, in which I hear the sound of wood-chopping. The sun goes down behind a low cloud, and the world is darkened. The partridge is budding on the apple-tree, and bursts away from the pathside. Before I got home, the whole atmosphere was suddenly filled with a mellow, yellowish light equally diffused, so that it seemed much lighter around me than immediately after the sun sank behind the horizon-cloud fifteen minutes before. Apparently not till the sun had sunk thus far, did I stand in the angle of reflection.

Dec. 5, 1856. P. M. As I walk along the side of the hill, a pair of nuthatches flit by toward a walnut tree, flying low in mid course, and then ascending to the tree. I hear one's faint *tut-tut* or *quah-quah* (no doubt heard a good way off by its mate, now flown to the next tree), as it is ascending the trunk or branch of a walnut in a zigzag manner, wriggling along, prying into the crevices of the bark; and now it has found a savory morsel which it pauses to devour, then flits to a new bough. It is a chubby bird, white, slate-color, and black.

It is a perfectly cloudless and simple winter sky. A white moon half full in the pale or dull-blue heaven, and a whiteness like the reflection of the snow extending up from the horizon all around, a quarter of the way up to the zenith. I can imagine that I see it shooting up like an aurora now at 4 P. M. About the sun it is only whiter than elsewhere, or there is only the faintest possible tinge of yellow there.

My themes shall not be far-fetched. I will tell of homely, every-day phenomena and adventures. Friends, society! It seems to me that I have an abundance, there is so much that I rejoice in and sympathize with, and men, too, that I never speak to, but only know and think of. What you call bareness and poverty is to me simplicity. God could not be unkind to me, if he should try. I love the winter with its imprisonment and its cold, for it compels the prisoner to try new fields and resources. I love to have the river closed up for a season, and a pause put to my boating, to be obliged to get my boat in. I shall launch it again in the spring with so much more pleasure. This is an advantage in point of abstinence and moderation compared with the seaside boating, where the boat ever lies on the shore. I love best to have each thing in its season only, and enjoy doing without it at all other times. It is the greatest of all advantages to enjoy no advantage at all. I find it invariably true, the poorer I am, the richer I am. What you consider my disadvantage, I consider my advantage ; while you are pleased to get knowledge and culture, I am delighted to think I am getting rid of them. I have never got over my surprise that I should have been born into the most estimable place in all the world, and in the very nick of time, too.

Dec. 5, 1858. How singularly ornamented is that salamander. Its brightest side, its yellow belly, sprinkled with fine dark spots, is turned downwards. Its back is indeed ornamented with two rows of bright vermilion spots, but they can only be detected on the very closest inspection, and poor eyes fail to discover them even then, as I have found.

Dec. 6, 1854. To Providence to lecture. After lecturing twice this winter, I feel that I am in danger of cheapening myself by trying to become a successful lecturer, that is, to interest my audiences. I am disappointed to find that most that I am, and value myself for, is lost, or worse than lost, on my audience. I fail to get even the attention of the mass. I should suit them better if I suited myself less. You cannot interest them except as you are like them, and sympathize with them. I would rather that my audience should come to me, than I go to them ; that so they should be sifted ; that is, I would rather write books than lectures. To read to a promiscuous audience, who are at your mercy, the fine thoughts you solaced yourself with, far away, is as violent as to fatten geese by cramming, and in this case they do not get fatter.

Dec. 6, 1856. 2 p. m. To Hubbard's Bridge and Holden Swamp, and up river on ice to Fair Haven pond crossing, just below pond ; back on east side of river. Skating is fairly begun. I can walk through the spruce swamp now dryshod amid the water andromeda and *Kalmia glauca.* How handsome every one of these leaves that are blown about over the snow crust, or lie neglected beneath, soon to turn to mould ! Not merely a matted mass of fibres like a sheet of paper, but a perfect organism and system in itself, so that no mortal has ever yet discerned or explored its beauty. Over against this swamp, I take to the river-side where the ice will bear. White snow-ice it is, but pretty smooth. It is quite glare close to the shore, and wherever the water overflowed yesterday. Just this side of

Bittern Cliff, I see the very remarkable track of an otter, made undoubtedly December 3d, when the snow-ice was mere slush. It had come up through a hole (now black ice).by the stem of a button-bush, and apparently pushed its way through the slush, as through snow on land, leaving a track eight inches wide, more or less, with the now frozen snow shoved up two inches above the general level on each side. Where the ice was firmer were seen only the track of its feet. At Bittern Cliff I saw where these creatures had been playing, sliding or fishing, apparently to-day, on the snow-covered rocks, on which for a rod upwards and as much in width, the snow was trodden and worn quite smooth, as if twenty had trodden and slid there for several hours. Their droppings are a mass of fishes' scales and bones, loose, scaly, black masses. At this point, the black ice approached within three or four feet of the rock, and there was an open space just there a foot or two across, which appeared to have been kept open by them. I continued along on that side, and crossed on white ice just below the pond. The river was all tracked up with otters from Bittern Cliff upward. Sometimes one had trailed his tail edgewise, making a mark like the tail of a deer-mouse; sometimes they were moving fast, and there was an interval of five feet between the tracks. I saw one place where there was a zig-zag piece of black ice two rods long and a foot wide in the midst of the white, which I was surprised to find had been made by an otter pushing his way through the slush. He had left fishes' scales, etc., at the end. These very conspicuous tracks generally commenced and terminated at some button-bush or willow where black ice now marked the hole of that date. It is surprising that our hunters know no more about them. When I speak of the otter to our oldest village doctor, who should be ex officio a naturalist, he is greatly surprised, not knowing that such an animal is found in these parts, and I have to remind him that the Pilgrims sent home many otter skins in the first vessels that returned, together with beaver, mink, and black-fox skins, 1,156 pounds of other skins in the years 1631–36, which brought fourteen or fifteen shillings a pound, also 12,530 pounds of beaver skins.[1] In many places the otters appeared to have gone floundering along in the slushy ice and water.

On all sides in swamps and about their edges, and in the woods, the bare shrubs are sprinkled with buds more or less noticeable and pretty, their little gemmæ or gems their most vital and attractive parts now, almost all the greenness

[1] Vide Bradford's *History.*

and color left, greens and salads for the birds and rabbits. Our eyes go searching along the stem for what is most vivacious and characteristic, the concentrated summer gone into winter quarters. For we are hunters pursuing the summer on snow-shoes and skates all winter long, and there is really but one season in our hearts.

Dec. 7, 1838. Never do we live a quite free life, like Adam's, but are enveloped in an invisible network of speculations. Our progress is from one such speculation to another, and only at rare intervals do we perceive that it is no progress. Could we for a moment drop this by-play, and simply wonder without reference or inference !

Dec. 7, 1852. P. M. Perhaps the warmest day yet. True Indian summer. The walker perspires. The shepherd's - purse is in full bloom ; the andromeda not turned red. Saw a pile of snow-fleas in a rut in the wood-path, six or seven inches long, and three quarters of an inch high ; to the eye exactly like powder, as if a sportsman had spilled it from his flask, and when a stick was passed through the living and skipping mass, each side of the furrow preserved its edge, as in powder.

Dec. 7, 1856. Skate to Fair Haven pond. This is the first skating. It takes my feet a

few moments to get used to the skates. I see
the track of one skater who has preceded me
this morning. Now I go skating over hobbly
places, now shoot over a bridge of ice only a
foot wide between the water and the shore at a
bend. Now I suddenly see the trembling surface of water where I thought were black spots
of ice only, around me. The river is rather
low, so that I cannot keep to it above the Clamshell bend. I am confined to a very narrow
edging of ice on the meadow, gliding with unexpected ease through withered sedge, but slipping
sometimes on a twig, again taking the snow to
reach the next ice, but this rests my feet ; strad-
dling the bare black willows, winding between
the button-bushes, and following narrow thread-
ings of ice amid the sedge, which bring me out
to clear fields unexpectedly. Occasionally I am
obliged to take a few strokes over black and
thin-looking ice where the neighboring bank is
springy, and am slow to acquire confidence in it,
but returning, how bold I am ! Now I glide
over a field of white air-cells close to the surface, with covering no thicker than egg-shells,
cutting through with a sharp crackling sound.
There are many of those singular spider-shaped
dark places amid the white ice, where the surface-
water has run through some days ago. That
grand old poem called Winter is round again

without any connivance of mine. As I sit under Lee's Cliff, where the snow is melted, amid sere pennyroyal and frostbitten catnip, I look over my shoulder upon an arctic scene, and see with surprise the pond, a dumb white surface of ice speckled with snow, just as so many winters before, where so lately were lapsing waves or smooth, reflecting water. I see the holes which the pickerel fisher has made, and I see him, too, retreating over the hills drawing his sled behind him. The water is already skimmed over again, and I hear the familiar belching voice of the pond. It seemed as if winter had come without any interval since midsummer, and I was prepared to see it flit away by the time I again looked over my shoulder. It was as if I had dreamed it. The winters come now as fast as snowflakes. It is wonderful that old men do not lose their reckoning. It was summer, and now again it is winter. Nature loves this rhyme so well that she never tires of repeating it. So sweet and wholesome is the winter, so simple and moderate, so satisfactory and perfect, that her children will never weary of it. What a poem, an epic in blank verse, enriched with a million tinkling rhymes! It is solid beauty. It has been subjected to the vicissitudes of millions of years of the gods, and not a superfluous ornament remains. The severest and coldest of the immortal critics have shot their arrows at it, and pruned it, till it cannot be amended.

You will see full-grown woods where the oaks and pines and birches are separated by right lines, growing in squares or other rectilinear figures, because different lots were cut at different times.

Dec. 7, 1857. Running the long northwest side of Richardson's Fair Haven lot. It is a fine, sunny, and warm day *in the woods* for the season. We eat our dinner in the middle of the line, amid the young oaks in a sheltered and unfrequented place. I cut some leafy shrub oaks, and cast them down for a dry and springy seat. As I sit there amid the sweet fern, talking with my man, Briney, I observe that its recent shoots (which like many larger bushes and trees have a few leaves in a tuft still at the extremities) toward the sun are densely covered with a slight silvery down which looks like frost, so thick and white. Looking the other way, I see none of it, but the bare reddish twigs. Even this is a cheering and compensating discovery in my otherwise barren work. I get thus a few positive values answering to the bread and cheese which makes my dinner. I owe thus to my week's surveying a few such slight, but positive discoveries.

Dec. 8, 1838. Nothing in Nature is sneak-

ing or chap-fallen, as somewhat maltreated or
slighted, but each is satisfied with its being, and
so is as lavender and balm. If skunk-cabbage
is offensive to the nostrils of men, still has it
not drooped in consequence, but trustfully un-
folded its leaf of two handsbreadth. What was
it to Lord Byron whether England owned or
disowned him, whether he smelled sour and was
skunk-cabbage to the English nostril, or, vio-
let-like, the pride of the land and ornament of
every lady's boudoir. Let not the oyster grieve
that he has lost the race ; he has gained as an
oyster.

Dec. 8, 1850. It snowed in the night of the
6th, and the ground is now covered ; our first
snow, two inches deep. I see no tracks now of
cows or men or boys beyond the edge of the
wood. Suddenly they are shut up. The remote pastures and hills beyond the woods are
closed to cows and cowherds, aye, and to cowards. I am struck by this sudden solitude and
remoteness which these places have acquired.
The dear privacy and retirement and solitude
which winter makes possible, carpeting the
earth with snow, furnishing more than woolen
feet to all walkers ! From Fair Haven I see the
hills and fields, aye and the icy woods in the
Corner, gleam with the dear old wintry sheen.
Those are not surely the cottages I have seen all

summer. They are some cottages which I have
in my mind.

It is interesting to observe the manner in
which the plants bear their snowy burden. The
dry calyx-leaves, like an oblong cup, of the
Trichostéma dichotomum in the woodpath, have
caught the rain or melting snow, and so this
little butter-boat is filled with a frozen pure
drop which stands up high above the sides of
the cup, so many pearly drops covering the
whole plant. The pennyroyal there also retains
its fragrance under the ice and snow.

Dec. 8, 1852. One cannot burn or bury even
his old shoes without a feeling of sadness and
compassion, much more his own body, without a
slight sense of guilt.

Dec. 8, 1853. 7 A. M. How can we spare to
be abroad in the morning red, to see the forms
of the eastern trees against the dun sky, and hear
the cocks crow, when a thin low mist hangs over
the ice and frost in meadows. I have come
along the river-side in Merrick's pasture to collect for kindling the fat pine roots and knots
which the spearers dropped last spring, and
which the floods have washed up. Get a heaping bushel-basket full.

Dec. 8, 1854. P. M. Up river and meadow
on ice to Hubbard's Bridge, and thence to Walden. Winter has come unnoticed by me, I

have been so busy writing. This is the life most lead in respect of nature. How different from my habitual one! It is hasty, coarse, and trivial, as if you were a spindle in a factory. The other is leisurely, fine, and glorious, like a flower. In the first case, you are merely getting your living. In the second, you live as you go along. You travel only on roads of the proper grade, without jar or running off the track, and sweep around the hills by beautiful curves.

Here is the river frozen over in many places. The skating is all hobbled like a coat of mail or thickly bossed shield, apparently sleet frozen in water. How black the water where the river is open, when I look from the light, by contrast with the surrounding white, the ice and snow! a black artery, here and there concealed under a pellicle of ice. Went over the fields on the crust, to Walden, over side of Bear Garden. Already foxes have left their tracks. How the crust shines afar, the sun now setting. There is a glorious clear sunset sky, soft and delicate and warm, even like a pigeon's neck. Why do the mountains never look so fair as from my native fields?

Dec. 8, 1855. This afternoon I go to the woods down the railroad, seeking the society of some flock of little birds, or some squirrel, but in vain. I only hear the faint lisp of probably a

tree sparrow. I go through empty halls, apparently unoccupied by bird or beast. Yet it is
cheering to walk there, while the sun is reflected
from far through the aisles with a silvery light
from the needles of the pine. The contrast of
light or sunshine and shade, though the latter
is now so thin, is food enough for me. In a
little busy flock of lisping birds, chickadees or
lesser red-polls, even in a nuthatch or downy
woodpecker, there would have been a sweet
society for me. But I did not find it. Yet I
had the sun penetrating into the deep hollows
through the aisles of the wood, and the silvery
sheen of its reflection from masses of white pine
needles.

Jacob Farmer brought me the head of a mink
to-night, and took tea here. He says he can
call a male quail close to him by imitating
the note of the female, which is only a faint
whistle.

Dec. 8, 1856. 8° above zero. Probably the
coldest day yet.

Bradford, in his history of the Plymouth Plantation, remembering the condition of the Pilgrims on their arrival in Cape Cod Bay the 11th
of November, 1620, O. S., says (p. 79), " Which
way so ever they turned their eyes (save upward to the heavens) they could have little solace or content in respect of any outward objects,

for, summer being done, all things stared upon them with a weather beaten face, and the whole country, full of woods and thickets, represented a wild and savage hue." Such was a New England November, in 1620, to Bradford's eyes, and such no doubt it would be to his eyes in the country still. It required no little courage to found a colony here at that season of the year. The earliest mention of anything like a glaze in New England that I remember is in the same History, p. 83, where Bradford describes the second expedition from Cape Cod Harbor in search of a settlement, the 6th of December, O. S. : " The weather was very cold, and it froze so hard as the spray of the sea lighting on their coats, they were as if they had been glazed." Bradford was one of the ten principal persons. That same night they reached the bottom of the Bay, and saw the Indians cutting up a black-fish. Nature has not changed one iota.

Dec. 8, 1857. S—— says he came to Concord twenty-four years ago, a poor boy, with a dollar and three cents in his pocket, and he spent the three cents for drink at Bigelow's tavern, and now he is worth " twenty hundred dollars clear." He remembers many who inherited wealth whom he could buy out to-day. I told him that he had done better than I, in a pecuniary respect, for I had only earned my living. " Well," said he, "that 's all I 've done, and I don't know as I 've got much better clothes than you." I was particularly poorly clad then, in the woods ; my hat, pants, boots, rubbers, and gloves would not have brought fourpence, and I told the Irishman that it was n't everybody could afford to have a fringe round his legs, as I had, my corduroys not preserving a selvage.

Dec. 8, 1859. How is it that what is actually present and transpiring is commonly perceived by the common sense and understanding only, is bare and bald, without halo, or the blue enamel of intervening air ? But let it be past or to come, and it is at once idealized. The man dead is spiritualized, the fact remembered is idealized. It is ripe and with the bloom on it. It is not simply the understanding now, but the imagination that takes cognizance of it. The imagination requires a long range. It is the faculty of the poet to see present things as if in this sense past and future, as if distant or universally significant. We do not know poets, heroes, and saints for our contemporaries, but we locate them in some far off vale ; the greater and better, the farther off we are accustomed to consider them. We believe in spirits, we believe in beauty, but not now and here. They have their abode in the remote past, or in the future.

Dec. 9, 1852. p. m. To A. Smith's hill. Those little ruby-crowned lesser red-polls still about. They suddenly flash away from this side to that, in flocks, with a tumultuous note, half gurgle, half rattle, like nuts shaken in a bag, or a bushel of nutshells, soon returning to the tree they had forsaken on some alarm. They are oftenest seen on the white birch, apparently feeding on its seeds, scattering the scales about.

A fresh dandelion. The chestnuts are about as plenty as ever, both in the fallen burrs and out of them. There are more this year than the squirrels can consume. I picked three pints this afternoon, and did not find one mouldy one among those which I picked from under the wet and mouldy leaves. They are plump and tender. I love to gather them, if only for the sense of the bountifulness of nature they give me. A few petals of the witch hazel still hold on. A man tells me he saw a violet to-day.

In the " Homes of American Authors," it is said of most that at one time they wrote for the " North American Review." It is one of my qualifications that I have not written an article for the " North American Review."

Dec. 9, 1856. p. m. Railroad to Lincoln bridge and back by road. From a little east of Wyman's I look over the pond westward. The sun is near setting, away beyond Fair Haven.

A bewitching stillness reigns through all the woodland, and over all the snow-clad landscape. Indeed, the winter day in the woods or fields has commonly the stillness of twilight. The pond is perfectly smooth and full of light. I hear only the strokes of a lingering woodchopper at a distance and the melodious hooting of an owl, which is as common and marked a sound as that of the axe or the locomotive whistle ; yet where does the ubiquitous hooter sit? and who sees him? In whose wood-lot is he to be found? Few eyes have rested on him hooting, few on him silent on his perch even, yet cut away the woods never so much year after year, though the chopper has not seen him, and only a grove or two is left, still his aboriginal voice is heard indefinitely far and sweet, mingled oft in strange harmony with the newly invented din of trade, hooting from his invisible perch at his foes, the woodchoppers who are invading his domains. As the earth only a few inches beneath the surface is undisturbed and what it was anciently, so are heard still some primeval sounds in the air. Some of my townsmen I never see, and of a great proportion I do not hear the voices in a year, though they live within my horizon ; but every week almost, I hear the loud voice of the hooting owl, though I do not see the bird more than once in ten years.

I perceive that more or other things are seen in the reflection than in the substance. As I look over the pond westward, I see in substance the now bare outline of Fair Haven Hill, a mile beyond ; whereas in the reflection I see not this, only the tops of some pines which stand close to the shore, but are invisible against the dark hill beyond, and these are indefinitely prolonged into points of shadow.

The sun is set, and over the valley which looks like an outlet of Walden toward Fair Haven, I see a burnished bar of cloud stretched low and level, as if it were the bar over that passage-way to Elysium, the last column in the train of the sun. When I get as far as my bean-field, the reflected white in the winter horizon of the perfectly cloudless sky is being condensed at the horizon's edge, and its hue deepening into a dun golden, against which the tops of the trees, pines and elms, are seen with a beautiful distinctness, and a slight blush begins to suffuse the eastern horizon, and so the picture of the day is done, and set in a gilded frame. Such is a winter eve. Now for a merry fire, some old poet's pages, or else serene philosophy, or even a healthy book of travels, to last far into the night, eked out perhaps with the walnuts which we gathered in November.

The worker who would accomplish much these

short days, must shear a dusky slice off both ends of the night. The chopper must work as long as he can see, often returning home by moonlight, and set out for the woods again by candle-light.

The northwest wind meeting the current in an exposed place produces that hobbly ice which I described at Cardinal Shore day before yesterday. Such is the case in this place every year, and no doubt the same phenomenon occurred annually at this point in the river, a thousand years before America was discovered. This regularity and permanence make these phenomena more interesting to me.

Dec. 9, 1858. At New Bedford. See a song sparrow and a pigeon woodpecker. Dr. Bryant tells of the latter pecking holes in blinds, and also in his barn roof and sides in order to get into it, holes in the window sashes or casings, as if a nail had been driven into them.

Dec. 10, 1837. Not the carpenter alone carries his rule in his pocket. Space is quite subdued to us. The meanest peasant finds in a hair of his head, or the white crescent upon his nail, the unit of measure for the distance of the fixed stars. His middle finger measures how many *digits* into space. He extends a few times his thumb and finger, and the continent is *spanned.* He stretches out his arms, and the sea is fathomed.

Dec. 10, 1840.   I discover a strange track in
the snow, and learn that some migrating otter
has made across from the river to the wood, by
my yard and the smith's shop, in the silence of
the night.   I cannot but smile at my own wealth
when I am thus reminded that every chink and
cranny of nature is full to overflowing.   Such
an incident as this startles me with the assurance that the primeval nature is still working,
and makes tracks in the snow.   It is my own
fault that he must thus skulk across my premises by night.   Now I yearn toward him, and
heaven to me consists in a complete communion with the otter nature.   He travels a more
wooded path by watercourses and hedgerows, I
by the highways, but though his tracks are now
crosswise to mine, our courses are not divergent,
but we shall meet at last.

Mere innocence will tame any ferocity.

Dec. 10, 1853.   Another still more glorious
day, if possible.   Indian summer, even.   These
are among the finest days in the year, on account
of the wholesome bracing coolness and clearness.
Paddled up Assabet.   Passed in some places between shooting ice crystals extending from both
sides of the stream.   Upon the thinnest black
ice crystals, just cemented, was the appearance
of broad fern leaves or ostrich plumes, or flat
fir-trees with branches bent down.   The surface

was far from even, rather in sharp-edged plaits
and folds. The form of the crystals was oftenest that of low flattish or three-sided pyramids.
When the base was very broad, the apex was
imperfect, with many irregular rosettes of small
and perfect pyramids, the largest with bases
two or three inches long. All this appeared to
advantage only while the ice (one twelfth of an
inch thick, perhaps), rested on the black water.

What I write about at home, I understand so
well comparatively, and I write with such repose and freedom from exaggeration.

Dec. 10, 1854. P. M. To Nut Meadow.
Weather warmer. Snow softened. Saw a large
flock of snow-buntings (quite white against
woods, at any rate), though it is quite warm.
Snow-fleas in paths ; first I have seen. Hear
the small woodpecker's whistle ; not much else,
only crows and partridges and chickadees. How
quickly the snow feels the warmer wind. The
crust, which was so firm and rigid, is now suddenly softened, and there is much water in the
road.

Dec. 10, 1856. A fine, clear, cold winter
morning, with a small leaf-frost on trees, etc.
The thermometer at 7.15 and 7.30 A. M., 3° +

It is remarkable how suggestive the slightest
drawing is as a memento of things seen. For a
few years past I have been accustomed to make

a rude sketch in my journal, of plants, ice, and various natural phenomena, and though the fullest accompanying description may fail to recall my experience, these rude outline drawings do not fail to carry me back to that time and scene. It is as if I saw the same thing again, and I may again attempt to describe it in words, if I choose.

Yesterday I walked under the murderous Lincoln bridge, where at least ten men have been swept dead from the cars within as many years. I looked to see if their heads had indented the bridge, if there were sturdy blows given as well as received, and if their brains lay about. The place looks as innocent as " a bank whereon the wild thyme grows." The bridge does its work in an artistic manner. We have another of exactly the same character in another part of the town, which has killed one, at least, to my knowledge. Surely the approaches to our town are well guarded. These are our modern dragons of Wantley. Buccaneers of the Fitchburg Railroad, they lie in wait at the narrow passes, and decimate the employees. The Company has signed a bond to give up one employee at this pass annually. The Vermont mother commits her son to their charge, and when she asks for him again, the directors say, " I am not your son's keeper ; go look beneath the ribs of the Lincoln bridge." It is a monster which would not have minded Perseus with his Medusa's head. If he could be held back only four feet from where he now crouches, all travelers might pass in safety, and laugh him to scorn. This would require but a little resolution in our legislature, but it is preferred to pay tribute still.

Dec. 11, 1840. A man who had failed to fulfill an engagement, and grossly disappointed me, came to me to-night with a countenance radiant with repentance, and so behaved that it seemed as if I was the defaulter and could not be satisfied till he would let me stand in that light. How long a course of strict integrity might have come short of such confidence and good will! The crack of his whip was before attractive enough, but such conciliatory words from that shaggy coat and coarse comforter I had not expected. I saw the meaning which lurked far behind eye, all the better for the dark, as we see some faint stars better when we do not look directly at them with the full light of the eye. A true contrition, when witnessed, will humble integrity itself.

Dec. 11, 1853. To Heywood's Pond and up brook. Almost a complete Indian-summer day, clear and warm. I am without greatcoat. Ch. says he saw larks yesterday, a painted tor-

toise the day before, under ice at White Pond,
and a ground robin (?) last week. He conjectures, I am told, that the landscape looks fairer
when we turn our heads upside down, because
we behold it with nerves of the eye unused
before. Perhaps this reason is worth more for
suggestion than explanation. It occurs to me
that the reflection of objects in still water is in
a similar manner fairer than the substance, and
yet we do not employ unused nerves to behold
it. Is it not that we let much more light into
our eyes (which in the usual position are shaded
by the brows), in the first case, by turning them
more to the sky, and in the case of the reflections, by having the sky placed under our feet?
that is, in both cases we see terrestrial objects,
with the sky or heavens for a background or
field ; accordingly they are not dark or terrene,
but lit and elysian.

Dec. 11, 1854. P. M. To Bare Hill. We
have now those early, still, clear winter sunsets
over the snow. It is but mid-afternoon when I
see the sun setting far through the woods, and
there is that peculiar, clear, vitreous, greenish
sky in the west, as it were, a molten gem. The
day is short. It seems to be composed of two
twilights merely. The morning and the evening
twilight make the whole day. You must make
haste to do the work of the day before it is dark.

I hear rarely a bird except the chickadee, or perchance a jay or a crow. A gray rabbit scuds away over the crust in the swamp on the edge of the Great Meadows beyond Peters's. A partridge goes off, and coming up, I see where she struck the snow with her wings, making five or six, as it were, finger-marks.

Dec. 11, 1855. P. M. To Holden Swamp, Conantum. For the first time I wear gloves, but I have not walked early this season. I see no birds, but hear, I think, one or two tree sparrows. No snow, scarcely any ice to be detected ; it is only aggravated November. I thread the tangle of the spruce swamp, admiring the leaflets of the swamp pyrus which had put forth again, now frost-bitten, the great yellow buds of the swamp pink, the round red buds of the high blueberry, and the firm sharp red ones of the panicled andromeda. Slowly I worm my way amid the snarl, the thicket of black alder, blueberry, etc., see the forms, apparently of rabbits, at the foot of maples, and cat-birds' nests now exposed in the leafless thicket. Standing there, though in this bare November landscape, I am reminded of the incredible phenomenon of small birds in winter, that erelong, amid the cold, powdery snow, as it were a fruit of the season, will come twittering a flock of delicate, crimson-tinged birds, lesser red-polls, to sport and feed on the seeds and buds just ripe for them on the sunny side of a wood, shaking down the powdery snow there in their cheerful social feeding, as if it were high midsummer to them. These crimson aerial creatures have wings which would bear them quickly to the regions of summer, but here is all the summer they want. What a rich contrast! tropical colors, crimson breasts, on cold white snow! Such etherealness, such delicacy in their forms, such ripeness in their colors, in this stern and barren season! It is as surprising as if you were to find a brilliant crimson flower which flourished amid snow. They greet the hunter and the chopper in their furs. Their maker gave them the last touch, and launched them forth the day of the Great Snow. He made this bitter imprisoning cold, before which man quails, but he made at the same time these warm and glowing creatures to twitter and be at home in it. He said not only, let there be linnets in winter, but linnets of rich plumage and pleasing twitter, bearing summer in their natures. The snow will be three feet deep, the ice will be two feet thick, and last night, perchance, the mercury sank to thirty degrees below zero. All the fountains of nature seem to be sealed up. The traveler is frozen on his way, but under the edge of yonder birch wood will be a little flock of crimson-breasted lesser

red-polls, feeding on the seeds of the birch, as
if a flower were created to be now in bloom, a
peach to be now first fully ripe on its stem. I
am struck by the perfect confidence and success
of Nature. There is no question about the existence of these delicate creatures, their adapt-
edness to their circumstances. There is added
superfluous painting and adornment, a crystalline, jewel-like health and soundness, like the
colors reflected from ice-crystals. When some
rare northern bird, like the pine grossbeak, is
seen thus far south, in the winter, he does not
suggest poverty, but dazzles us with his beauty.
There is in them a warmth that is akin to the
warmth that melts the icicle. Here is no im-
perfection suggested. The winter with its snow
and ice is not an evil to be corrected. It is as
it was designed and made to be, for the artist
has had leisure to add beauty to use. I had
a vision thus prospectively, as I stood in the
swamp, of these birds, my acquaintances, angels
from the north. I saw this familiar, too familiar
fact, at a different angle, and I was charmed and
haunted by it.* I had seen into paradisaic regions with their air and sky, and I was no longer
wholly or merely a denizen of this vulgar earth.
Yet I had hardly a foothold there. It is only
necessary to behold thus the least fact or phenomenon, however familiar, from a point a hair's

breadth aside from our habitual path or routine, to be overcome, enchanted by its beauty and significance.   Only what we have touched and worn is trivial, our scurf, repetition, tradition, conformity.   To perceive freshly, with fresh senses, is to be inspired.   Great winter itself looked like a precious gem reflecting rainbow colors from one angle.   My body is all sentient.   As I go here or there, I am tickled by this or that I come in contact with, as if I touched the wires of a battery.   I can generally recall, have fresh in my mind, several scratches last received. These I continually recall to mind, reimpress and harp upon.   The age of miracles is each moment thus returned ; now it is wild apples, now river reflections, now a flock of lesser red-polls.   In winter, too, resides immortal youth and perennial summer.   Its head is not silvered, its cheek is not blanched, but has a ruby tinge in it.   If any part of nature excites our pity, it is for ourselves we grieve, for *there* is eternal health and beauty.   We get only transient and partial glimpses of the beauty of the world. Standing at the right angle, we are dazzled by the colors of the rainbow in colorless ice.   From the right point of view, every storm and every drop in it is a rainbow.   Beauty and music are not mere traits and exceptions ; they are the rule and character.   It is the exception that we see and hear. Then I try to discover what it was in the vision that charmed and translated me. What if we could daguerreotype our thoughts and feelings ! — for I am surprised and enchanted often by some quality which I cannot detect. I have seen an attribute of another world and condition of things. It is a wonderful fact that I should be affected, and thus deeply and powerfully, more than by aught else in all my experience, that this fruit should be borne in me, sprung from a seed finer than the spores of fungi floated from other atmospheres ! finer than the dust caught in the sails of vessels a thousand miles from land ! Here the invisible seeds settle, and spring, and bear flowers and fruits of immortal beauty.

Dec. 11, 1856. Minott tells me that his and his sister's wood-lot contains about ten acres, and has, with a very slight exception at one time, supplied all their fuel for thirty years, and he thinks would constantly continue to do so. They keep one fire all the time, and two some of the time, and burn about eight cords in a year. He knows his wood-lot, and what grows in it, as well as an ordinary farmer does his cornfield, for he has cut his own wood till within two or three years, knows the history of every stump on it, and the age of every sapling, knows how many beech-trees and black birches there are, as another knows his pear or cherry trees. It is more economical as well as more poetical to have a wood-lot, and cut and get your own wood from year to year than to buy it at your own door. Minott may say to his trees, " Submit to my axe ; I cut your father on this very spot." How many sweet passages there must have been in his life there, chopping all alone in the short winter days ! How many rabbits, partridges, foxes he saw ! A rill runs through the lot where he quenched his thirst, and several times he has laid it bare. At last rheumatism has made him a prisoner, and he is compelled to let a stranger, a vandal it may be, go into his lot with an axe. It is fit that he should be buried there.

Dec. 12, 1837. There are times when thought elbows her way through the underwood of words to the clear blue beyond : —

> " O'er bog or steep, though strait, rough, dense, or rare,
> With head, hands, wings, or feet, pursues her way,
> And swims, or sinks, or wades, or creeps, or flies."

But let her don her cumbersome working-day garment, and each sparkling dewdrop will seem a " Slough of Despond."

When we speak of a peculiarity in a man or a nation, we think sometimes to describe a mere mathematical point. But in fact it pervades the whole, as a drop of wine in a glass of water tinges the whole glass. Some parts may be further removed than others from the centre, but not a particle so remote as not to be shined on or shaded by it.

No part of man's nature is formed with a useless or sinister intent. In no respect can he be wholly bad, but the worst passions have their root in the best. So a spine is proved to be only an abortive branch " which, notwithstanding, even as a spine, bears leaves, and in *Euphorbia heptagona,* sometimes flowers and fruit."

Dec. 12, 1840. Society seems very natural and easy. Can I not walk among men as simply as in the woods ? I am greeted everywhere with mild looks and words, and it seems as if the eaves were running, and I heard the sough of melting snow all around me.

The young pines springing up in the cornfields from year to year are to me a much more refreshing fact than the most abundant harvests. My last stronghold is the forest.

Dec. 12, 1851. In regard to my friends, I feel that I know and have communion with a finer and subtler part of themselves which does not put me off when they put me off, which is not cold to me when they are cold, not till I am cold. I hold by a deeper and stronger tie than absence can sunder.

Ah, dear nature, the mere remembrance, after

a short forgetfulness, of the pine woods! I come to it as a hungry man to a crust of bread.

I have been surveying for twenty or thirty days, living coarsely, even as respects my diet (for I find that will always alter to suit my employment), indeed leading a quite trivial life, and to-night, for the first time, made a fire in my chamber and endeavored to return to myself. I wished to ally myself to the powers that rule the universe. I wished to dive into some deep stream of thoughtful and devoted life which meanders through retired and fertile meadows far from towns. I wished to do again, or for once, things quite congenial to my highest, inmost, and most sacred nature, to lurk in crystalline thought like the trout under verdurous banks where stray mankind should only see my bubble come to the surface. I wished to live, ah, as far away as a man can think. I wished for leisure and quiet to let my life flow in its proper channels, with its proper currents, when I might not waste the days, might establish daily prayer and thanksgiving in my family, might do my own work, and not the work of Concord and Carlisle, which would yield me better than money. I bethought myself, while my fire was kindling, to open one of Emerson's books, which it happens that I rarely look at, to try what a chance sentence out of that could do for me, thinking at the same time of a conversation I had with him the other night, I finding fault with him for the stress he had laid on some of Margaret Fuller's whims and superstitions, but he declaring gravely that she was one of those persons whose experience warranted her attaching importance to such things as the *Sortes Virgilianæ,* for instance, of which her numerous friends could give remarkable accounts. At any rate, I saw that he was disposed to regard such things more seriously than I. The first sentence which I opened upon in his book was this, " If, with a high trust, he can thus submit himself, he will find that ample returns are poured into his bosom, out of what seemed hours of obstruction and loss. Let him not grieve too much on account of unfit associates," etc. ; " in a society of perfect sympathy, no word, no act, no record would be. He will learn that it is not much matter what he reads, what he does. Be a scholar, and he shall have the scholar's part of everything," etc. Most of this corresponded well enough with my mood, and this would be as good an instance of the *Sortes Virgilianæ* as most, to quote. But what makes this coincidence very little, if at all, remarkable to me, is the fact of the obviousness of the moral, so that I had perhaps thought the same thing myself twenty times during the day, and yet had not been contented with that account of it, leaving me thus to be amused by the coincidence, rather than impressed as by an intimation out of the deeps.

How much forbearance, aye, sacrifice and loss, goes to every accomplishment! I am thinking by what long discipline and at what cost, a man learns to speak simply at last.

Nothing is so sure to make itself known as the truth, for what else waits to be known.

Dec. 12, 1852. Colder at last. Saw a violet on the C. Miles road where the bank had been burned in the fall. *Beomyces rosea*, also. Tansy still fresh yellow, by the lower bridge. From Cliffs, I see snow on the mountains. Last night's rain was then snow there. They now have a parti - colored look, like the skin of a pard, as if they were spread with a saddle-cloth for Boreas to ride. I hear of a cultivated rose blossoming in a garden in Cambridge within a day or two. The buds of the aspen are large, and show wool in the fall.

Dec. 12, 1856. Wonderful, wonderful is our life, and that of our companions! That there should be such a thing as a brute animal, not human! that it should attain to a sort of society with our race! Think of cats, for instance ; they are neither Chinese nor Tartars, they neither go to school, nor read the Testament. Yet how near they come to doing so, how much they are like us who do so. At length without having solved any of these problems, we fatten and kill and eat some of our cousins !

Where is the great natural historian ? Is he a butcher ? or the patron of butchers ? As well look for a great anthropologist among cannibals or New Zealanders.

Dec. 12, 1858. Up river on ice to Fair Haven Hill. I see an immense flock of snow buntings, I think the largest I ever saw. There must be a thousand or two, at least. There is but three inches at most of crusted and dry frozen snow, and they are running . amid the weeds that rise above it. They are very restless, and continually changing their ground. They will suddenly rise again a few seconds after they have alighted, as if alarmed, but after a short wheel, settle close by. As they fly from you in some positions, you see only or chiefly the black part of their bodies, and then as they wheel, the white comes into view, contrasted prettily with the former, and in all together at the same time. Seen flying higher against a cloudy sky, they look like snowflakes. When they rise all together, their note is like the rattling of nuts in a bag, as if a whole bin-full were rolled from side to side. They also utter from time to time, that is, individuals do, à clear rippling note, perhaps an alarm or call. It is remarkable that their note, above described, should resemble the lesser red-polls'. Away goes the great wheeling, rambling flock, rolling through the air, and you cannot easily tell where they will settle. Suddenly the pioneers, or a part not foremost, will change their course, when in full career, and, when at length they know it, the rushing flock on the other side will be fetched about, as it were, with an undulating jerk, as in the boys' game of snap-the-whip, and those that occupy the place of the snapper are gradually off after their leaders on the new track. Like a snowstorm, they come rushing down from the north. They are unusually abundant now. I should like to know where all these snowbirds will roost to-night, for they will probably roost together. What havoc an owl might make among them! So far as I observe, they confine themselves to the uplands, not alighting in the meadows. But Melvin tells me he saw a thousand feeding a long time in the Great Meadows, he thinks on the seeds of the wool grass, about the same time I saw those above described.

Dec. 13, 1851. Surveying to-day. We had one hour of most Indian-summer weather in the middle of the day. I felt the influence of the sun. It softened my stoniness a little. The pines looked like old friends again. Cutting a path through swamp where was much brittle dogwood, etc., I wanted to know the name of every bush. This varied employment to which my necessities compel me serves instead of foreign travel and the lapse of time. If it makes me forget some things which I ought to remember, it no doubt makes me forget many things which I ought to forget. By stepping aside from my chosen path so often, I see myself better, and am enabled to criticise myself better. It seems an age since I took walks and wrote in my journal, and when shall I revisit the glimpses of the moon? To be able to see ourselves, not merely as others see us, but as we are, that service a variety of absorbing employments does us.

I would not be rude to the fine intimations of the gods for fear of incurring the reproach of superstition.

Saw Perez Blood in his frock, — a stuttering, sure, unpretending man, who does not speak without thinking, does not guess. When I reflected how different he was from his neighbors, I saw that it was not so much outwardly, but that I saw an inner form. We do indeed see through and through each other, through the veil of the body, and see the real form and character, in spite of the garment. Any coarseness or tenderness is seen and felt under whatever garb.

How nakedly men appear to us, for the spiritual assists the natural eye.

Dec. 13, 1852. Walk early through the woods to Lincoln to survey. Winter weather may be said to have begun yesterday. Why have I ever omitted early rising and a morning walk? As we walked over the Cedar Hill, Mr. Weston asked me if I had ever noticed how the frost formed about a particular weed in the grass, and no other. It was a clear cold morning. We stooped to examine, and I observed about the base of the cistus the frost formed into little flattened trumpets or bells, an inch or more long, with the mouths down about the base of the stem. They were very conspicuous, dotting the grass white. But the most remarkable thing about it was that though there were plenty of other dead weeds and grasses about, no other species exhibited this phenomenon. I think it can hardly be because of the form of its top, and that therefore the moisture is collected and condensed, and flows down its stem. It may have something to do with the life of the root, which I noticed was putting forth shoots beneath. Perhaps the growth generates heat and so steam.

Dec. 13, 1855. Sanborn tells me that he was waked up a few nights ago in Boston about midnight by the sound of a flock of geese passing over the city, probably about the same night I heard them here. They go honking over cities where the arts flourish, waking the inhabitants, over state-houses and capitols, where legislatures sit, over harbors where fleets lie at anchor, — mistaking the city, perhaps, for a swamp or the edge of a lake, about settling in it, not suspecting that it is preoccupied by greater geese than themselves.

Dec. 13, 1857. In sickness and barrenness, it is encouraging to believe that our life is dammed, and is coming to a head, so that there seems to be no loss, for what is lost in time is gained in power. All at once, unaccountably, as we are walking in the woods, or sitting in our chamber, after a worthless fortnight, we cease to feel mean and barren.

Dec. 13, 1859. My first true winter walk is perhaps that which I take on the river, or where I cannot go in the summer. It is the walk peculiar to winter, and now first ·I take it. I see that the fox has already taken the same walk before me, just along the edge of the button-bushes where not even he can go in the summer. We both turn our steps hither at the same time.

Now at 2.30 P. M., the melon-rind arrangement of the clouds, really parallel columns of fine mackerel sky reaching quite across the heavens from west to east, with clear intervals of blue sky ; and a fine-grained vapor like spun glass extending in the same direction beneath the former. In half an hour, all the mackerel sky is gone.

What an ever-changing scene is the sky, its drifting cirrus and stratus! The spectators are not requested to take a recess of fifteen minutes while the scene changes, but, walking commonly with our faces to the earth, our thoughts revert to other objects, and as often as we look up, the scene has changed. Now I see it is a column of white vapor reaching quite across the sky from west to east, with locks of fine hair or tow that is carded, combed out on each side, surprising touches here and there which show a peculiar state of the atmosphere. No doubt the best weather signs are in these forms which the vapor takes. When I next look up the locks of hair are perfect fir-trees, with their recurved branches. These trees extend at right angles from the side of the main column. This appearance is changed all over the sky in one minute.

Again it is pieces of asbestos, or the vapor takes the curved form of the surf or breakers, and again, of flames.

But how long can a man be in a mood to watch the heavens? That melon-rind arrangement, so very common, is perhaps a confirmation of Wise the balloonist's statement that at a

certain height there is a current of air moving
from west to east. Hence we so commonly
see the clouds arranged in parallel divisions in
that direction. What a spectacle the subtle
vapors that have their habitation in the sky present these winter days ! You have not only un-
varying forms of a given type of cloud, but various types at different heights or hours. It is a
scene, for variety, for beauty and grandeur, out
of all proportion to the attention it gets. Who
watched the forms of the clouds over this part
of the earth a thousand years ago? who watches
them to-day ?

When I reach the causeway at the Cut, returning, the sun has just set, a perfect winter
sunset, so fair and pure, with its golden and
purple isles, I think the summer rarely equals it.
There are real damask-colored isles or continents
north of the sun's place, and further off northeast they pass into bluish purple. Hayden's
house, one which I see there, seems the abode of
the blessed. The eastern horizon also is purple.
But that part of the parallel cloud columns overhead is now invisible. At length, the purple
travels westward, as the sunk sinks lower below
the horizon, the clouds overhead are brought
out, and so the purple glow glides down the
western sky.

Dec. 14, 1840. How may a man most cleanly

and gracefully depart out of nature? At present his birth and death are offensive and unclean things. Disease kills him and his carcass smells to heaven. It offends the bodily sense only so much as his life offended the moral sense. It is the odor of sin. His carcass invites sun and moisture, and makes haste to burst forth into new and disgusting forms of life with which it already teemed. It was no better than carrion before, but just animated enough to keep off the crows. The birds of prey which hover in the rear of an army are an intolerable satire on mankind, and may well make the soldier shudder. The mosquito sings our dirge, he is Charon come to ferry us over the Styx. He preaches a biting homily to us. He says, put away beef and pork, small beer and ale, and my trump shall die away, and be no more heard. The intemperate cannot go nigh to any wood or marsh, but he hears his requiem sung. Man lays down his body in the field, and thinks from it, as a stepping-stone, to vault at once into heaven, as if he could establish a better claim, when he had left such a witness behind him on the plain. Our true epitaphs are those which the sun and wind write upon the atmosphere around our graves so conclusively that the traveler does not draw near to read the lie on our tombstones. Shall we not be judged rather by what we leave behind us, than by what we bring into the world ? The guest is known by his leavings. When we have become intolerable to ourselves, shall we be tolerable to heaven? Will our spirits ascend pure and fragrant from our tainted carcasses? May we not suffer our impurities gradually to evaporate in sun and wind with the superfluous juices of the body, and so wither and dry up, at last, like a tree in the woods, which possesses a sort of embalmed life after death, and is as clean as the sapling or fresh buds of spring? Let us die by *dry* rot at least. The dead tree still stands erect without shame or offense amidst its green brethren, the most picturesque object in the wood. The painter puts it into the foreground of his picture, for in its death it is still remembered. When Nature finds man returned on her hands, he is not simply the pure elements she has contributed to his growth, but with her floods she must wash away, and with her fires burn up the filth that has accumulated, before she can receive her own again. He poisons her gales, and is a curse to the land that gave him birth. She is obliged to employ her scavengers in self-defense to abate the nuisance. May not man cast his shell with as little offense as the mussel, and it, perchance, be a precious relic to be kept in the cabinets of the curious ? May we not amuse ourselves with it, as when we count the layers of a shell, and apply it to our ear, to hear the history of its inhabitant in the swells of the sea, the pulsation of the life which once passed therein still faintly echoed ? We confess that it was well done in Nature thus to let out her particles of lime to the mussel and coral, to receive them back again with such interest.

The ancients were more tidy than we, who subjected the body to the purification of fire before they returned it upon nature, for fire is the true washer ; water only displaces the impurity. Fire is thorough, water is superficial.

Dec. 14, 1851. As for the weather, all seasons are pretty much alike to one who is actively at work in the woods. I should say that there were two or three remarkably warm days, and as many cold ones in the course of the year, but the rest are all alike in respect to temperature. This is my answer to my acquaintances, who ask if I have not found it very cold being out all day.

I hear the small woodpecker whistle as he flies toward the leafless wood on Fair .Haven, doomed to be out this winter. The chickadees remind me of Hudson's Bay for some reason. I look on them as natives of a more northern latitude.

The now dry and empty, but clean-washed cups of the blue curls spot the half snow-covered grain-fields. Where lately was a delicate blue flower, now all the winter are held up these dry chalices. What mementos to stand above the snow!

Why not live out more yet, and have my friends and relatives altogether in nature? only my acquaintances among the villagers? That way diverges from this I follow, not at a sharp, but a very wide angle. Ah, nature is serene and immortal. Am I not one of the Zincali?

There are certain places where the ice will always be open, where, perchance, warmer springs come in. There are such places in every character, genial and open in the coldest seasons.

I come from contact with certain acquaintances, whom even I am disposed to look toward as possible friends. It oftenest happens that I come from them wounded. Only they can wound me seriously, and that perhaps without their knowing it.

Dec. 14, 1852. Ah, who can tell the serenity and clarity of a New England winter sunset? This could not be till the cold and the snow came. What isles those western clouds, in what a sea!

Dec. 14, 1854. P. M. With C. up north

bank of Assabet to Bridge. The river is open almost its whole length. It is a beautifully smooth mirror with an icy frame. It is well to improve such a time to walk by it. This strip of water of irregular width over the channel between broad fields of ice looks like a polished silver mirror, or like another surface of polished ice, and often is distinguished from the surrounding ice only by its reflections. I have rarely seen any reflections (of weeds, willows, and elms, and the houses of the village) so distinct, the stems so black and distinct, for they contrast not with a green meadow, but clear white ice, to say nothing of the silvery surface of the water. Your eye slides first over a plane surface of smooth ice of one color, to a watery surface of silvery smoothness, like a gem set in ice, and reflecting the weeds, trees, houses, and clouds with singular beauty. The reflections are particularly simple and distinct. These twigs are not referred to and confounded with a broad green meadow from which they spring, as in summer, but instead of that broad green ground absorbing the light, is the abrupt white field of ice.

Dec. 15, 1837. Jack Frost. As further confirmation of the fact that vegetation is a kind of crystallization, I observe that upon the edge of the melting frost on the windows, Jack is playing singular freaks, now bundling together his needle-shaped leaves so as to resemble fields waving with grain, or shocks of wheat rising here and there from the stubble. On one side, the vegetation of the torrid zone is presented, high-towering palms, and wide-spread banyans, such as we see in pictures of oriental scenery. On the other, are arctic pines, stiff-frozen, with branches downcast, like the arms of tender men in frosty weather. In some instances, the panes are covered with little feathery flocks where the particles radiate from a common centre, the number of radii varying from three to seven or eight. The crystalline particles are partial to the creases and flaws in the glass, and when these extend from sash to sash, form complete hedgerows, or miniature watercourses, where dense masses of crystal foliage " high over-arched embower."

Dec. 15, 1838. Silence is ever less strange than noise, lurking amid the boughs of the hemlock or the pine, just in proportion as we find ourselves there. The nuthatch tapping the upright trunks by our side is only a partial spokesman for the solemn stillness.

Silence is the communion of a conscious soul with itself. If the soul attend for a moment to its own infinity, then and there is silence. She is audible to all men, at all times, in all places.

If we will, we may always hearken to her admonitions.

Dec. 15, 1840. When most at one with nature I feel supported and propped on all sides by a myriad influences, as trees in the plain or on the hillside are equally perpendicular. The most upright man is he that most entirely reclines (the prone recline but partially) ; by his entire reliance he is most erect. Men of little faith stand only by their feet, or recline on the ground, having lost their reliance on the soul. Nature is right, but man is straight. She erects no beams, she slants no rafters, and yet she builds stronger and truer than he. Everywhere she preaches not abstract, but practical truth. She is no beauty at her toilet, but her cheek is flushed with exercise.

Dec. 15, 1856. 3 P. M. To Walden. I observe B———'s boat left out at the pond, as last winter. When I see that a man neglects his boat thus, I do not wonder that he fails in his business. It is not only shiftlessness or unthrift, but a sort of filthiness to let things go to wrack and ruin thus.

I still recall that characteristic winter evening of December 9th. The cold, dry, and wholesome diet my mind and senses necessarily fed on, — oak leaves, bleached and withered weeds that rose above the snow, the now dark green of

the pines, and perchance the faint metallic chip
of a single tree sparrow; the hushed stillness of
the wood at sundown, aye, all the winter day, the
short boreal twilight, the smooth serenity and
the reflections of the pond, still alone free from
ice; the melodious hooting of the owl, heard at
the same time with the yet more distant whistle
of a locomotive, more aboriginal, and perchance
more enduring here than that, heard above all
the voices of the wise men of Concord, as if
they were not (how little he is Anglicized!),
the last strokes of the woodchopper, who presently bends his steps homeward; the gilded bar
of cloud across the apparent outlet of the pond,
conducting my thoughts into the eternal west,
the deepening horizon glow, and the hasty walk
homeward to enjoy the long winter evening.
The hooting of the owl; that is a sound which
my red predecessors heard here more than a
thousand years ago. It rings far and wide, occupying the space rightfully, — grand, primeval,
aboriginal sound. There is no whisper in it of
the Bulkeleys, the Flints, the Hosmers, who recently squatted here, nor of the first parish, nor
of Concord Fight, nor of the last town-meeting.

Dec. 15, 1859. Philosophy is a Greek word,
by good rights, and it stands almost for a Greek
thing, yet some rumor of it has reached the
commonest mind. M. Miles, who came to col-

lect his wood-bill to-day, said, when I objected
to the small size of his wood, that it was necessary to split wood fine in order to cure it well;
that he has found that more than four inches in
diameter would not dry, and, moreover, a good
deal depended on the manner in which it was
corded up in the woods. He piled his high and
tight. If this were not well done, the stakes
would spread and the wood lie loosely, and so
the rain and snow find their way into it, and he
added, " I have handled a good deal of wood,
and I think that I understand the *philosophy*
of it."

Dec. 16, 1837. The woods were this morning covered with thin bars of vapor, the evap-
oration of the leaves, according to Sprengel,
which seemed to have been suddenly stiffened
by the cold. In some places it was spread out
like gauze over the tops of the trees, forming
extended lawns, where elves and fairies held
high tournament : —

> " Before each van
> Prick forth the aery knights, and couch their spears,
> Till thickest legions close."

The east was glowing with a narrow, but ill-
defined crescent of light, the blue of the zenith
mingling in all possible proportions with the
salmon color of the horizon. And now the
neighboring hilltops telegraph to us poor crawl-

ers of the plain, the monarch's golden ensign in
the east. •ͺ

How indispensable to a correct study of Nature is a perception of her true meaning. The
fact will one day flower out into a truth. The
reason will mature and fructify what the understanding had cultivated.

Dec. 16, 1840. Speech is fractional, silence
is integral.

Beauty is where it is perceived. When I see
the sun shining on the woods across the pond,
I think this side the richer which sees it.

The motion of quadrupeds is the most constrained and unnatural ; it is angular and
abrupt, except in those of the cat tribe, where
undulation begins. That of birds and fishes is
more graceful and independent. They move
on a more inward pivot, the former by their
weight or opposition to nature, the latter by
their buoyancy or yielding to nature. Awk-
wardness is a resisting motion, gracefulness is
a yielding motion. The line which would express the former is a tangent to the sphere,
that which would express the latter a radius.
But the subtlest, most ideal, and spiritual motion is undulation. It is produced by the most
subtle element falling on the next subtlest.
Rippling is a more graceful flight. If you consider it from the hilltop, you will detect in it

the wings of birds endlessly repeated. The two waving lines which express flight šeem copied from the ripple. There is something ·analogous to this in our most inward experience. In enthusiasm we undulate to the divine spiritus, as the lake to the wind.

Dec. 16, 1850. I noticed [last Sunday or the 14th] a bush covered with cocoons which were artfully concealed by two leaves wrapped round them, one still hanging by its stem, so that they looked like a few withered leaves left dangling. The worm, having first incased itself in another leaf, for greater protection folded more loosely around itself one of the leaves of the plant, taking care, however, to incase the leaf-stalk and the twig with a thick and strong web of silk. So far from its depending on the strength of the stalk, which is now quite brittle, the strongest fingers cannot break it, and the cocoon can only be got off by slipping it up and off the twig. There they hang themselves secure for the winter, proof against cold and the birds, ready to become butterflies when new leaves push forth.

The snow everywhere was covered with snow-fleas, like pepper. When you hold a mass in your hand, they skip and are gone before you know it. They are so small that they go through and through the new snow. Sometimes, when collected, they look like some powder which the hunter has spilled in the path.

Dec. 16, 1852. Observed the reflection of the snow on Pine Hill from Walden extending far beyond the true limits of a reflection quite across the pond. Also, less obviously, of pines. The sky overcast with thick scud, which in the reflection, the snow ran into.

Dec. 16, 1853. The elms covered with hoar frost seen in the east, against the morning light, are very beautiful. These days, when the earth is still bare and the weather is so warm as to create much vapor by day, are the best for these frost works.

Would you be well, see that you are attuned to each mood of nature.

Dec. 16, 1859. A. M. To Cambridge, where I read in Gerard's Herbal. His admirable though quaint descriptions are to my mind greatly superior to the modern more scientific ones. He describes not according to rule, but according to his natural delight in the plants. He brings them vividly before you, as one who has seen and delighted in them. It is almost as good as to see the plants themselves. It suggests that one cannot too often get rid of the assumption that is in our science. His leaves are leaves; his flowers, flowers; his fruit, fruit. They are colored and fragrant. It is a man's knowledge added to a child's delight. Modern botanical descriptions approach ever nearer to the dryness of an algebraic formula, as $x + y = a$ love-letter. It is the keen joy and discrimination of a child who has just seen a flower for the first time, and comes running in with it to his friends. How much better to describe your object in fresh English words than in these conventional Latinisms ! He has really seen, and smelled, and tasted, and reports his sensations.

Dec. 17, 1837. In all ages and nations we observe a leaning towards a right state of things. This may especially be seen in the life of the priest, which approaches most nearly to that of the ideal man. The druids paid no taxes, and " were allowed exemption from warfare and all other things." The clergy are even now a privileged class. In the last stage of civilization, poetry, religion, and philosophy will be one, and there are glimpses of this truth in the first.

Dec. 17, 1840. The practice of giving the feminine gender to all ideal excellences personified is a mark of refinement observable in the mythologies of even the most barbarous nations. Glory and victory even are of the feminine gender, but it takes manly qualities to gain them. Man is masculine, but his manliness (*virtus*) feminine. It is the inclination of brute force to moral power.

Dec. 17, 1850. I noticed, when the snow first came, that the days were very sensibly lengthened by the light reflected from the snow. Any work which required light could be pursued about half an hour longer, so we may well pray that the ground may not be laid bare by a thaw in these short winter days.

Dec. 17, 1851. The pitch-pine woods on the right of the Corner road. A piercing cold afternoon ; wading in the snow. The pitch pines hold the snow well. It lies now in balls on their plumes, and in streaks on their branches, their low branches rising at a small angle and meeting each other. A sombre twilight comes through this roof of pine leaves and snow, yet in some places the sun streams in, producing the strongest contrasts of light and shade.

The winter morning is the time to see in perfection the woods and shrubs wearing their snowy and frosty dress. Even he who visits them half an hour after sunrise will have lost some of their most delicate and fleeting beauties. The trees wear their morning burden but coarsely after midday, and it no longer expresses the character of the tree. I observed that early in the morning every pine needle was covered with a frosty sheath, but soon after sunrise it was all gone. You walk in the pitch-pine woods as under a pent-house. The stems and branches of the trees look black by contrast. You wander zigzag through the aisles of the wood, where stillness and twilight reign. I do not know but a pine wood is as substantial and as memorable a fact as a friend. I am more sure to come away from it cheered than from those who are nearest to being my friends.

Improve every opportunity to express yourself in writing, as if it were your last.

When they who have aspired to be friends cease to sympathize, it is the part of religion to keep asunder.

To explain to a friend is to suppose you are not intelligent of one another. If you are not, to what purpose will you explain?

One of the best men I know often offends me by uttering made words, the very best words, of course, most smooth and gracious and fluent, a dash of polite conversation, a graceful bending, as if I were Master Kingsley, of promising parts, from the university. Oh, would you but be simple and downright, would you but cease your palaver. The conversation of gentlemen after dinner, — no words are so tedious. Never a natural or simple word or yawn. It produces an appearance of phlegm and stupidity in me, the auditor. I am suddenly the closest and most phlegmatic of mortals, and the conversation comes to naught.

My acquaintances sometimes wonder why I will impoverish myself by living aloof from this or that company, but greater would be the impoverishment if I should associate with them.

Dec. 17, 1853. While surveying in Lincoln, to-day, saw a great many, may be a hundred, silvery brown cocoons of some great moth, wrinkled and flattish, on young alders in a meadow, three or four inches long, fastened to the main stem and branches at the same time, with dry alder and fragments of fern leaves attached to and partially concealing them.

Dec. 17, 1856. P. M. Cold, with a piercing northwest wind and bare ground still. It is pretty poor picking outdoors to-day. There's but little comfort to be found. You go stumping over bare frozen ground, sometimes clothed with curly, yellowish, withered grass, like the back of half-starved cattle late in the fall, now beating this ear, now that, to keep them warm. It is comparatively summer-like on the south side of woods and hills.

When I returned from the south the other day, I was greeted by withered shrub-oak leaves which I had not seen there. It was the most homely and agreeable object that met me. I found that I had no such friend as the shrub oak hereabouts. A farmer once asked me what

they were made for, not knowing any use they
served. But I can tell him that they do me
good. They are my parish ministers, regularly
settled. They never did any man harm that I
know. Now you have the foliage of summer
painted in brown. Go through the shrub oaks.
All growth has ceased, no greenness meets the
eye, except what there may be in the bark of
this shrub. The green leaves are all turned to
brown, quite dry and sapless, the little buds are
sleeping at the base of the slender shrunken
petioles. Who observed when they passed from
green to brown? I do not remember the transition. But these leaves still have a kind of life
in them. They are exceedingly beautiful in
their withered state. If they hang on, it is like
the perseverance of the saints. Their colors are
as wholesome, their forms as perfect as ever.
Now that the crowd and bustle of summer is
passed, I have leisure to admire them. Their
figures never weary my eye. Look at the few
broad scallops in their sides. When was that pat-
tern first cut? With what a free stroke the curve
was struck! With how little, yet just enough,
variety in their forms! Look at the fine bristles
which arm each pointed lobe, as perfect now as
when the wild bee hummed about them, or the
chewink scratched beneath them. What pleasing and harmonious colors above and below!

The smooth, delicately brown-tanned upper surface, acorn-color, and the very pale, some silvery
or ashy, ribbed under side. How poetically, how
like saints, or innocent and beneficent beings
they give up the ghost! How spiritual! Though
they have lost their sap, they have not given up
the ghost. Rarely touched by worm or insect,
they are as fair as ever.

Dec. 17, 1859. P. M. To Walden. I see on
the pure white snow what looks like dust for
half a dozen inches under a twig. Looking
closely I find that the twig is hardhack, and the
dust its slender, light-brown, chaffy-looking seed,
which falls still in copious showers, dusting the
snow, when I jar it, and here are the tracks of a
sparrow which has jarred the twig, and picked
the minute seeds a long time, making quite a
hole in the snow. The seeds are so fine that it
must have got more snow than seed at each pick.
But they probably look large to its microscopic
eyes. I see, when I jar it, that a meadow-sweet
close by has quite similar, but larger seeds.
This is the reason, then, that these plants rise
so high above the snow, and retain their seed,
dispersing it, on the least jar, over each successive layer of snow beneath them ; or it is carried
to distant places by the wind. What abundance
and what variety in the diet of these small
graminivorous birds, while I find only a few

nuts still. These stiff weeds which no snow can break down, hold their provender. What the cereals are to men, these are to the sparrows. The only threshing they require is that the birds fly against their spikes or stalks. A little further I see the seed-box, *Ludwigia*, full of still smaller yellowish seeds. On the ridge, north, is the track of a partridge amid the shrubs. It has hopped up to the low clusters of smooth sumac berries, sprinkled the snow with them, and eaten all but a few. Also, here only, or where it has evidently jarred them down (whether intentionally or not, I am not sure), are the large oval seeds of the stiff-stalked lespedeza, which I suspect it ate with the sumac berries. There is much solid food in them. When the snow is deep, the birds can easily pick the latter out of the heads, as they stand in the snow.

Dec. 18, 1852. P. M. To Anursnack. Very cold, windy day. Loring's Pond beautifully frozen. (This the first skating.) So polished the surface, I took many parts of it for water. It was waved or watered with a slight dust, nevertheless. Cracked into large squares, like the faces of a reflector, it was so exquisitely polished that the sky and dun-colored scudding clouds, with mother-o'-pearl tints, were reflected in it as in the calmest water. I slid over it with a little misgiving, mistaking the ice before me for water. Still the little ruby-crowned birds about.

Dec. 18, 1856. 12 M. Start for Amherst, N. H. A very cold day. Thermometer at eight A. M., 8°, and I hear of others very much lower at an earlier hour, 2° at 11.45. The last half the route from Groton Junction to Nashua is along the Nashua river mostly. This river looks less interesting than the Concord. It appears even more open, that is, less wooded (?). At any rate, the banks are more uniform, and I notice none of our meadows on it. At Nashua, hire a horse and sleigh, and ride to Amherst, eleven miles, against a strong northwest wind, this bitter cold afternoon. At my lecture, the audience attended closely, and I was satisfied. That is all I ask or expect generally. Not one spoke to me afterward, nor needed they. I have no doubt they liked it in the main, though none of them would have dared say so, provided they were conscious of it. Generally, if I can only get the ears of an audience, I do not care whether they say they like my lecture or not. I think I know as well as they can tell. At any rate, it is none of my business, and it would be impertinent for me to inquire. The stupidity of most of these country towns, not to include the cities, is in their infantile innocence. Lectured in basement (vestry) of the orthodox church, and, I trust, helped to undermine it. I was told to stop at the United States Hotel ; an old inhabitant had never heard of it, but I found the letters on a sign without help. It was the ordinary, unpretending (?), desolate - looking country tavern. The landlord apologized to me because there was to be a ball there that night, which would keep me awake, and it did.

Dec. 18, 1859. Rain. It rains but little this afternoon, though there is no sign of fair weather. It is a lichen day. The pitch pines are very inspiriting to behold. Their green is as much enlivened and freshened as that of the lichens. It suggests a sort of sunlight on them, though not even a patch of clear sky is to be seen to-day. As dry and olive or slate-colored lichens are of a fresh and living green, so the already green pine needles have acquired a far livelier tint, as if they enjoyed this moisture as much as the lichens do. They seem to be lit up more than when the sun falls on them. Their trunks and those of trees generally, being wet, are very black, and the bright lichens on them are so much the more remarkable. Apples are thawed now, and are very good. Their juice is the best kind of bottled cider that I know. They are all good in this state, and your jaws are the cider press. The oak woods a quarter of a mile off appear more uniformly red than ever. The withered leaves, being thoroughly saturated with moisture, are of a livelier color, and they are not only redder for being wet, but through the obscurity of the mist one leaf runs into another, and the whole mass makes one impression.

Dec. 19, 1837. Hell itself may be contained within the compass of a spark.

Dec. 19, 1840. This plain sheet of snow which covers the ice of the pond is not such a blankness as is unwritten, but such as is unread. All colors are in white. It is such simple diet to my senses as the grass and the sky. There is nothing fantastic in them. Their simple beauty has sufficed men from the earliest times. They have never criticised the blue sky and the green grass.

Dec. 19, 1850. The witch hazel is covered with fruit, and droops over gracefully, like a willow, the yellow foundation of its flowers still remaining.

Dec. 19, 1851. In all woods is heard now, far and near, the sound of the woodchopper's axe ; a twilight sound now in the night of the year, as if men had stolen forth in the arctic night to get fuel to keep their fires a-going.

The sound of the axes far in the horizon is like the dropping of the eaves. Now the sun sets suddenly without a cloud, and with scarcely any redness following, so pure is the atmosphere, only a faint rosy blush along the horizon.

Dec. 19, 1854. P. M. Skated half mile up Assabet, and then to foot of Fair Haven Hill. This is the first tolerable skating. I am surprised to find how rapidly and easily I get along, how soon I am at this brook, or that bend in the river, which it takes me so long to reach on the bank or by water. I can go more than double the usual distance before dark.

Near the island I saw a muskrat close by, swimming in an open reach. He was always headed up stream, a great proportion of the head out of water, and his whole length visible, though the root of the tail is about level with the water. It is surprising how dry he looks, as if that back was never immersed in the water. Off Clamshell, I heard and saw a large flock of *Fringilla linaria* over the meadow. Suddenly they turn aside in their flight, and dash across the river to a large, white birch, fifteen rods off, which plainly they had distinguished so far. I afterward saw many more in the Potter swamp up the river. They were commonly brown, or dusky above, streaked with yellowish white or ash, and more or less white or ash beneath. Most had a crimson crown or frontlet, and a few a crimson neck and breast, very handsome.

Some, with a bright crimson crown, had clean white breasts. I suspect that these were young males. They keep up an incessant twittering, varied from time to time with some mewing notes. Occasionally, for some unknown reason, they will all suddenly dash away with that universal loud note (twitter), like a bag of nuts. They are busily clustered in the tops of the birches, picking the seeds out of the catkins, and sustain themselves in all kinds of attitudes, sometimes head downwards, while about this. Common as they are now, and were winter before last, I saw none last winter.

Dec. 19, 1859. When a man is young, and his constitution and body have not acquired firmness, that is, before he has arrived at middle age, he is not an assured inhabitant of the earth, and his compensation is that he is not quite earthy. The greater uncertainty of his fate seems to ally him to a nobler race of beings, to whom he in part belongs, or with whom he is in communication. The young man is a demigod, he is but half here, he knows not the men of this world, the powers that be. They know him not. Prompted by the reminiscence of that other sphere from which he has so lately arrived, his actions are unintelligible to his seniors. He bathes in light. He is interesting as a stranger from another sphere. He really

thinks and talks about a larger sphere of existence than this world.   It takes him forty years
to accommodate himself to the conditions of this
world.   This is the age of poetry.   Afterward
he may be the president of a bank, and go the
way of all flesh.   But a man of settled views,
whose thoughts are few and hardened like his
bones, is truly mortal, and his only resource is
to say his prayers.

Dec. 20, 1840.   My home is as much of nature as my heart embraces.   If I only warm my
house, then is that only my home.   But if I
sympathize with the heats and colds, the sounds
and silence of nature, and share the repose and
equanimity that reign around me in the fields,
then are they my house, as much as if the kettle
sang and fagots crackled, and the clock ticked
on the wall.

I rarely read a sentence which speaks to my
muse as nature does.   Through the sweetness
of his verse, without regard to the sense, I
have communion with Burns.   His plaint escapes through the flexure of his verses.   It was
all the record it admitted.

Dec. 20, 1851.   To Fair Haven Hill and
plain below.   Saw a large hawk circling over a
pine wood below me, and screaming, apparently
that he might discover his prey by their flight.
Traveling ever by wider circles, what a symbol

of the thoughts ; now soaring, now descending, taking larger and larger circles, or smaller and smaller. It flies not directly whither it is bound, but advances by circles, like a courtier of the skies. No such noble progress! How it comes round, as with a wider sweep of thought! But the majesty is in the imagination of the beholder, for the bird is intent on its prey. Circling and ever circling, you cannot divine which way it will incline, till perchance it drives down straight as an arrow to its mark. It rises higher above where I stand, and I see with beautiful distinctness its wings against the sky, primaries and secondaries, and the rich tracery of the outline of the latter (?), its inner wings or wing-linings, within the outer, like a great moth seen against the sky ; a will-o'-the-wind, following its path through the vortices of the air ; the poetry of motion, not as preferring one place to another, but enjoying each as long as possible, most gracefully thus surveying new scenes, and revisiting the old. How bravely he came round one of those parts of the wood which he had not surveyed, taking in a new segment, annexing new territories. Without " Heave yo," it trims its sail. It goes about without the creaking of a block. That America, yacht of the air, that never makes a tack, though it rounds the globe itself ; takes in and shake out its reefs without a flutter, its sky-scrapers all under its control; holds up one wing, as if to admire, and sweeps off this way, then holds up the other, and sweeps off that way. If there are two concentrically circling, it is such a regatta as Southampton waters never witnessed. Flights of imagination! Coleridgean thoughts! So a man is said to rise. in his thought ever to fresh woods and pastures new.

Red, white, and green, and in the distance dark brown, are the colors of the winter landscape. I view it now from the cliffs. The red shrub oaks on the white ground of the plain beneath make a pretty scene. Most walkers are pretty effectually shut up by the snow.

It is no doubt a good lesson for the woodchopper, his long day in the woods, and he gets more than his half-dollar a cord.

Say the thing with which you labor. It is a waste of time for the writer to use his talents merely. Be faithful to your genius. Write in the strain that interests you most. Consult not the popular taste.

A clump of white pines seen far westward over the shrub-oak plain which is now lit up by the setting sun, a soft feathery grove, with their gray stems indistinctly seen, like human beings come to their cabin door, standing expectant on the edge of the plain, inspires me with a mild humanity. The trees indeed have hearts. The sun seems to send its farewell ray far and level over the copses to them, and they silently receive it with gratitude, like a group of settlers with their children. The pines impress me as human. A slight vaporous cloud floats high over them, while in the west the sun goes down apace behind glowing pines and golden clouds which like mountains skirt the horizon. Nothing stands up more free from blame in this world than a pine-tree.

The dull and blundering behavior of clowns will as surely polish the writer at last, as the criticism of men of thought.

Our country is broad and rich, for here within twenty miles of Boston I can stand in a clearing in the woods, and look a mile or more over the shrub oaks to the distant pine copses and horizon of uncut woods, without a house or road or cultivated field in sight.

Go out before sunrise, or stay out till sunset.

It is wonderful, wonderful, the unceasing demand that Christendom makes on you, that you speak *from a moral point of view*. Though you be a babe, the cry is, repent, repent. The Christian world will not admit that a man has a just perception of any truth unless at the same time he cries, " Lord, be merciful to me, a sinner."

What made the hawk mount? Did he not fill himself with air? Before you were aware of it, he had mounted by his spiral path into the heavens.

Dec. 20, 1854. 9 A. M. To Hill. Said to be the coldest morning as yet. The river appears to be frozen everywhere. Where was water last night, is a firm bridge of ice this morning. The snow which has blown upon the ice has taken the form of regular star-shaped crystals an inch in diameter. Sometimes these are arranged in the form of a spear three feet long, quite straight. I see the mother-o'-pearl tints now at sunrise on the clouds high over the eastern horizon, before the sun has risen above the low bank in the east. The sky in the eastern horizon has that same greenish, vitreous, gem-like appearance which it has at sundown, as if it were of perfectly clear glass, with the green tint of a large mass of glass. Here are some crows already seeking their breakfast in the orchard, and I hear a red squirrel's reproof. The woodchoppers are hastening to their work afar off, walking fast to keep warm, before the sun has risen, their ears and hands well covered, the dry cold snow squeaking under their feet. They will be warmer after they have been at work an hour. P. M. Skated to Fair Haven with C. C's skates are not the best, and beside, he is far from an easy skater, so that, as he said, it was killing work for him. Time and again the perspiration actually dropped from his forehead upon the ice, and it froze in long icicles on his beard. Yet he kept up his spirits and his fun. It has been a glorious winter day; its elements so simple, the sharp, clear air, the white snow everywhere covering the earth, and the polished ice. Cold as it is, the sun seems warmer on my back even than in summer, as if its rays met with less obstruction. And then the air is so beautifully still, not an insect in it, hardly a leaf to rustle. If there is a grub out, you are sure to detect it on the snow or ice. The shadows of the Clamshell hills are beautifully blue, as I look back half a mile at them, and in some places where the sun falls on it, the snow has a pinkish tinge.

INDEX.

ACADEMY of Natural Sciences, 302.
Acorn, 83, 84, 86, 87, 172, 173, 325.
Acquaintances, 433, 445.
Advantages, 390.
Æschylus, 216, 217.
African seeds, 285.
Afternoon, 21, 28, 181, 182.
Alcott, Mr., 150.
Alder, 307.
Alternate reproduction, 107.
Amherst, N. H., 449.
Amusements, 178, 179, 180, 196.
Andrewsii, 35.
Andromeda, 391, 394, 413.
Andromeda Ponds, 290.
Andromeda Swamp, 391.
Andropogon scoparius, 117.
Anemone, 323, 324.
Antiquity, 267.
Ants, 211, 275, 280.
Anursnack, 206, 448.
Apple blossoms, 228.
Apples, 83, 95, 96, 134, 135, 212, 250.
Ardea minor, 70, 78, 159.
Arrowheads, 84, 117, 120, 173, 174, 344.
Art, 89 ; works of, 9.
Arum berries, 25.
Asclepias cornuti, 50, 51.
Ash, 41.
Ash, black, 41.
Ash, white, 41, 210.
Ashes, 79.
Aspens, 57, 422.
Aspidium cristatum, 186.
Aspidium spinulosum, 186.   See Ferns.
Aspirations, 154.
Assabet, 89, 114, 137, 167, 193, 240, 250, 288, 310, 345, 408, 434, 452.
Associates, 320.
Aster, 42, 70, 79, 147.
Aster multiflorus, 29.
Aster tradescanti, 29.

Aster undulatus, 239, 318.
Atmosphere, 24, 248.
Aubreys, 349.
Author, 19.
Authorship, 164.
Autumn, 108, 248.
Autumn afternoons, 21, 28.
Autumnal tints, 16, 19, 55, 58, 79, 102, 110, 143, 147, 312.

BACON, leg of, 356.
Ball's Hill, 147, 373, 374.
Banks, Sir Joseph, 104.
Barberries, 136.
Bare Hill, 412.
Bark of trees, 199, 234, 235.
Barn, 332.
Barrett's Mill, 127, 186.
Bateman's Pond, 59, 199, 200, 226.
Battle-ground, 370.
Bays, 357.
Baywings, 68.
Beanfield, 376.
Bear Garden, 400.
Beauty, 439.
Bee hunting, 42, 43, 44, 45.
Beech leaves, 198.
Beeches, 199.
Bees, 42, 43, 44, 45, 46, 47.
Beggar ticks, 39, 53.
Bell, 97, 98, 362, 363.
Beomyces rosea, 422.
Berries, 26, 27, 136, 320.
Bible, 116.
Bidens, 38, 39, 53, 70.
Bidens connata, 239, 318.
Bigelow, 322.
Bigelow's " Plants of Boston and vicinity," 386.
Billerica, 370, 372, 373.
Birch, 190, 191, 198.
Birch groves, 353.
Birch, white, 41.
Birches, 297, 310.
Birches, white, 29, 169, 220, 297.

Birches, yellow, 37, 148.
Birds, 13, 69, 70, 79, 80, 127, 190, 230, 252, 319, 400, 401, 413, 449.
Birds, collection of, 303.
Birds, diet of, 447, 448.
Birds, motions of, 252.
Birds' nests, 239.
Bittern, 70, 193, 199.
Bittern cliff, 392.
Blackberry leaves, 17.
Blackberry vines, 29.
Blackbirds, 70, 88.
Blackfish, 402.
Blake, 240.
Bleat of sheep, 148.
Blood, Perez, 425.
Bloom, 213, 214, 368.
Blueberry buds, 283.
Blueberry bushes, 118, 413.
Blueberry twigs, 314.
Bluebirds, 28, 79, 80, 91, 192, 224.
Bluets, 37.
Boat, 355, 388, 389, 436.
Body, 56, 430, 431, 432.
Bones, 247.
Book of autumn leaves, 312.
Book : "A Week on the Concord and Merrimack Rivers," 163, 339.
Books, 303.
Books, Indian, 355.
Boomer, 70.
Boots, 378.
Botanists, 5.
Botany, 386, 387.
Boulder field, 35, 204, 234.
Boulders, 204, 205.
Box-trap, 85.
Boys and horse, 54.
Bradford, 401, 402.
Breams, 360, 361, 362.
British naturalists, 104.
Broker, 140.
Brook, 278.
Brooks, Abel, 341, 342.
Broom pods, 2.
Brown, Capt. John, 260, 277, 278, 290, 363, 382.
Brown creeper, 335.
Brown, Simon, 362.
Brown's, James P., Pond, 344, 257.
Buds, 283, 340, 364, 377.
Bull-frog, 23.
Bullocks, 305, 306.
Bumblebees, 42, 46.
Bunker Hill Monument, 71.
Burns, 454.
Business dealings, 274.
Buttercup, 217, 265, 318, 321.
Butterflies, 42, 197.

Button-bushes, 182.
Buttonwoods, 41.
Buttons, 122.
Byron, Lord, 398.

C., W. E., 18, 239, 357, 370, 458, 459.
Caddis-worms, 136, 137, 317.
Cambridge, 343, 349, 350, 441.
Canoe birch, 190, 191, 198.
Cape Ann, 4, 48.
Cardinal shore, 265, 407.
Carlisle road, 10, 12, 59, 134.
Cat, 36, 52, 180, 328, 385.
Cat-birds' nests, 413.
Cato, 88.
Cat-owl, 7, 292, 293.
Cats, 422.
Cattle, 235, 259, 328.
Cattle on Sundays, 100.
Causeway, 429.
Cedar Hill, 426.
Cerastium, 318.
Cerastium viscosum, 283.
Change, 121.
Character, 252, 253, 350, 351.
Cheney's shore, 114.
Chestnut-tree, 123.
Chestnuts, 94, 95, 110, 113, 124, 144, 146, 404.
Chickadees, 69, 92, 95, 102, 103, 114, 119, 187, 198, 210, 211, 226, 227, 229, 234, 335, 340, 365, 380, 409, 432.
Chickweed, 318.
Chipbirds, 68.
Chips, 341, 342.
Cholmondeley, 355.
Chords, 130.
Christ, 281, 380, 382, 383.
Christendom, 457.
Christians, 14.
Church, 281, 282, 284.
Church of England, 180.
Cicindela, 340.
Circus, 18.
Cistus, 426.
Clam, 250.
Clamshell, 21, 23, 28, 117, 156, 157, 199, 286, 304, 332, 352.
Clamshell bank, 21.
Clamshell Hill, 174, 376, 459.
Clamshell meadow, 157.
Clamshell reach, 17.
Clamshells, colors of, 376, 377.
Clark, Brooks, 134.
Cledonia, 324.
Clematis Virginiana, 228.
Clergy, 442.
Clethra, 233.

Cliffs, 17, 70, 97, 101, 152, 191, 257, 343, 364, 388, 422.
Clock, 57.
Clothes, 403.
Cloud, 96, 117, 257, 258, 269, 270, 294, 328, 358, 359, 406, 427, 428, 429, 437.
Clover, 198.
Clowns, 457.
Cobwebs, 183, 184, 185, 190, 381.
Cochituate, 230.
Cocks, 51, 52, 183, 319, 385.
Cocoanut, 203.
Cocoons, 440, 445.
Coincidences, 309.
Colburn farm woodlot, 335.
Cold, 52, 329, 445.
Color, 147, 158, 308, 359, 366, 367, 383, 384, 456.
Comet, 52, 74, 197.
Comfort, 327.
Committee, 362.
Common-sense, 217.
Communities, 126.
Companion, 235.
Conant's grove, 33.
Conant's meadow, 8.
Conantum, 7, 8, 33, 34, 66, 86, 126, 154, 169, 189, 256, 296, 308, 413.
Conantum Cliff, 8.
Concord River, 157.
Concord woods, 372.
Connecticut, 301.
Conversation, 444.
Copan, 347.
Corner spring, 66, 77 109.
Cornus florida, 221, 222.
Corydalis, 55.
Cottages, 398.
Country, 457.
Country tavern, 450.
Country towns, 449.
Cowpath, 371.
Cows, 72.
Cranberries, 183, 299.
Creeds, 365.
Cress, 311.
Cricket-frog, 27.
Crickets, 21, 22, 23, 28, 96, 181, 189, 230, 246, 256, 258, 276.
Crotalaria, 58.
Crowfoot, 297.
Crows, 333, 337, 347, 409, 458.
Crystallization, 434, 435.
Currency, 348.

DANDELION, 33, 79, 108, 189, 211, 239, 279, 318, 404.
Days ripened like fruits, 3.

Deafness, 268.
Deep cut, 17, 107.
Deer-mouse, 368.
Dennis's Hill, 83, 85.
De Quincey, 255.
Descriptions, 104, 105, 106.
Desmodium, 38, 39, 53.
Desmodium paniculatum, 38.
Desmodium rotundifolium, 38.
Desor, 297.
Dew, 300, 301.
Dicksonia fern, 10, 66, 125.
Diet, 378, 379.
Dipper, 30, 31, 290.
Discourse with nature, 55.
Discovery, 333.
Diver, Great Northern, 251, 252.
Dog, 90.
Dogwood, 16.
Domestication, 191.
Donati, 285.
Douglas, 266.
Doves, 191, 192, 270.
Down on plants, 307, 308, 314.
Drawings, 409, 410.
Dreamland, 309.
Dreams, 19,150, 151,175,176,318, 343.
Driftwood, 131, 132, 139.
Druids, 442.
Ducks, 30, 31, 161, 169, 170, 371.
Dudley Pond, 239.
Dumb-bells, 94.
Duty, 10.

EAGLE Head, 4.
East India Marine Hall, 9.
Easterbrook, 2, 94, 134, 136.
Elephant, 193.
Elms, 41, 79, 99, 441.
Eloquence, 291, 292.
Emerson, Miss Mary, 264, 265.
Emerson, R. W., 362, 381, 382, 420, 421.
Emerson's Cliff, 18.
Emmonds, 372.
Employment, 425.
Encouragement, 383, 427.
English plants, 181.
Enjoyment, 316.
Entertainment, 81.
Enthusiasm, 36, 37.
Euphorbia heptagona, 419.
Evergreens, 234, 290.
Everlasting, 19, 48, 368.
Ex-plenipotentiary, 2.
Eye, 38, 56, 147.

FACES, 59.
Facts, 51, 189, 237.

464   *INDEX.*

Fair Haven, 182, 249, 335, 398, 404, 406, 432.
Fair Haven Bay, 222.
Fair Haven Hill, 39, 52, 80, 112, 239, 257, 261, 357, 358, 406, 423, 452, 454.
Fair Haven lot, 397.
Fair Haven Pond, 41, 53, 75, 101, 102, 113, 191, 309, 391, 394.
Fairies, 69, 71.
Falcons, 192.
Fall, 161.
Farmer, Jacob, 226, 227, 242, 336, 401.
Farmer, 365, 366, 375.
Farmer's life, 60, 61, 62, 316, 332.
Farmer's pleasure, 232.
Farming, 178, 179.
Feminine gender, 442.
Fern, climbing, 322, 354.
Fern, Dicksonia, 10, 66, 125.
Fern, sweet, 289, 307, 314, 397.
Fern tree, 20.
Ferns, 20, 24, 67, 68, 186, 187, 211.
Fields, 295, 377.
Finches, 189.
Fine days precious, 212.
Fire, 377, 432.
Fishermen, 75, 76, 139, 141.
Fishes, 362.
Fishing, 64, 65.
Fitchburg Railroad, 410.
Flannery, 295.
Flies, 42.
Flint's Bridge, 35.
Flint's Pond, 57, 92, 110, 142.
Flood, 232.
Flower cups, 433.
Flowers, 70, 79, 108, 318, 386.
Forest, 58.
Fossil turtle, 9.
Fox, 331, 400, 427.
Fragrance, 11.
Fragrant thoughts, 125.
Frame of landscape, 222, 223.
Friend, 91, 126, 129, 197, 206, 207, 389, 419.
Friends, 321, 322, 444.
Friendship, 118, 207.
Fringed gentian, 16, 94, 119, 206, 356.
Fringilla hiemalis, 17, 157, 383.
Fringilla linaria, 37, 452, 453.
Frogs, 186, 200.
Frost, 95, 426.
Frost weed, 154.
Frost work, 337, 338.
Fruits, 320, 321, 325.
Fuel, 140, 141, 142, 216, 241, 242, 342.

Fugitive slave, 49, 50.
Fuller, Margaret, 265, 421.
Fungus, 93, 104, 220.
Fungi, 218.
Furness, 302.
Furniture, 57.

Garden of Eden, 220.
Gavel, 61.
Geese, 146, 161, 231, 232, 250, 265, 269, 294, 312, 320, 327, 356, 357, 426, 427.
Genius, 217, 373.
Gentian, 16, 35, 94, 119, 206, 356.
Gentian Lane, 35.
Gentlemen, 133.
Gerard, 5, 106.
Gerard's Herbal, 441, 442.
Gerardia purpurea, 54, 70.
Gesta gallorum, 385.
Giant, 162.
Gloucester, 48, 49.
Glow-worms, 256, 257, 318, 340.
Gold, 294.
Golden eggs, 90.
Golden-rod, 42, 46, 70, 79, 152, 239, 318.
Goldfinches, 114.
Goodwin, John, 139, 140, 141, 215, 216, 251, 380.
Goose Pond, 328.
Gossamer, 183, 184, 185, 190, 277.
Grackles, 47, 68.
Granite, 100.
Grape Cliff, 38.
Grass, 118, 182, 189, 228, 246, 295, 368.
Grasshoppers, 197, 276.
Great Fields, 35, 58, 294.
Great Meadows, 79, 413.
Grebe, 290.
Greeley, 303.
Green mountains, 131.
Grisi, 303.
Grist-mill, 381.
Grossbeak, 415.
Ground nuts, 40.
Growth, 222.

Haden's, 152, 366.
Halo, 308.
Happiness, 280.
Hard times, 108.
Hardhack seeds, 447.
Harper's Magazine, 300.
Harris, Dr., 340.
Harvest time, 109.
Hat, 386.
Hawks, 16, 29, 30, 192, 255, 455, 456, 458.

Hazel, 159, 315, 367.
Health, 296.
Hell, 451.
Hemlocks, 164, 165, 210, 211, 226, 240.
Hermann, 282.
Herons, 156, 193.
Heywood's Peak, 57.
Heywood's Pond, 411.
Hickeses, 349.
Hickories, 37, 65, 364.
Hieracium Canadense, 53.
Hill, 71, 346, 458.
Hills, 371, 373.
Historical facts, 29.
Hoar frost, 338.
Holden swamp, 275, 391, 413.
Holden wood, 68.
Home, 454.
Homer, 380.
Homes, 60, 61.
Honey, 338.
Hooper, Harry, 223.
Hoosac mountains, 131.
Hop hornbeam, 159.
Horizon, 249.
Hornbeams, 364.
Hornets' nest, 15, 34.
Horse, 55.
Horse chestnuts, 173.
Hosmer, Mr. Edmund, 309.
Hosmer, Mr. Joseph, 267, 268, 299, 344.
Hosmer's field, 311.
Hosmer's meadow, 227, 277.
Hour variously spent, 242.
Houses, 34.
Houstonia, 37, 79, 198, 217.
Howell, Francis, 198.
Hubbard, Cyrus, 365.
Hubbard's bridge, 283, 391, 399.
Hubbard's Close, 328.
Hubbard's Grove, 108.
Hubbard's woods, 250, 255, 369.
Hubbardston, 131.
Huckleberries, 8, 79, 307.
Hylodes, 57, 144, 258, 319, 363.
Hypericum, 54, 210.
Hypnum, 169.

Ice, 316, 317, 384, 391, 407, 433, 434, 448.
Ice crystals, 408, 409, 435, 458.
Ice foliage, 339.
Ichthyolites, 32.
Illusion, 206, 207.
Imagination, 403.
Imaginings, 195, 196, 197.
Indian books, 355.
Indian gouge, 83, 84.

Indian mind, 148.
Indian relics, 173.
Indian summer, 102, 103, 110, 181, 197, 226, 233, 290, 319, 325, 394, 408, 423.
Indians, 297, 298, 344, 402.
Insane man, 381.
Inspection, 197.
Irishman, 402, 403.

Jay, 16, 73, 205, 206, 226, 229, 236, 245, 246, 279, 371.
Jenny's desert, 20.
John's-wort, 286.
Journal, 280.
Joy, 383.
Juniper repens, 39.

Kalmia glauca, 391.
Keyes, John, 362.
Kirby and Spence, 184, 185
Knowledge, 31, 38.

Labaume, 288.
Labor, 298.
Lake Superior Indians, 297, 298.
Lakes, 53.
Lambkill, 35, 37.
Landscape, 80, 81, 191, 330, 364, 412.
Larks, 20, 68, 79, 199, 411.
Last words, 379.
Laurus sassafras, 86.
Law, 99, 100.
Leaves, 163, 200, 252, 259, 295, 312, 365, 391.
Leaves of oaks, 295, 367.
Leaves of trees, 88, 109.
Leaves, radical, 285, 286.
Lecture, 390, 391.
Lecturer, 449.
Ledum swamp, 115, 276.
Lee's Bridge, 7, 282.
Lee's Cliff, 37, 283, 396.
Lee's farm swamp, 85, 186.
Lee's hillside, 87.
Leisure, 260.
Le Jeune, 113.
Lespedeza, 307, 314, 448.
Lesson, 252.
Library, 350.
Lichens, 211, 213, 323, 324, 367, 450.
Life, 124, 146, 193, 219, 245, 319.
Life a failure, 347.
Life, springs of, 96, 400.
Life in winter, 100.
Life-everlasting, 70, 246, 279, 286.
Light, 98, 117, 120, 170, 171, 248, 256, 289, 307, 312, 345, 388.
Lily, 354.

Linaria Canadensis, 314.
Lincoln, 445.
Lincoln Bridge, 379, 404, 410, 411.
Lincoln Hills, 9.
Linnæus, 273, 282, 285.
Linnets, 414.
Lion, 36.
Littorales, 294.
Living, 219.
Locust, 87.
Loon, 57, 251.
Loring's Pond, 448.
Lotus, 302.
Love, 272, 323.
Lover, 3.
Ludwigia, 448.
Luxuries, 333.
Lyceum lectures, 274, 275.
Lycopodiums, 187.
Lygodium palmatum, 322, 354.
Lynx, 9.
Lynx, Canada, 39, 121, 347, 348.

MACHINE work, 129.
Magazines, 284.
Maiden, 217, 252.
Maiden-hair fern, 69.
Malthus, 304.
Man, 191, 192.
Man's nature, 419.
Man's worth, 303.
Manchester, 4.
Manners, 58, 65.
Maples, 8, 21, 28, 37, 41, 53, 57, 79, 89, 102, 148, 169, 297, 345.
Marlboro' road, 83, 84, 247.
Marsh-hawk, 21, 89, 171, 172, 306.
Martin, 192.
Maynard's, 315, 316.
Meadow grass, 169, 170.
Meadow-sweet, 447.
Meadows, 346.
Meander, 117.
Medeola berries, 25.
Melody, 298.
Melvin, 375, 380, 423.
Melvin's Preserve, 9.
Memorial book, 313.
Men, 153.
Merrick's pasture, 21, 35, 399.
Merrimack, 117.
Migration, 270.
Migratory birds, 156, 157.
Miles, C., 232.
Miles, Martial, 306, 437, 438.
Miles Swamp, 29, 275.
Milkweed, 143.
Mill, cobweb drapery of, 128.
Miller, Hugh, 32, 33.
Min, 385.

Ministerial lot, 292.
Ministerial Swamp, 19, 136, 304, 322.
Mink, 265, 266, 372, 401.
Minott, 55, 57, 61, 62, 63, 223, 226, 250, 255, 256, 355, 376, 380, 417, 418.
Minott, George, 309, 376.
Minott's house, 334, 335.
Mint, 148.
Mole crickets, 22, 27, 29.
Monadnock, 25, 26.
Moods, 209, 210.
Moon, 260.
Moonlight, 376.
Moore's Swamp, 57.
Moose, 193.
Moses, 281.
Moss, 169, 227, 234, 293, 324, 363, 364.
Motion, 439.
Mountain, 131, 176, 177.
Mountain ash, 16, 181.
Mountain peak, 25, 26.
Mountains, 130, 131, 143, 214, 215, 263, 264, 301.
Mouse, 297, 385.
Mouse-ear chickweed, 318.
Mulleins, 279.
Munroe, J. & Co., 163, 339.
Mus leucopus, 276.
Music, 35, 36, 97, 119, 120, 252, 291, 378.
Musical sand, 4.
Musketaquid, 117, 174, 193.
Muskrats, 371, 372, 373, 376, 452.
Muskrats' diet, 354.
Muskrats' houses, 77, 78, 79, 111, 116, 118, 218, 224, 225, 228, 239, 240, 249, 250, 251, 255.
Mussels, 78.
Myrtle birds, 137.

NAMES, 273.
Nashua river, 449.
Nature, 76, 77, 180, 212, 213, 234, 436, 454.
Nature, changes in, 204.
Nature genial to man, 315.
Nature, gradation in, 266.
Nature, home in, 258.
Nature the only panacea, 13.
Nature, phases of, 11.
Nature serene, 433.
Nature, success of, 415.
Nature's pensioners, 134, 135, 136.
Nawshawtuck, 3, 174, 198.
Neighbors, 169, 379.
New Bedford, 407.
New England, 402.

New England winter sunsets, 433.
Night, 69, 85, 159.
Night-shade, 47, 48.
Non-producers, 5, 6.
North America discovered, 30.
"North American Review," 404.
Northeast storm, 146, 156.
Novelty, 195, 196.
November, 158, 183, 189, 191, 196, 233, 262, 269, 270, 295, 297, 314.
November afternoon, 261, 290, 307, 328.
November evening, 194, 195.
November in New England, 402.
Nut meadow, 409.
Nuthatch, 236, 335, 369, 370, 388, 389, 435.

OAK, black, 114, 148, 346.
Oak leaves, 59, 114, 122, 204, 297, 308, 345, 346, 364, 384, 436, 451.
Oak, red, 114, 148, 201, 202.
Oak, scarlet, 114.
Oak, white, 114, 138, 139, 148, 346.
Oak wood, 236, 346.
Oaks, 37, 146, 169, 315, 323, 373.
Oar, 147.
Obstacles, 159.
October, 143, 312.
Old shoes, 399.
Olive oil, 338.
Order or system, 106.
Osmundas, 66.
Otters, tracks of, 392, 393, 408.
Out-doors, 212.
Owls, 86, 165, 166, 167, 168, 405, 437.
Owl's nest, 275.
Oxen, 366.
Oyster, 398.

PAGODA, 18.
Pails, 128, 129.
Panicum crus-galli, 23.
Panicum filiforme, 23.
Panicum sanguinale, 23.
Partridge, 229, 231, 293, 352, 388, 409, 413, 448.
Partridge berries, 311.
Partridge berry leaves, 279.
Party, 267, 268.
Passenger pigeon, 30.
Peabody, 70.
Pears, 6, 95, 96.
Peculiarity, 418.
Pelagii, 294.
Pelham's Pond, 111.
Pencils, 299, 300.
Pennyroyal, 399.
Pestle, 344.

Peterboro' Hills, 263.
Philadelphia, 302.
Philosophy, 437, 438.
Phosphorescent wood, 63, 64, 74.
Pickerel, 183, 278.
Pickerel fisher, 396.
Picture-frame, 204, 205, 406.
Pigweed, 23.
Pilgrims, 39, 401.
Pine Hill, 58, 110, 212, 214, 328, 330, 354.
Pine log, 355.
Pine needles, 18, 115, 401.
Pine roots and knots, 399.
Pine warblers, 68.
Pine wood, 109, 309, 346, 419, 443, 444.
Pines, 37, 57, 146, 148, 192, 193, 226, 283, 343, 419.
Pines, pitch, 53, 87, 109, 139, 152, 443, 450.
Pines, white, 52, 109, 191, 198, 247, 256, 312, 314, 353, 456, 457.
Pitch-pine cones, 269, 306.
Pitcher plant, 33, 34, 275, 283.
Plants, 70, 386, 387.
Pliny, 274.
Ploughing, 243, 244.
Ploughman, 305.
Plymouth plantation, 401.
Poet, 192, 204, 304, 319, 322.
Poetry, 360.
Poetry, ancient Scotch, 261.
Poetry, English, 349.
Poet's life, 161, 162.
Poet's thoughts, 294.
Politics, 244.
Polygonum articulatum, 20.
Polygonum aviculare, 198.
Polygonums, 84.
Polygula sanguinea, 108.
Polypody, 199, 200, 201, 220, 221.
Pond, 237, 357, 383, 396, 404, 405.
Pontederia, 239, 240.
Poplar Hill, 79, 102, 215.
Poplars, 37.
Populus grandidentata, 41, 312.
Populus tremuloides, 354, 364.
Porter, Commodore, 321.
Potatoes, 219, 220, 287.
Potentilla argentea, 239, 318.
Potentilla Canadensis, 35.
Poverty, 265.
Pratt, Minott, 356.
Prayer, 100, 369.
Preacher, 281, 284.
Preaching, 283, 284.
Presents, 220.
Priest, 442.
Primrose, 286.

Prinos berries, 53, 233.
Prinos verticillata, 297.
Prosperity, 13.
Providence, 390.
Public opinion, 94.
Puffballs, 71, 72.
Puffer, 380.
Pyramids, 303.

QUAIL, 401.
Questions, 122.

RABBIT, 85, 86, 187, 293, 324, 325, 336, 413.
Railway journeys, 301, 302.
Rainbow, 257.
Rana palustris, 11, 27.
Rana sylvatica, 11.
Ranunculus bulbosus, 305.
Ranunculus repens, 79, 239, 318.
Redpolls, 404, 413–416.
Redwings, 47, 68.
Reflections, 406, 412, 434, 441.
Reflections in water, 183, 199, 202, 238, 319, 373, 374.
Regrets, 260.
Reminiscence, 153, 154.
Repentance, 411.
Rhexia, 53.
Rice, 286, 287, 288, 380.
Richardson, 376, 380, 397.
Ripe, 259.
Rising generation, 223.
River, 7, 111, 112, 119, 147, 157, 160, 182, 183, 190, 249, 283, 339, 370, 371, 372, 384, 388, 389, 400, 434, 458.
River scenery, 8.
Robin, 198.
Rocks, 201, 211, 274.
Roots, 354, 355.
Rose, 422.
Routine, 416.
Ruskin, 180.
Ruskin's " Modern Painters," 76.

S———, a poor boy, 402, 403.
Sabbath, 281.
Safford, 162,
Saffron-Walden, 376.
Salamander, 390.
Sanborn, 426.
Sand, 98.
Sand banks, 108.
Sarracenia purpurea, 33.
Sassafras, 86, 88.
Saw Mill Brook, 24, 209, 210, 310.
Science, 105, 131, 361, 374.
Science, man of, 221.
Scott's " Lady of the Lake " quoted, 254.

Screech-owl, 5, 86, 165, 166, 167, 168.
Seasons, 74, 154, 157, 158, 289, 432.
Second Division Brook, 136.
Seeds transported by birds, 2.
Selectmen, 363.
Self knowledge, 182.
Sentences, 254.
Serenity, 270.
Shad-bush, 103, 227, 228.
Shad frogs, 79.
Shakespeare, 161, 380.
Shattuck, 376.
Shells, 294.
Shepherd's purse, 318, 394.
Shiners, 58, 59.
Shrub oak, 309, 314, 345, 368, 369, 397, 445, 446, 456.
Shrub oak leaves, 87, 327, 367, 383, 445, 446, 447.
Shrub oak plain, 17, 102, 308, 456.
Shrubs, buds on, 393.
Shrubs reflected, 82, 83.
Side-saddle flower, 33.
Side view, 221.
Sight, 195.
Silence, 435, 439.
Sin, 260, 291.
Skating, 391, 394, 395, 400, 452, 458.
Skeleton, 374.
Skies, 285.
Skinner, 340.
Skins, 393.
Skunk cabbage, 187, 188, 189, 398.
Sky, changes of, 428, 429.
Small things, 83.
Smith's Hill, 24, 25, 404.
Smoke, 59, 60, 61, 79, 102, 272, 315.
Snake, 22, 23, 87.
Snapdragon, Canada, 113.
Snapping turtle's eggs, 285.
Snipes, 157, 159.
Snow, 113, 158, 230, 243, 346, 317, 318, 323, 324, 398, 443, 451.
Snowbirds, 328, 366.
Snow-buntings, 227, 347, 409, 423, 424.
Snow-fleas, 161, 183, 394, 409, 440.
Snowstorm, 341, 359.
Social virtues, 144.
Society, 401, 419.
Solanum, dulcamara, 23, 24.
Solidago cæsia, 46.
Solidago speciosa, 54.
Solomon's seal, 25.
Song-sparrow, 79, 407.
Sortes Virgilianæ, 421.
Sounds, 101.
Space, 407.
Spanish book, 212.

Sparrows, 23, 68, 70, 126, 127, 157, 158, 189, 230, 305, 328, 407.
Spear-head, 372.
Species, 298.
Speculations, 394.
Speech, freedom of, 284.
Spencer, Brook, 59.
Spiders, 133, 184, 185, 186, 275.
Spine, 419.
Sprague, 308.
Sprengel, 438.
Spring, 91, 159, 160, 370, 371.
Spring, a second, 35, 144, 279, 319.
Spruce swamp, 413.
Squash, 6.
Squirrel, 73, 74, 155, 211, 230, 231, 236, 299, 352, 353, 369, 458.
Star, 159, 336.
Statements, 188, 189.
Stellaria media, 318.
Stillness, 228, 229, 405.
Still water, 111, 120.
Stranger, 144.
Stream, ascent and descent of, 202, 203.
Stumps, 169, 215, 216.
Succory, 20, 53, 108.
Sudbury, 314, 316.
Sudbury men, 316.
Sumac, 16, 448.
Summer, 394.
Summer duck, 240, 241.
Sun, reflected heat of, 22.
Sunlight, 289.
Sun-sparkles, 229.
Sunset, 3, 17, 90, 112, 152, 214, 259, 311, 327, 330, 331, 345, 388, 429.
Sunsets, New England winter, 433.
Superstition, 421, 425.
Swallow, 192, 242, 243.
Swallow holes, 383.
Swallows' nests, 304.
Swamp, 33, 186, 187, 231, 232, 331, 387, 425.
Swamp Bridge Brook, 174, 319.
Swamp pink, 233, 283, 364, 413.
Swamp pyrus, 233, 413.
Sweetbriar, 86.
Sweet fern, 289, 307, 314, 397.
Sword, 9.
Syriaca, 143.

Tahatawan, 174, 360.
Tansy, 108, 239, 268, 294, 318, 422.
Tarbell's, 332, 371.
Tastes, 155.
Tears, 248.
Teeth, 381.
Telegraph harp, 107.
Tent, 18.

Thanksgiving afternoon, 331.
Theme, 124, 125.
Theophrastus, 274.
Therien, 250.
Thimbleberry shoots, 213, 330, 368.
Thinking, 280.
Thistles, 149.
Thoughts, 158, 212, 262, 333, 334.
Thoughts, old ruts of, 12, 418.
Threshing, 61.
Ticks, 38, 39.
Tiger, 316.
Toad-flax, 314.
Tools, 287.
Tortoise, 3, 79, 412.
Touch-me-not seed vessels, 24.
Tournefort, 282.
Towns, 367.
Tracks, 384, 385, 408.
Trade, 140.
Trail, 341.
Travel, 304.
Tree fern, 20.
Tree, injury to, 145.
Tree sparrows, 103, 181, 199, 328, 340, 383, 401, 413.
Treetoads, 153.
Trees, 210, 222, 338, 377, 379.
Trees, character of, 41.
Trees, dead, 431.
Trichostema dichotomum, 399.
Truth, 189, 203, 218, 260, 422.
Turnips, 311.
Turtle-dove, 25.
Twilight, 374, 412.

Uncannoonuc, 243.
Undulations, 439, 440.

Valor, 342, 343.
Valparaiso squash, 321.
Values, 348, 349.
Vanessa Antiopa, 197.
Vapor, 107, 428, 429, 438.
Varro, 148.
Verses, 223, 224, 253, 297, 351, 352.
Vestiges of creation, 33.
Vice an aid to success, 1.
Viola lanceolata, 57.
Viola ovata, 79, 108.
Viola pedata, 230, 237.
Violet, hood-leaved, 35.
Violets, 35, 237, 279, 422.
Virgin's Bower, 228.
Visiting, 65, 386.

Wachusett, 131, 354, 359.
Walden, 57, 110, 152, 209, 327, 354, 357, 360, 365, 399, 400, 436, 441, 447.

Walden in Essex, 376.
Walden Pond, 37, 42, 82, 83, 214, 226, 253, 380.
Walk, 235, 328, 329.
Walking, 328, 329.
Walnuts, 148, 173.
Ware, Dr., Jr., 208, 209.
Wasps, 42.
Water, 160, 373.
Water bugs, 95.
Water the centre of landscape, 102.
Water, colors of, 152.
Waterloo, 6.
Weather, 92, 93, 225, 269, 314, 343.
Weeds, 6.
" Week on the Concord and Merrimack Rivers," 163.
Weird Dell, 358.
Well Meadow Brook, 283.
Well Meadow Field, 358.
Weston, Mr., 326.
Whale, 193.
Wheeler's pasture,'305, 307.
Wheeler's Owl wood, 358.
Whippoorwill, 70.
White mountains, 71.
White pine needles, 18.
White Pond, 108.
White-weed, 113.
Wild apples, 212.
Wild-cat, 340.
Wild flowers, 7.
Wild pig, 313, 314.
Williams, Henry, 49.
Williams, Oliver, 223.
Willow Bay, 115.
Willow catkins, 297.
Willows, 182, 184, 354.
Wind, 35, 71, 253, 330, 332.
Wind, self-registering, 208.
Window, 214, 337, 338, 354.

Winter, 158, 161, 244, 249, 346, 395, 396, 415, 416.
Winter, love for, 389.
Winter day, 459.
Winter eve, 406.
Winter evening, 436, 437.
Winter morning, 443.
Winter scenes, 125, 324, 326, 357, 358, 359.
Winter sky, 389.
Winter walk, 427.
Winter weather, 332.
Wisdom, 36, 317.
Wise, the balloonist, 428.
Wishes, 420.
Witherel Glade, 117, 277.
Wolves, 336, 337.
Women, 265, 267.
Woodbine, 29.
Wood-choppers, 293, 388, 405, 407, 437, 451, 456, 458.
Woodchuck, 69.
Woodcock, 159, 310, 311.
Wooden trays, 128, 129.
Wood-lot, 379, 417, 418.
Wood-path, 366.
Woodman, 293.
Woodpecker, 407, 409, 432.
Woods, 85, 203, 204, 271, 326, 397.
Woods, drama in, 279.
Words, 207.
Wordsworth, 293.
World, beauty of, 416, 417.
Wormwood, 368.
Writer, 456.
Writing, 331, 444.
Wyman, John, 223.

Yarrow, 108, 211, 239, 268, 294, 318.
Young men, 453, 454.
Youth, 322.

14 DAY USE
RETURN TO DESK FROM WHICH BORROWED
LOAN DEPT.

This book is due on the last date stamped below, or
on the date to which renewed.
Renewed books are subject to immediate recall.

31 Aug'64 SB

REC'D LD

AUG 17 '64 -7 PM

ImTheStory.com

WS - #0025 - 010923 - C0 - 229/152/28 - PB - 9781314131475 - Gloss Lamination